SOUL HEALING

SOUL HEALING

A Spiritual Orientation in Counseling and Therapy

DOROTHY S. BECVAR

BasicBooks
A Division of HarperCollins*Publishers*

Library of Congress Cataloging-in-Publication Data

Becvar, Dorothy Stroh.

    Soul healing : a spiritual orientation in counseling and therapy /

  by Dorothy S. Becvar. — 1st ed.

      p. cm.

    Includes bibliographical references and index.

    ISBN 0-465-09552-6

    1. Psychotherapy—Religious aspects.   2. Counseling—Religious aspects. 3. Spirituality.   I. Title.

RC489.R46B43   1997

158'.3—dc21   96-45051
                                                    CIP

97 98 99 00 ❖/HC 9 8 7 6 5 4 3 2 1

for all that is

Contents

Foreword

At a recent conference on "Spirituality and Healing" sponsored by Harvard Medical School, David Larson, M.D., summarized the findings of more than 200 studies researching the association between spirituality and mental health by noting that "Individuals with a spiritual commitment showed lower levels of substance abuse, stress, depression, and suicide and reported increased overall marital, sexual, and life satisfaction." A spiritual orientation—a commitment to living according to beliefs that transcend the immediate here-and-now and provide a meaningful and hopeful perspective on life and living—is, it seems, just what the doctor might order! It also appears to be what our field is yearning for.

Until recently, with some notable exceptions, we therapists tended to ignore and at times pathologize the role of spirituality and religion in our clients' lives. Discussions on this topic generally overemphasized the harm and suffering that religious/spiritual dogmatism and fanaticism have caused through the centuries and underemphasized the health-promoting elements at the heart of spirituality within or outside organized religion. Lately, however, there has been a marked shift. Maybe as a backlash to our field's preoccupation with adjusting to the demands of managed care and developing ever briefer treatment models designed to alleviate strictly behavioral symptoms, the call for renewed emphasis on what has been termed the "soul of therapy" is being widely heard. The number of articles in the lay and professional literature as well as of well-attended workshops dedicated to addressing issues of values and spirituality at professional conferences has increased significantly over the past few years. This interest, as my conversations with friends and colleagues indicate, is far from academic or merely theoretical. I continue to be amazed to learn how many of them meditate, explore Buddhist or Native American spiritual traditions, and intentionally address spiritual issues with their clients.

Many of us have come to a more spiritual orientation through the push of painful experiences and the pull of hope for better ways of living our lives. For example, I remember a profound experience 20 years ago when my mother was dying. I was sitting with her during the long, last night, holding her hand while she, writhing in pain, struggled for breath. With every moan I tensed up, anguished and at a loss regarding how to provide more comfort. Slowly it dawned on me that my reflexive responses only multiplied the suffering and tension in the room. I was gradually able to relax my breath, hold my mother's hand more gently, and visualize us both in a loving context. I began telling her how much she was loved and that she could let go, that I trusted that what came after her last breath would be safe and good and peaceful. Some minutes after I was able to feel calm, loving, and trusting, my mother's breathing became easier, and her moans softened and turned into sighs. A few hours later she drew her last breath, surrounded by her family. It felt like a sacred moment.

The experience of my mother's dying was instrumental in expanding my explorations of spirituality and in my seeking training to work with cancer patients and their families. In retrospect, I see that the experience already contained the elements Dorothy Becvar identifies as characterizing a spiritual orientation: acknowledging connectedness, suspending judgment, trusting the universe, creating realities, and walking the path with heart.

Out-of-the-ordinary experiences jolt us into the recognition of dimensions of our lives and minds that we might not otherwise have accessed. The challenge is, of course, to live a spiritual ordinary life. In this important book, Dorothy Becvar serves as an experienced guide to a journey of integrating a spiritual orientation into one's personal and professional life. Spirituality to Dorothy is not a set of dogmatic beliefs or a state of mind reserved for extraordinary moments; neither is it something we can possess or attain once and for all. Spirituality is a process, "a way of being in the world" (p. 29) to which we aspire. Traveling this path, we may discover for ourselves that we participate in "creating . . . the person we wish to be and the life we desire to lead" (p. 188). This is of far-reaching existential importance: our state of mind and spiritual beliefs and practices not only influence our personal lives but also impact the work we do and the individuals we wish to serve. A spiritual orientation may not only be good for us but for our clients as well.

Many colleagues from all over the country have reported personal experiences with the sacred and with spiritual practices—mostly in private, however. Not so the author of this book. I am awed by my friend Dorothy's courage and generosity in writing this volume and "going public" with her understandings. Fully aware that her "views . . . are outside the mainstream and . . . to express them is risky" (p. 59), she proceeds to elaborate and operationalize her perspective on the place of spirituality in our lives and of therapy as a spiritual path toward healing and personal growth.

This book is unique in several ways: The author uses a systemic lens and social constructionist framework to explore the context, meaning, and function of therapist/client spiritual values and beliefs. She provides a context for her perspective and translates her scholarship into specific processes that therapists might consider in helping dis-spirited clients make choices toward a more hopeful, "spirited" future. In addition, Dorothy does so with an integrity and a style that are rare in professional literature. Congruent with her profound belief that we always communicate our personal construction of "reality"—even when couched in abstract or analytical language—she enters into self-revealing dialogue with her readers. In the tradition of Virginia Satir, she modestly proposes that readers reflect on the issues with her, take from the discourse what fits, and discard what does not.

Throughout history, individuals who lived and proposed a spiritual path have courageously dared to be nonconformist and to challenge the prevailing orthodoxy. Dorothy stands in the tradition as a trailblazer and innovator. This book no doubt will stimulate vigorous discussion and dialogue; it may also prompt dissent. Whatever its reception, I believe that Dorothy proposes a redirection for the field that will be fully accepted and integrated in the years to come.

At the 1996 annual conference of the American Association for Marriage and Family Therapy, Monica McGoldrick reminisced about the field's past resistance to considering the importance of gender and diversity issues in people's lives. "How could we not see that it mattered?!" she exclaimed emphatically. I similarly believe that in the very near future the field will embrace the importance of spiritual issues in the work we do. I picture a time when professional education will include helping trainees clarify their own and explore their clients' spiritual orientation, and therapy will focus on an intentional utilization of the spiritual dimensions of fostering hope, meaning, and connectedness in everyday living. Ten, maybe 15 years from now, we very likely will be astounded by how we ever could have thought that spirituality did not matter. I expect that we will then return to this book as a pioneering classic.

—INGEBORG E. HAUG, D.MIN.

Preface

It has been said that life is what happens to you when you are making other plans. I must admit that I have similar feelings about this book. That is, although I have stayed with the original format, there is much about the proposed contents that has evolved and changed in the course of writing. In particular, I found that in order to be consistent with my own frame of reference I had to share a great deal more of my personal story than I originally had intended. Thus, in answer to a question posed to me by a friend about midway through the process regarding whether it would be a scholarly or an autobiographical account, I acknowledged that, in fact, it was both. Certainly this may seem strange in a book describing a therapeutic approach. However, it is logical given my belief that, in order to fully understand this approach, it is appropriate that you have an understanding not only of how it came to be but also of the many influences on its continuing evolution.

To explain, as a constructivist and a social constructionist, I operate from the perspective that we each create our own reality as a function of the larger socially constructed realities within which we live and work. Therefore, I believe it is necessary for me to make the lens through which I view the world and according to which I operate very clear. And as a systems theorist, one who sees interconnectedness and all behavior as logical within a given frame of reference, I also believe it is important to describe the context within which my story emerged and thus within which it fits or makes sense. In addition, as a therapist, I understand how important it is to provide concrete examples whenever possible. Accordingly, I have drawn case examples from my own experience to illustrate my ideas and to give you a sense of what my version of soul healing looks like in practice.

As you may have noticed, I use the word *story* to refer to the viewpoint I am presenting. Indeed, I would like you to know that, in my view, all that this book can represent is one story, mine, about the domain referred to as counseling/therapy. Similarly, I would like you to be aware from the outset that I consistently emphasize my belief that we create our reality as a function of our stories, and that as we tell different stories, we perceive a different reality. With that in mind, it is now time to provide you with a brief summary of what lies ahead.

Part I, "Theoretical Framework," which includes chapters 1, 2, and 3, describes the underpinnings of my view of counseling/therapy with a spiritual orientation. In chapter 1, "Pathways to the Present," I outline the important events and influences that have gone into the creation of my story. I begin with an overview of significant moments in my personal life. This discussion is followed by a consideration of influences derived from my professional training. In this chapter I also consider characteristics of the larger society at various points throughout my life as well as in terms of the current context within which we live and work. Of particular note is the development of a renewed interest in spirituality and greater acceptance of discussions of the soul in both professional writing and in lay literature. Finally, I offer some thoughts about where the conclusions that I have reached take me relative to a spiritual orientation in counseling/therapy—the process I think of as soul healing.

In chapter 2, "The Spiritual Path," I examine the meaning of various related ideas, considering spirituality as a concept distinct from that of religion and providing definitions of relevant terms. Also included in this chapter is a review of several spiritual perspectives on healing and a summary of the assumptions underlying a focus on soul healing. This is followed by the presentation of a model for understanding the interactions between belief system and experience for both client and therapist, the interactions between the client's spirituality and that of the therapist, and the impact of the larger therapeutic/spiritual context on the therapeutic relationship. This model provides a framework for weaving information from various perspectives into a coherent whole that therapists and counselors may understand and embrace without feeling they or their clients must abandon their particular belief systems. Finally, I explore specific ideas and behaviors relative to counseling/therapy with a spiritual orientation.

In chapter 3, "The Road to Soul Healing," I consider what caring for one's soul and the souls of others requires. Included in this discussion is an exploration of the ways in which we may enhance our knowledge and understanding in the realm of spirituality. I also examine the challenges associated with the use of diagnostic labeling and of a metaphoric understanding of illness. Emphasis is given to the ramifications of viewing problems as opportunities for learning, growth, and perhaps for achieving one's highest potential. Further, I discuss how to help clients become aware of the ability they may have to influence their own healing while at the same time avoiding guilt and self-blame about ill health, emotional problems, or both. This chapter concludes with a brief overview of the basic principles of soul healing that form the basis of Part II: acknowledging connectedness, suspending judgment, trusting the universe, creating realities, and walking the path with heart.

Part II, "Clinical Strategies," which includes chapters 4 through 8, provides descriptions of specific means by which therapists and counselors may incorporate a spiritual orientation, either implicitly or explicitly, in their work with clients. Strategies examined include the use of stories and storytelling, the creative arts, dream work, meditation and guided imagery, sensory exploration, dialogue with illness, and conversations about death and the meaning of life. Suggestions for helping clients create contexts that nurture and support wellness are provided, as are typical homework assignments that might be used. The explanations of these strategies are consistent with the basic principles of soul healing articulated at the end of chapter 3. Each chapter provides detailed descriptions of various situations drawn from practice that illustrate the incorporation of a spiritual orientation in counseling/therapy. Potential challenges and ethical issues also are discussed. Examples of work relative to a broad range of presenting problems and client configurations are utilized in order to offer helpful information to therapists and counselors operating from many different perspectives and working in many different kinds of settings.

The case examples and suggestions presented in chapter 4, "Acknowledging Connectedness," focus on ways in which therapists and counselors may enhance the experience of connectedness with their clients and thus cocreate a therapeutic relationship infused with a spiritual dimension, regardless of whether or not this dimension is explicitly acknowledged. Specific strategies discussed include learning to hear as well as engaging in self-disclosure and the sharing of one's own journey. Additional discussions focus on when and how to introduce the topic of spirituality into the conversation and how to proceed depending upon where the client is. The chapter concludes with a consideration of the ramifications, for therapy, of relationships in which connectedness is acknowledged.

In chapter 5, "Suspending Judgment," I discuss the utility of operating according to the systemic notion that all behavior, including that labeled as problematic, makes sense in context. I also describe some of the basic concepts and contributions of constructivist and social constructionist perspectives. While implicitly attending to the spiritual dimensions of altruism and the sacredness of all life, I give particular attention to the importance of accepting people where they are, assuming good intentions on the part of all, being in the moment, and helping clients to suspend judgment in order to support the cocreation of a context within which soul healing may be achieved.

The focus of chapter 6, "Trusting the Universe," is on the use of nonlocal, or universal, mind to provide guidance for the counseling/therapy process. Therapists and counselors are encouraged to access gut-level feelings and intuitive information, or both, about their clients. They also are provided with case material and exercises designed to help them learn how to facilitate faith in the process, educate intuition, explore dreams, integrate shamanic practices, and make use of oracles. The notion of balance between the physical and spiritual realms is addressed throughout the chapter and also comprises the topic of the closing discussion.

Considering a variety of ways in which counselors/therapists may participate in the creation of contexts to meet the unique needs of each client system is the goal of chapter 7, "Creating Realities." The issues of system perturbation, or mutual interaction and influence, as well as having recourse to sources of the random, or new information, particularly as related to spirituality, are thus discussed. As a crucial part in this process, I consider the ability to frame questions and offer reflections that provide different windows through which problems may be viewed and understood. Attention also is given to a focus on solutions, the importance of the role played by the counselor/therapist in the creation of realities, and ways to support clients in these processes. I conclude the chapter with a discussion of ethics and moral/ethical behavior.

Chapter 8, "Walking the Path with Heart," focuses on understanding, discerning, and choosing a life journey that is experienced as fulfilling at a soul level. Included are discussions of such issues as finding the meaning of life and death, the soul's purpose, facing terminal illness, dealing with grief and loss, and making difficult choices. The chapter closes with a consideration of the tension involved with living at two levels—the material and the spiritual—and of the challenge to integrate both in a meaningful way in order to experience a measure of ultimate satisfaction.

In Part III, "Conclusion," I consider the ramifications of counseling and therapy focused on healing at a soul level. That is, according to Maturana and Varela (1987, p. 245), "The *knowledge of knowledge* compels. . . . It compels us to see that the world will be different only if we live differently." Thus, if we practice counseling/therapy differently, we inevitably will create a different world for ourselves, for our clients and for society. Indeed, consideration of the potential outcomes may be the strongest argument for an incorporation of a spiritual orientation into counseling and therapy.

In chapter 9, "Continuing the Journey," I explore what might happen for both individuals and society if more of us were to undertake consciously, both in our professional and our private lives, the journey toward wholeness, which may be conceived of as a process of soul healing. Possible pitfalls that may be encountered along the spiritual path as well as suggestions for how to avoid or overcome them also are considered. A summary of the major themes in the book is provided as a map for those readers who wish to venture further into the territory referred to as soul healing. By way of conclusion, some final thoughts on the ramifications of a soul healing, spiritual orientation, both as we discuss the process of counseling/therapy and as we work with our clients, are presented.

Finally, in the afterword, I offer some further reflections on the process of writing this book and on including spirituality in the therapeutic conversation. Also included are acknowledgments of some very important people whose support has been invaluable to me. But more about that later. For now, I would like you to be aware that the perspective with which you are about to be presented represents a synthesis of ideas that have informed my work for a number of years. And it is very gratifying indeed that interest in and permission to discuss spirituality has increased to the point that it has become a credible topic within the mental health professions. Therefore, it is with great delight that I have engaged in the process of creating this book. My hope is that you will find that it informs your life and practice in ways that are meaningful for you as well.

—DOROTHY S. BECVAR, PH.D.
JUNE 1996

PART I

Theoretical Framework

Words lead to deeds. . . . They prepare the soul, make it ready, and move it to tenderness.

—SAINT THERESA

CHAPTER 1

Pathways to the Present

INTRODUCTION

W henever I meet with a new client I am keenly aware of how essential it is to establish a meaningful relationship. As I often remind my students, despite all the knowledge and skill a therapist may acquire, he or she can be helpful only if the client chooses to return. And that choice to return is based largely, I believe, on the experience the client has during the initial contact with the therapist. For similar reasons, I am mindful that the way in which I begin my story about spirituality and counseling/therapy is extremely important if you, the reader, are going to continue beyond the first few pages. While we obviously cannot meet face to face, you are ever present as I think about how to proceed. So, I ask myself what *you* would like to hear first. I wonder what *you* would find the most interesting and meaningful place to begin. And in this imaginary dialogue I speculate that you would prefer to learn initially about my personal background as it relates to spirituality in order to have it as a context within which to understand the professional and more theoretical aspects of my story. And so I begin with the personal narrative. Following this account, I provide you with an overview of the development of my professional/theoretical belief system. Finally, I conclude this chapter with a survey of the larger context and a look at aspects of society that have influenced the development of a renewed interest in spirituality and greater acceptance of discussions of the soul and spirituality in conjunction with the healing of both mental and physical problems.

As noted in the preface, I use the word *story* rather than theory, and I use it to refer not only to my perspective but also to those of others. I also sometimes use *story* as a verb. For it is my belief that all I or anyone else can offer about any topic is a personal construction, whether of events, experiences, ideas, beliefs, theories, or truth—with a lower-case *t*. Further, I believe that how we story, or create, our reality is done as a function of our personal narratives, and thus that believing is seeing. All of this will be discussed more fully as we proceed. At this point, however, let me invite you to have a brief look at my world.

THE PERSONAL PATH

Although I will spare you the long and detailed version of my history, I do want to start at the beginning and share some highlights that I believe provide important information. I grew up in suburban Philadelphia, the third of four children of very traditional parents—my father worked outside the home; my mother, except for brief periods of "rebellion," worked inside the home. My ethnic heritage is largely Germanic, and life in our household tended to be structured. Tasks were divided along gender lines, with my two brothers doing such things as emptying the trash and taking care of the yard and my sister and I having responsibility for doing the dishes and other household tasks. There was tremendous emphasis on the importance of the family, and although I wouldn't describe the relationship between my mother and father as particularly happy, divorce was unthinkable. When my father died at the age of 85, my parents had been married for 55 years.

In terms of religion, we were Lutheran, and regular church attendance was a family rule. Apparently this had a profound effect on me, for I can remember from my earliest years having a sense of faith in a transcendent phenomenon, known to me at that time as God. And three events related to spirituality particularly stand out in my mind as I think back on my childhood. One was a sermon in which the minister told of how the parents of a sick child had prayed repeatedly for healing, but to no avail. It was only when they were able to pray, "Thy will be done," that the child began to recover. I was truly moved by this story, which influenced my belief both in the power of prayer and in the importance of letting go of control.

The second event may well have followed this same sermon, although I am not sure. In any case, I had been intrigued by the service one Sunday morning, and that afternoon I went to my room and arranged it as best I could to look like a church. I then proceeded to pretend that I was a minister and began to deliver—to my dolls—a sermon I had written. When my father realized what I was doing, he scolded me, probably in the belief that my behavior was sacrilegious, for he had a strict code about what was right and wrong. Although that incident ended a rather brief career in the ministry, a strong spiritual orientation remained.

The third event is associated with my confirmation at the age of 13. I can remember that participation in confirmation preparation class was a far more serious undertaking for me than for many of my peers, and I felt a sense of great awe and mystery during my first experience of holy Communion. Thus, somehow, spirituality was an important aspect of my being from a very early age.

However, despite the fact that as a teenager I was a member of several church youth groups, my focus was largely on the more secular and social rather than the religious aspects of these associations. Indeed, my high school years proved to be a busy time for me, and my days were filled not only with homework but also with field hockey, women's lacrosse, tennis, basketball, swimming, the school newspaper, the yearbook, cheerleading, and spending time with my friends. I am one of the lucky ones in that, despite my share of the usual crises and problems, I had a good time during my early years and I would describe myself as having had a pretty "normal" childhood. At the same time, I was always in a hurry to grow up and was eager to go to college when the time finally came.

I entered Cornell University in 1959 and was so totally involved from day one that I regularly had to be reminded to call or write home. This was an interesting time to be going off to college, and I will never forget the professor of political science who harangued us incoming freshmen about being part of a generation that was too complacent about social issues. I believe he was correct in his assessment, and certainly I was a classic case in point. However, by the time I left, four years later, the civil rights movement was well under way, and I had participated not only in creating the mandate requiring all fraternities and sororities to do away with discriminatory practices but also in my sorority becoming the first on campus to revise its constitution accordingly. Nevertheless, my major in government notwithstanding, my days as a social activist also were short-lived.

Four months after graduation I married and within four years had two children, a son and a daughter. After a year in Boston, we moved to Philadelphia, near where I had grown up and where my sister and both brothers were still living. The traditional family pattern was repeating: my husband worked outside the home, and I was content to be a stay-at-home wife and mother. I was active in the PTA, alumni affairs, and community activities and thoroughly enjoyed spending time with my children. Believing that I had found my niche, I was totally and happily preoccupied with my domestic duties throughout the remainder of the '60s and early '70s and had little real involvement with the turbulent events that were unfolding around me. However, the ramifications of the changing social order literally were brought home when my husband decided that he wanted to leave the marriage.

Although divorce stories such as mine are rather common today, at the time it was still somewhat unusual and, given my background, was nearly beyond my comprehension. Further, although all three of my siblings ultimately experienced divorce, I was the first in my family to do so, and the task of breaking the news to my parents was an extremely difficult part of the process. But the greatest challenge was to figure out how to, first, just go on, and then, second, how to rebuild my life. My children were 7 and 9 years old and the only post-college job experience I had was 9 months as an executive secretary 11 years earlier. However, it soon became imperative for me to go to work, and I was fortunate in that at least I had a college degree.

My first paid employment was as a management trainee for Household Finance Corporation. It didn't take me long to realize that, despite my title, I was basically a glorified bill collector. While I despised having to try to collect money from people who didn't have it, I found I loved listening to their stories and helping them figure out ways to keep the wolves—like me—from their door.

After six months I was able to leave that job and instead took an assignment as an aide in the adolescent unit of a school for children with learning disabilities. This position was much more to my liking, but it also had its frustrations. I basically ran the unit for a talented but somewhat disorganized supervisor and at much less pay. In addition, there was little involvement with the families of the students, and few of the changes that occurred as a function of the school's work with the children were very long lasting. Aware that I needed further training but unsure of the specific direction in which to go, I began taking courses in both social work and education. At the same time I also became involved through my church with Family Clustering, which proved to be a significant turning point in my life.

To explain, while I was married, our church attendance had been sporadic at best and generally occurred only on holidays or other significant occasions, such as baptisms and weddings. However, after my divorce I switched my affiliation from the Lutheran church to the Episcopal church and became much more conscientious about attending in a more conscious way both to my own spirituality and to my children's religious education. I began to teach Sunday school and participated in the complete overhaul of the church's educational programming. It was not long before I was invited by the assistant rector to colead a Family Cluster.

Family Clustering is a model developed by Margaret Sawin (1979, 1982) for church-based work with groups of families aimed at enhancing their internal dynamics and ability to function. After I participated in coleading several clusters, the church underwrote my attendance at a weeklong training seminar led by Dr. Sawin. Although I didn't know it at the time, this was my first official preparation for a career as a family therapist, and it was through Family Clustering that I would meet my second husband, Ray.

In 1976 I was a member of a four-person team, which also included the assistant rector of the church I attended, his wife, and Margaret Sawin, who presented a preconference institute at the annual conference of the American Association for Marriage and Family Counselors, held that year in Philadelphia. Ray, a confirmed bachelor, attended the institute at the insistence of one of his closest friends, and at the end of the day asked me if I would be interested in having lunch with him sometime during the conference. I agreed, thinking I probably would never see him again since he lived in St. Louis and I was still living in Philadelphia. However, to use the words of C. S. Lewis, I was "surprised by joy," and lunch evolved into a two-year long-distance relationship. We now have been happily married for 18 years.

By the time that Ray and I were married, I had sorted out my professional goals and had decided to get a master's degree in social work and to become a family therapist. So, two weeks after marrying and moving with my children to St. Louis, I started graduate school at St. Louis University. While my desire to become a family therapist never changed, I was soon bitten by the teaching bug and ultimately decided to pursue a doctorate as well. I received my M.S.W. in 1980 and my Ph.D. in family studies in 1983. After a year in private practice, during which time I was an adjunct instructor at several colleges, I took a position as a visiting assistant professor at the University of Missouri–St. Louis. A year later I became an assistant professor at St. Louis University, working alongside my husband, who was a full professor there and the person responsible for starting a doctoral program in marriage and family therapy in the Department of Education.

St. Louis University is a Jesuit institution, and during my years as a graduate student and a faculty member there, I found it to be extremely supportive of spiritual explorations in a variety of areas. While at this point my views were generally rather traditional, I had been exposed during my master's degree program to Eastern metaphysical traditions. My multidisciplinary doctoral program also included course work in theology as a core component. When I became an instructor, students soon became aware that they could come and talk with me about their ideas in the spiritual realm, regardless of how different they might seem to be. They learned that, as a systems thinker, I espoused the notion of theoretical relativity, the idea that every theory has utility relative to con-text. They knew that I would not scoff at their beliefs however far they strayed from the traditional, although nontraditional spirituality was not part of my personal belief system at that time.

That is, I had done a fair amount of reading, including particularly the books of Carlos Castaneda, and I was always open to hearing and learning about new ideas. I also had a good friend who had been delving into the areas of hypnosis, self-hypnosis, and meditation. He had ventured into the realm of Jane Roberts and the "Seth" material and had begun exploring reincarnation, past lives, and other concepts that were certainly less than traditional in Western society. In addition, he had a gift, which today I would call psychic. However, although I knew of his curiosity and explorations in this area, about which he talked freely, I didn't pay a great deal of attention in terms of my personal pursuits. While it was certainly fine for him, it just wasn't where my interests lay.

An area that was of great interest to me was quantum physics. In fact, in 1986, I applied to the Kellogg Foundation for a fellowship that was offered in support of study in a discipline outside the faculty member's primary area of expertise. My desire was to focus on quantum physics, which for me parallels my study of systems theory. I didn't get the fellowship but I continued to read and explore the topic anyway, and as you will learn in later discussions, quantum physics plays an important part in my story about spirituality. For now, however, I will continue describing some of the major influences on the development of my personal frame of reference, particularly as they relate to spirituality.

I remember very distinctly being in a grocery store one day during this time in my life and wondering why it was that I never really had questioned my own traditional religious beliefs and what I considered to be a very strong faith. Despite having weathered the experience of divorce, which for me was traumatic, I hadn't felt compelled to doubt the existence of God. Rather, I had become more involved in the church and felt truly blessed, for I was now happier than I had ever been in my life. However, things changed, and ultimately I did do some rather serious questioning as a function of several other major upheavals in my life.

In July 1987, Ray and I decided to resign our positions at St. Louis University in order to join the faculty of Texas Tech University. This was to be a significant change, for at that point Ray had been at St. Louis University for 18 years, and I had been there two years. In addition to teaching, we both worked part-time as marriage and family therapists, and we were deeply rooted in St. Louis. Nevertheless, a career move seemed appropriate, and the opportunity to join the doctoral program in marriage and family therapy at Texas Tech seemed to warrant the change. At the time, my daughter, Lynne, was 20 and had just finished her sophomore year at the University of Connecticut. She was majoring in psychology and had just been made captain of the basketball team and been awarded a full scholarship. My son, John, who was 22 and had graduated from Cornell University the previous summer, was working full-time doing cancer research at St. Louis Children's Hospital, which is part of the Washington University Medical Center. Although John planned eventually to go to medical school, he had become a professional triathlete, and during nights, weekends and basically all of his spare time, he trained and competed in a sport he truly loved. We were all doing well, enjoying each other and our world and looking forward to what promised to be a very bright future. But life does not always turn out the way we think it will or should.

On Saturday, August 22, John got up early as usual, ate breakfast, and left with a friend to swim, bike, and then run. It was a beautiful sunny day and he was with a companion, so I felt a little less anxious than was normal for me when he didn't return in the early afternoon. At about 3 P.M., however, I received the phone call every parent dreads. Both young men were in the hospital, having been hit by a truck while biking on a backcountry road. Although John's friend was seriously injured, we quickly learned that he would be all right. John's situation was far more precarious as he had been biking in the lead when the accident occurred and was hit head-on. Following several hours of surgery he remained unconscious, and on Sunday afternoon he died.

During the 26 hours that John lived while in the hospital, mostly in intensive care, the friend whom I mentioned earlier—our psychic friend, who was into the Seth material and metaphysics—was with us. He never saw John during that time, but he was able to tell me what was going on with my son, things that were later validated by the doctors. He also was able to do some healing with me that allowed me to tolerate an almost unbearable experience. I don't know that I did it well, but I did tolerate it and I have survived it. However, it was still a devastating event for me, certainly the worst of my life, although today I have a somewhat different perspective on it as part of the shift in my thinking about spirituality.

For me, losing one of my beloved children seemed to be more than I could handle, and the days and months that followed were the darkest of my life. Somehow, initially, we completed all the appropriate arrangements but many of the decisions we subsequently made were less than brilliant, at least in hindsight. We had a vigil at the church on Tuesday evening and a memorial service celebrating John's life on Wednesday morning. On Friday we drove my daughter, Lynne, the 18 hours back to college in Connecticut. On Sunday we made the return trip to St. Louis. On Monday and Tuesday, with the help of friends, we loaded a rented moving van with many of our things and tried to tie up loose ends. On Wednesday and Thursday we drove, with our dog curled up at our feet, the 18 hours it took to get to Lubbock, Texas. We had the weekend to get settled in but the semester had already begun, so on the following Monday, we went back to work.

To say the least, it was not a good time to manage so much change. We had moved into a totally new situation—new city, new home, new jobs, new everything—and had little energy for any of it. Ray set about doing things, anything. My pattern was to teach my classes and come home and cry. I slept very little. Nothing made sense anymore and I could find no answers. I had a brief moment of peace following a conversation with the rector of my church just before moving. Contrary to some of the things I had been hearing, he shared his belief that God didn't want my son to die, that in fact, he thought, "God is crying with you." However, I still had some big questions about how this could have happened. I searched for answers in books, reading everything I could get my hands on. I also started writing a journal, which at least provided me with an outlet for my feelings. While I didn't get angry at God, I sure didn't have a story that allowed me to make sense of what was for me a totally unbeliev-able experience.

At the end of six weeks Ray and I went back to St. Louis for our first visit. Despite the change in circumstances, we had stayed with our origi-nal plan, which was to keep our house and return once a month to check in on things. And the second night we were in St. Louis, we visited with the same friend who had been with us in the hospital, the man whom I described as being psychic. After dinner, he came and sat directly in front of me and in a very deliberate manner said, "I have a message for you."

I said, "OK," although I had no idea what he was talking about or what to expect. With that, however, he began to talk to me about other levels of reality, saying some rather bizarre things. As you may recall, I had had a nodding acquaintance with Eastern religions and meta-physics, but little meaningful experience in these areas. Nevertheless, the words of my friend were, "What has happened, John's death, is something that the four of you—you and Ray and Lynne and John—have agreed to at another level, at a soul level. You have agreed that this is an appropriate path for each of you to take and that what it's about is growth, for all of you. And your challenge"—here, he looked at me—"is to stay here, to make sense out of this, to grow, and to go on. One day, you have the potential to rediscover great joy in your life."

Although it all sounded strange to me, and I certainly didn't feel very joyful, my experience was that I began to yawn and to relax. And that night I slept, deeply, for the first time since John's death. Somehow, at an intuitive level, what I was hearing made sense and seemed right. I imme-diately wanted to know more, and so it was that I began what I think of today as a spiritual quest for understanding. In the process, I made signif-icant shifts in my personal belief system. However, it took one more ma-jor life event to complete this move into different ways of thinking.

Although I finally had found a story that was helpful, for the most part I was still in the depths of despair. I was too far away from my daughter, who I knew was suffering desperately. Ray and I were very much alone, separated as we were from the wonderful network of sup-port we had left behind in St. Louis. There was no peace in our lives, and it was a challenge to get through each day. The months passed, and we managed to struggle through John's birthday as well as our first Thanks-giving and Christmas without him. But everything had lost its meaning and, I now believe, I was giving up on life, although not consciously.

In February 1988, just six months from the day that John died, I found a lump in my breast. As I shared my discovery and my fears with Ray, I lay on the bed crying. But in that moment I also made a crucial decision. I realized that I did not want to die, and I told Ray that I truly wanted to live. I asked him to help me do just that, even if I had cancer. It didn't take long for us to go into action. We found a doctor who examined me and suggested I get a mammogram. Waiting for the results was one of the most nerve-racking times I can remember. However, the radiologist reported, "No sign of malignancy," and my doctor concluded that it must be a cyst, just as he had suspected. Needless to say, I experienced incredible relief. I also decided that I would begin a process of trying to heal myself. I had a lot of support in this area from friends who provided me with tapes, sessions in guided imagery, and books to read. Although the lump didn't go away, I am sure that I had begun the journey back to health.

Two months later I returned to the doctor's office with a horrible case of the flu. The doctor also rechecked the lump and said that since it hadn't changed, I needed to see a surgeon. After that, things began to move very quickly. When the surgeon's attempt to remove the lump by aspiration was unsuccessful, he scheduled me for a biopsy the following week, assuring me that although he didn't think it was malignant, the growth needed to be removed. When I awoke in the recovery room, I could hear the nurses telling other patients that their lumps had been benign and everything was fine. When I asked for the results of my biopsy, I was told that I would have to ask my doctor. I knew the diagnosis. But I also knew I would be fine, too.

I knew I would be fine because about a month previously I had had a dream which, at the time, I had not been able to decipher but which now, suddenly, made perfect sense. In the dream John and I were swimming together, something we had often done during the last year of his life. This time, however, it was nighttime and we were making our way across a dark channel. Although I couldn't see John, I knew he was there, behind me, urging me on. It was rough going, and I had to dodge large ships that were navigating through the channel we were trying to cross. Eventually, after an arduous workout, I got to the other side. It was now bright daylight, and a large crowd of people was waiting for me and cheering my success because I had made it!

Having had this dream, I was the one who, ironically, wound up reassuring my family and friends that I wasn't going to die and telling them they could put aside their fears and long faces. And it didn't take long for me to demonstrate the truth of my conviction. When I went into the Methodist hospital in Lubbock, Texas, on Tuesday morning, I still was recovering from the flu. That afternoon, following the biopsy, I developed a bladder infection. The next day, Wednesday, I had a modified radical mastectomy. However, my surgeon immediately reported that I had come through it all beautifully, and he agreed with me that I probably was going to have nothing more than a sore chest. I chose not to hear the pathologist's report, informing him that I was not a statistic. On Saturday morning I was discharged from the hospital. Ten days later, I flew back to St. Louis in order to undergo chemotherapy and continue to heal myself with the help of my very loving and caring spouse and friends.

The six months of chemotherapy definitely were challenging, but I used the time to continue, in earnest, my exploration into other realms of consciousness, and into different belief systems and various religious and spiritual traditions. I read constantly and started attending workshops related to my new interests. I gradually began to see clients again, something I hadn't been inclined to do since John's death. I swam and did my exercises, and it wasn't long before I had regained full mobility in my arm, which had been impaired by the surgery. I began meditating. I also had regular sessions of hypnosis and guided imagery, and my experience of side effects from the chemotherapy was minimal. Above all, I embraced healing, perfect health, and life, which became my mantra whenever I felt myself becoming afraid. Each of these pursuits helped me create a new story which has facilitated my going on in a way that feels meaningful, and which I am able to share with my clients as appropriate. It is that story which I describe to you in this book, along with ideas which, I hope, may be helpful to you in your life and in your work. Although I will expand on this idea, the summary version of where all of this has taken me, both personally and professionally, is to the belief that not only therapy, but all of life, is a spiritual experience. While this may seem a great leap, it was for me a rather small step given my theoretical orientation, the evolution of which I describe in the following section.

THE PROFESSIONAL PATH

The theoretical foundation that guides my professional work has evolved over many years and as a function of a variety of learning experiences, both in and out of the classroom. Once again, however, I will merely touch on the highlights, this time of significant aspects of my formal education. Following this discussion I will provide a delineation of the basics of my personal paradigm, the epistemological lens through which I view the world and according to which I currently live and work.

As an undergraduate student, I experienced a true liberal arts education, majoring in government and minoring in history. While I was not prepared for a career in a specific area, I was exposed to a variety of disciplines and came away with a love for both the process of learning and the academic environment, although at the time I never entertained the thought that I might one day return as a professor. I find it worthy of note that as I was completing my graduate education and making plans to join a university faculty I realized I also had come full circle in another way. That is, I was once again dealing with crucial issues related to the larger social context, the area that had been my primary focus during my bachelor's degree program. However, there was a 15-year hiatus between my undergraduate and graduate schooling and my education during that period of time, though of no less value, was of a very different nature. Indeed, I found returning to the university context as a "mature" student to be both exciting and challenging, and I felt myself to be at a distinct advantage as a function of the life experience I had acquired in the interim.

I chose to pursue a master's degree in social work at St. Louis University, with the goal of being able to work with families. Thus I was on a direct practice, or clinical track, from the outset. I had few elective options, but one of my most crucial curriculum decisions was to take a course in the philosophy of the behavioral sciences during my first semester as a graduate student. It was in this course that I was introduced to Gregory Bateson and the systemic/cybernetic paradigm. Although I was often scoffed at by my social work professors because of my interest in systems theory and family therapy, it was a conceptual framework that was immediately comfortable to me. Along with all of its other basic assumptions, it provided me with a "both/and" perspective from which it was possible to acknowledge the importance and validity of many different ways of knowing, a view that continues to be essential to my belief system.

Toward the end of my master's degree program I was given the assignment, which I experienced as extremely meaningful, to describe the theoretical influences on the development of my epistemology and to articulate my personal and professional frame of reference. In rereading it today I find that much of what I wrote at that time continues to describe my current belief system. However, further additions certainly have been made as a function of both my doctoral studies and subsequent explorations on my own following completion of my Ph.D.

My decision to pursue a doctoral degree was clinched when I fell in love with teaching. While still a student in the master's degree program, I was hired as an adjunct faculty member, and it didn't take me long to realize that a career in academia, which would also allow me to continue my clinical work, was what I wanted. For a variety of reasons, I chose a multidisciplinary program that enabled me to create my own curriculum in family studies and to select as my faculty advisers and doctoral committee a representative of each of the five disciplines included in my program: education, social psychology, sociology and anthropology, social work, and theology. Although certainly not the short way to do things, this provided an enormously rich and varied experience that allowed me to focus on the areas of greatest interest to me with some of the best faculty at St. Louis University. My doctoral dissertation was a philosophical exploration entitled "The Relationship Between the Family and Society in the Context of American Ideology: A Systems Theoretical Perspective."

Following graduation, I continued to teach at several universities on an adjunct basis and worked full-time as a marriage and family therapist. In 1984, I received my first full-time academic appointment and continued doing therapy on a part-time basis. Now, 11 years and five academic positions later, I am once again doing therapy on a full-time basis and teaching on a part-time basis. While most of my learning in the intervening years has come through the process of teaching, I also have participated in a wide variety of training experiences. In the early years of my career the focus of the workshops I attended was primarily marriage and family therapy. In more recent years, I have shifted to an emphasis on holistic health and healing and the mind/body connection, the newly emerging field of psychoneuroimmunology. In addition, I have explored the area of non-drug-induced altered states of consciousness and also have spent two years doing formal study on the subject of metaphysics. The following is an attempt to articulate, in summary fashion, my basic assumptions and beliefs as they have evolved to this point.

Indeed, I must begin this overview by saying that perhaps my primary goal has always been that my theoretical framework be an ongoing, emergent process rather than a static entity, with continued growth and openness to change the most sought-after constants. On the other hand, with the passage of time and the assimilation of each new bit of learning, I am increasingly aware that there is nothing new under the sun. Hence, to represent my personal and professional philosophy, I would choose the metaphor of a tree, which grows and develops while also responding in an ever-recurring cycle of death and life—one of the "patterns that connect" (Bateson, 1979). Since I am by my own admission an idealist as well as an optimist (I refer to my idealism and optimism as an inherent ability to positively reframe), it seems only fitting that while my philosophical roots are well planted in terra firma, my upper extremities be a bit in the clouds. Finally, not far in the background of my metaphorical tree, and represented for me by a sun/smiley face, is humor, that essential ingredient which warms and unites and makes the impossible possible—a representative of as well as a solution to the paradoxes of existence.

I am and have been for many years a proponent of a postmodernist, cybernetics of cybernetics, constructivist, social-constructionist perspective. To explain, rather than seeing the world as something "out there" that can be understood in terms of independent and objectively observed linear, cause-effect sequences, I think in terms of circularity and recursion, of patterns and process, and acknowledge the inevitable subjectivity of my perceptions and their influence on the creation of my reality. For me, the observer is part of the observed. My story took root early on in the notion of a "constantly conjoined universe" (Bronowski, 1978), according to which an ultimate truth is not accessible to us. Thus I understand a fundamental paradox of existence to be that while we may know "truth," assuming that it exists, we are doomed to know that what we know may not be the truth or that while it may be the truth, we cannot assert it as such in an absolute sense. In Bateson's words, "[W]e shall never be able to claim final knowledge of anything whatsoever" (1979, p. 27). Rollo May has called this the "human dilemma," or "the capacity of man to see himself as both subject and object" (1967, p. 20).

Accordingly, I do not believe in the possibility of absolute objectivity, but rather see all knowledge as personal (Polanyi, 1958) and all experience as subjective (Bateson, 1979). I believe that we make distinctions based on our own frames of reference and that we punctuate reality according to these epistemological premises (Keeney, 1983). I subscribe to the notion of reality as personally constructed in the context of consensual domains (Maturana & Varela, 1987) that are structured in and by language (Gergen, 1991). That is, language is understood as the means by which individuals come to know their world and, in their knowing, simultaneously to create it. Thus, for me, mind and nature become inseparable.

An important early influence on the development of my perspective was the work of George Kelly, author of *The Psychology of Personal Constructs*. Kelly (1955) proposed that "man-the-scientist" be seen as construing his world in a continual process of successive approximations. According to this process of "constructive alternativism" by which development occurs, the individual chooses between alternatives and tests his construct system in order to determine its predictive efficiency. The individual, therefore, is not bound to the past but rather becomes a bridge between the past and the future. That is, one may learn from past experience, and present representations are all subject to revision or replacement as one anticipates the future. I have found this process strikingly similar to that described by Thomas Kuhn (1970) regarding paradigm change in the scientific community. As Kuhn notes in his book *The Structure of Scientific Revolutions*:

> But paradigm debates are not really about relative problem-solving ability, though for good reasons they are usually couched in those terms. Instead, the issue is which paradigm should in the future guide research on problems many of which neither competitor can yet claim to resolve completely. A decision between alternate ways of practicing science is called for, and in the circumstances that decision must be based less on past achievement than on future promise. (pp. 157–158)

Kelly's basic assumption was that both the universe and the individual must be viewed along the dimension of time, and that each of us has the creative capacity to represent that universe rather than being doomed to respond to it. Kelly regarded all individuals as scientists whose ultimate aim is to predict and control their world by placing alternate constructions on it. Today these views seem consistent with the conceptions of those mental health professionals who espouse what has been termed a postmodern perspective.

As I have noted here, another fundamental aspect of my story, arrived at fairly early on, is the concept of theoretical relativity. That is, in thinking about counseling/therapy, I do not judge any theoretical framework, personal or otherwise, in terms of whether it is right or wrong, good or bad. The more important consideration is the usefulness of a theory, which for me is something that can be decided only relative to context. In the manner of Richard Bernstein (1978), I prefer not to make exclusive either/or choices and instead choose to integrate what I perceive to be useful, and to reject, based on my perceptions, what is not, while striving for more comprehensive understanding of the whole.

As Bateson has cautioned, I remain concerned with presuppositions in an effort to avoid "pathologies of epistemology" (Bateson, 1972) or logical inconsistencies. And the methodology of transcendental phenomenology has provided me with a format for self-referential argumentation by means of which I may do just that. Thus the key issue for me is to discern the basic assumptions upon which a given theory is based and to delineate those knowledge claims made by that theory which are or are not justifiable. To the extent that our attention is directed to conditions of possibility, I therefore concur with Husserl (1965, p. 122), who wrote: "The critical separation of the psychological and phenomenological methods shows that the latter is the true way to a scientific theory of reason."

I am a systems theorist through and through and have even been referred to as a systems purist. While I believe in the dignity and worth of the individual, my focus is on the relationships of individuals to one another and on their context. I do not believe it is fruitful to consider only individuals and groups in isolation. Rather, I support a view (Bertalanffy, 1968) that includes all the societies of the earth, and perhaps beyond. And yet I acknowledge the importance of every individual, for each has an impact on and feels the impact of the system as a whole. Further, for me the whole is defined as a multiverse (Maturana & Varela, 1987) of individual perspectives rather than as a universe, and thus the importance of each person is retained.

I believe that individual identities emerge in the context of interactions and that it is our perception-determining beliefs that define and participate in the creation of reality. Thus an analysis of behavior change from a metaperspective, a view whose focus is on the level of process, which bypasses "why" and focuses on "what" (Watzlawick, Weakland, & Fisch, 1974), is basic to my philosophical framework. Similarly, I am concerned with the levels of communication and learning as well as the way in which information is perceived and processed. Operating, as I do, from the framework of second-order cybernetics, I believe that the observer and the observed are inseparable, and that the most I may do is participate in the perturbation of the system. For me, change in context is a cocreation of all participants. Consistent with my systemic perspective, I see causality as circular or reciprocal, as residing in the interface between individuals and systems. Similarly, I perceive responsibility as mutual, and control as a bilateral process. In sum, I believe we are all involved in each other's destinies.

Professionally, all of this translates into a concern for families, as the basic unit of socialization, with an emphasis on the ecology of human development (Bronfenbrenner, 1979), which takes into consideration "interactions between learning environments and human growth and development" (Blocher, 1974, p. 17). I operate with a strengths-based, solution-oriented focus, and my emphasis is on enrichment, or an enhancement of the quality of life of all individuals, especially as this is played out within the context of the family and other systems. An overriding concern and caution throughout my career has been the extent to which we social scientists and mental health professionals may be a part of the problem rather than of its solution (Becvar, Becvar, & Bender, 1982).

My beliefs about change have been most influenced by the Bateson group in Palo Alto and their studies of schizophrenic communication (Bateson, 1972). Indeed, it was Bateson, an anthropologist, who provided the link between systems theory and human development by focusing on schizophrenia as an interpersonal phenomenon rather than viewing it as an intrapsychic disorder of the individual that secondarily influences interpersonal relationships. The concept of the double bind, which describes communicational dynamics characterizing the families of persons diagnosed with schizophrenia and which emerged from the work of the Bateson group, represented a monumental breakthrough in the behavioral sciences, despite the elements of linearity it retained. Further, the investigations of its creators into the workings of hypnosis, the role of logical typing, and paradox formation and resolution in human communication spawned a wealth of research into and information about problem solving and behavioral change (Bateson, 1972; Haley, 1963, 1973; Lederer & Jackson, 1968; Watzlawick, 1978; Watzlawick et al., 1974) that I have found exceedingly valuable as I strive for greater understanding and effectiveness as a helper and as a facilitator of change. For me, a guiding principle continues to be the assumption that change equals a change in context and that fundamental to this process is the role of perception in the creation of contexts, and hence in the construction of reality.

I also have been influenced heavily by the stories about consciousness that grew out of split-brain research and a heightened interest in Eastern philosophy and altered states of consciousness. Robert Ornstein (1976) was the social scientist who provided for me the initial bridge between Western psychology and the so-called esoteric traditions. In so doing, he opened up many new doors with the challenge that we direct our attention to such things as the "education of intuition" and right-brain, nonlogical modes of learning and understanding. More recently, work in the area of psychoneuroimmunology

(Maier, Watkins, & Fleshner, 1994) has provided scientific validation for my belief that the mind and body are inseparable and that rather than referring to each separately, it is more appropriate to speak of the body/mind. Indeed, Candace Pert (1986; Horrigan, 1995), whose research has focused on neuropeptides and who sees consciousness as residing in all of our cells, states that she is no longer able to make a distinction between the brain and the body. Thus, as I have moved further and further into this area, I have found myself in agreement with the following principles, which outline a holistic perspective on health and healing:

1. There is a continuous interplay between our thoughts, emotions, and our physical and emotional state of health and well-being.
2. Each of us has primary responsibility for our life and thus for our health.
3. Since the mind and the emotions play a large part in the creation of dis-ease, they also can be employed in the healing process.
4. The body/mind has an intelligence of its own. Each cell has the wisdom and inclination to carry out its particular function, which may be negatively or positively influenced consistent with the messages received.
5. The body/mind speaks to us and can be our teacher if we are willing to learn. Pain, discomfort, and disease provide information about conflict and disharmony.
6. It is important to consider the symptoms of illness at a variety of levels, including the mental, the physical, the emotional and the spiritual/soul levels.
7. The inner self, or the self at the spiritual/soul level, is always seeking to grow.
8. Harmony and the reduction or elimination of conflict are facilitated by desire, by a willingness actively to pursue these states, and by self-awareness.
9. What appears to be an illness may actually be the necessary by-product of a deeper level of healing. As we heal holistically, we go through periods of detoxification that may be experienced as temporary discomfort.
10. Each of us knows his or her body/mind better than anyone else. By learning to listen within, we also become our own greatest healers. (Adapted from an unpublished paper by Rhonda Leifheit.)

All of these principles will be discussed at greater length in subsequent chapters. For now, however, it is important to note that it was quantum physics which, for me, provided the link between my systemic perspective and conclusions such as those I have enumerated. That is, from a systems perspective, one views the universe and all of its components as a continuum of nested and interconnected holons (Koestler, 1978). From the smallest particle to the level of the entire cosmos, interdependence and mutual influence are the rule, and consciousness is understood as all pervasive. The news from quantum physics is that perhaps this is indeed the way the universe may accurately be described. Further, the findings of researchers not only validate this perspective but move us into the realm of spirituality. The following is a brief summary of arguments in support of this conclusion.

According to Paul Davies (1983), the universe is creative and has organized its own self-awareness. Erwin Schrodinger (1967) speaks of the hidden oneness of all human minds. John Wheeler (1973) describes a symbiosis of mind and matter and the notion that "the universe is preselected by consciousness." The uncertainty principle of Werner Heisenberg (1971) would have us be aware that the observer's consciousness influences what is being observed. David Bohm (1980) writes that the information of the entire universe is contained in each of its parts. Karl Pribram (1971) sees the brain as a hologram which perceives and participates in a holographic universe. Ilya Prigogine (1980) describes the capacity for self-transcendence exhibited by all self-organizing systems. Rupert Sheldrake (1981) speaks of a memory process in nature, which he terms "morphic resonance." And the Gaia (1979) hypothesis of James Lovelock defines the earth as a living entity. All of which can be summed up in the notion that there is an overarching pattern to the universe and that there is something divine about the way it all fits together:

> [T]he new scientific worldview that has emerged in the twentieth century agrees with what mystics and spiritual masters have been telling us for thousands of years. We are One. Not in just some trivial sense, but at the essential core of our beings. Everything is alive. Matter is not the solid stuff it appears to be; it is a stable form of energy. We are dynamic patterns of cosmic energy, connected to the whole of life in some wonderfully mysterious way. (Fields, Taylor, Weyler, & Ingrasci, 1984, p. 203)

It is therefore my conclusion that, whether looking at the separation of mind and body, competing epistemologies, relationship splits, divisions between nations, or failure to recognize the connections between people and their environments, it is possible to transcend dichotomies, to think holistically, and to see the pattern that connects. A closer look at this perspective reveals its spiritual dimensions, or in Bateson's words, "sacred unity" and "the peculiarities of the god whom we might call Eco" (Bateson & Bateson, 1987, p. 142).

I do not believe in accidents. I do believe that mind is nonlocal (Dossey, 1989), or universal, and that we dwell in consciousness. Echoing the words of Alan Watts (1972), for me, body is in soul. Our challenge as human beings is to evolve and grow through the recognition and living in awareness of the divine essence of which each of us is an expression. Hence my belief that all of life, including therapy, is a spiritual process in which each of us is engaged, whether consciously or not. However, I will postpone further discussion of these conclusions at this point. For now, having presented you with an overview of my personal and professional history, as well as the basics of my belief system, I would like to consider the social context within which the latter evolved, including a look at some of the developments in the larger society relative to spirituality.

THE SOCIAL CONTEXT

I was born just a few months before the bombing of Pearl Harbor to parents who had come of age during the Great Depression. I entered college during the Eisenhower era and graduated and married just as the civil rights, the "hippie," and the women's liberation movements had gotten under way. I bore my children and was focused primarily on parenting during the period of the Vietnam war and the protests against it. I was divorced at a time when women still could not get credit cards in their own name if they were married, and it was not yet commonplace to be a single parent. I became a social worker and a family therapist just as the country entered the Reagan era, with its cuts in public spending. I began investigating the connections between science and spirituality during the period when the two were still considered to be separate realms, and Freud's view that religion is the neurosis of the masses prevailed. I became a professor at the same time that colleges and universities were forced by economic conditions and changing demographics to think of themselves primarily as business enterprises. And I lost a child, experienced serious illness, and began my explorations into metaphysics shortly after the 1987 "harmonic convergence" gave official notice that the New Age was already well upon us.

It is only recently that public acknowledgment of explorations such as mine in the realm of spirituality has become acceptable. Today, however, articles abound regarding renewed interest in both traditional religions and nontraditional spiritual quests. Similarly, dissatisfaction with traditional, allopathic medicine and widespread exploration into alternative forms of healing are well documented. Further, the views of the researchers noted here permeate the media. The December 18, 1992, cover of *Time* magazine posed the question, "What Does Science Tell Us About God?" A year later, Bill Moyers aired a TV special entitled "Healing and the Mind." Themes of reincarnation, as well as out-of-body and near-death experiences, have found their way onto movie and TV screens and into popular fiction and nonfiction. At the same time, we have become aware of broader ecological issues and the threat posed by technology that is insensitive to its impact on the environment. Indeed, as I write, we are but five years from the turn of the century, and theories regarding impending earth changes as well as a variety of millennial prophesies are receiving greater and greater attention.

While I have barely skimmed the surface, obviously, much has changed during my lifetime, to the point that this book is just one of many dealing with spiritual issues and the soul currently on the market. However, if I were to tell myself (and you) a story about the above overview of my history relative to the social context, I would probably have to note that for most of my life I have been out of sync with events in the larger society. Indeed, despite greater acceptance today of a world view like mine, it certainly is not consistent with the prevailing paradigm, or way of thinking. Nevertheless, while having often experienced myself as being outside the mainstream, I have not storied my life in a negative manner. Rather, I prefer to think of myself as a "paradigm pioneer," an advance scout, perhaps, who thoroughly enjoys navigating new territory and is excited to report back on what I have found. And what I have found, finally, is not only permission but perhaps pressure to explore existence in terms of its spiritual dimensions. Given my story, I cannot do otherwise. In the final section of this chapter, I will discuss where all of this has taken me in terms of my professional practice.

SOUL HEALING

I operate on the assumption that each of us experiences, to greater or lesser degrees, an urge toward wholeness. Consistent with my second-order cybernetics, constructivist, and social constructionist perspectives, I believe that each of us participates in the creation of his or her own reality. Indeed, I also believe that at some level we choose all of our experiences, including our physical and emotional problems, which provide opportunities for learning lessons essential to our personal growth, or for becoming whole at a soul level. While I do not believe these are choices of which we typically are conscious, I do think we participate in them. Further, what may be experienced as a problem at the physical or emotional level also may be viewed as a necessary process related to a deeper level of healing—soul healing. It is this growth that counselors/ therapists may actively participate in facilitating as they incorporate a spiritual orientation into their work with clients.

From my perspective, spirituality transcends specific religious traditions and accommodates the full range of belief systems. Counseling/ therapy with a spiritual orientation focuses on the whole of the client/system and is aimed at the cocreation of a new context within which healing at a soul level is achieved. And it includes a conscious awareness both of the connectedness of client and counselor/therapist and of the sacred trust that is bestowed upon counselors and therapists by their clients.

Although the word *psychology* literally means study of the spirit, or the soul, mainstream mental health practice traditionally has deemed the realm of spirituality inappropriate. However, consistent with the shifts within the larger society, there seems to be a growing acceptance of the spiritual dimension, and a variety of contemporary approaches to counseling/therapy now explicitly focuses on this realm. Such approaches include past-life therapy, pastoral counseling, shamanic counseling, Jungian analysis, Christian psychotherapy, moral psychotherapy, personal mythology dream work, guided fantasy encounter, attitudinal healing, logotherapy, existential psychotherapy, humanistic psychotherapy, and transpersonal psychotherapy (Krippner & Welch, 1992).

I'm not sure where my approach would fall among those just listed for, as I have indicated, I am not speaking only of a counseling or therapy model that focuses on or includes the spiritual dimension. Rather, I speak of counseling/therapy as a spiritual process, regardless of whether this is or is not an explicit focus in terms of my interactions with clients. That is, my spiritual orientation evolves out of my systemic perspective regarding the interconnectedness of all that is. What is more, it is my belief that, as noted by Thomas Moore (1992, p. 270), "the fields of psychology and ecology overlap, because care of the world is a tending to the soul that resides in nature as well as in human beings." According to Moore, the word *ecology* is derived from the Greek word *oikos*, meaning home. Thus we are called upon to nurture the world, and the things of the world, as aspects of our home and out of true affection for them. In a similar vein, in a conversation regarding the overlap of science and religion, the following observations were made:

> Ecological awareness and ecological consciousness go far beyond science, and at the deepest level, ecological awareness is an awareness of the fundamental interconnectedness and interdependence of all phenomena and of this embeddedness in the cosmos. And, of course, the notions of being embedded in the cosmos, and of belonging to the cosmos, are similar. This is where ecology and religion meet. And this is also why the new-paradigm thinking in science has these surprising parallels to thinking in spiritual traditions; for example, the parallels to Eastern mysticism. (Capra & Steindl-Rast, 1991, p. 70)

Indeed, the words of Gregory Bateson, one of the earliest proponents of such "new-paradigm thinking in science," sum up the fundamental assumptions of my orientation:

> I surrender to the belief that my knowing is a small part of a wider integrated knowing that knits the entire biosphere or creation. (Bateson & Bateson, 1979, p. 88)
>
> Mind and nature form a necessary unity, in which there is no mind *separate from* body and no god separate from his creation. (Bateson, 1987, p. 12)

At this point, it is my hope that you have a good sense not only of where I am coming from but also how I got there. By way of conclusion to this chapter, I would like you to be aware that soul healing is a process in which I am actively engaged on a personal as well as a professional level and it has ramifications for every part of my life. Further, it is my belief that we have only begun to scratch the surface of what is possible in terms of our ability to facilitate healing for ourselves and others, and that a spiritual orientation moves us in a direction that offers great hope for all of us. Indeed, mine is an optimistic story, the details of which you will find in the chapters that follow.

For I do nothing but go about persuading you all, old and young alike, not to take thought for your persons or your properties, but first and chiefly to care about the greatest improvements of the soul.

—PLATO

CHAPTER 2

The Spiritual Path

INTRODUCTION

As you certainly are aware now if you weren't before, until very recently it generally has not been permissible to talk about either spirituality or the soul in the context of counseling or therapy. Although we, as clinicians, may have realized how difficult it can be to try to exclude this dimension of people's lives from our work, it typically has been seen as outside the purview of science. However, that there are several paradoxes inherent in such a position becomes apparent as we consider and define exactly what it is that we are talking about. Therefore, the first order of business will be to take a closer look at the root meaning of the word *psychology* as well as the reality of this field as it has evolved to the present. Next, I believe it is important to explain the distinctions I make between spirituality and religion and to define the concept of soul. This is followed by a discussion of several approaches to therapy from a spiritual perspective as well as a further look at what it means to focus on soul healing. A consideration of the interaction of belief systems from the perspective of the client, the therapist, and the larger context is then provided. I conclude the chapter with an overview of counseling/therapy with a spiritual orientation.

PSYCHOLOGY, RELIGION, SPIRITUALITY, AND SOUL

The literal definition of psychology, you may recall, has little relationship to the field as we generally think of it today. That is, "Psychology means soul knowledge. It means the study of the spirit, but has never been that. Psychology is the study of cognition, perceptions and affects. It is the study of the personality" (Zukav, 1990, p. 193). Indeed, the only place in the psychology story that explicitly has allowed for or acknowledged spirituality and the soul is that known as the Third Force, or transpersonal psychology. For the most part, however, psychology has chosen to ally itself with the medical model and with the pursuit of credibility based on empirical research, thus excluding the intangible and unmeasurable aspects of people's lives. Such a stance has had tremendous ramifications for clinical practice. In fact, for Gary Zukav, the separation of soul and spirit from the realm of psychology undermines the ability of the latter to facilitate healing:

> Because psychology is based upon the perceptions of the five-sensory personality, it is not able to recognize the soul. It is not able to understand the dynamics that underlie the values and behaviors of the personality. Just as medicine seeks to heal the body without recognizing the energy of the soul that lies behind the health or illness of the body and, therefore, cannot heal the soul, psychology seeks to heal the personality without recognizing the force of the soul that lies behind the configuration and experiences of the personality, and, therefore, also cannot heal. (1990, pp. 193–194)

Thomas Moore, a Jungian analyst with a background in theology and the author of the best-selling book *Care of the Soul*, makes a similar observation:

> If we have a psychology rooted in a medical view of human behavior and emotional life, then the primary value will be health. But if our idea of psychology is based on the soul, then the goal of our therapeutic efforts will be beauty. I will go so far as to say that if we lack beauty in our lives, we will probably suffer familiar disturbances in the soul— depression, paranoia, meaninglessness, and addiction. (1992, p. 278)

Indeed, we have so divorced soul and spirituality from psychology that, until very recently, we have defined most approaches that included this dimension as belonging to another world. We have referred to this as the world of the shaman, or the realm of spirit. According to one view, "conventional psychotherapy [is seen] as living outside the realm of spirit, operating from a model of illness and emphasizing interpretation and analysis while counseling labeled as Shamanic sees spirit and empowerment as crucial and understanding as secondary" (Krippner & Welch, 1992, p. 63).

As we begin to rethink and to rewrite our stories about counseling and therapy to include spirituality, it thus becomes apparent that both our process and our goals also may need revising. As indicated in the just-cited observations, our focus shifts to the facilitation of health and wellness, to approaches that enable the client to feel empowered, to discussions of that which is experienced as meaningful and beautiful. Further, considerations of the religious and spiritual dimensions of people's lives are invited or at least welcomed.

It is appropriate at this point to articulate the distinction I am making between religion and spirituality. For me, religion refers to a specific, institutionalized belief system that may or may not be an expression of spirituality as practiced by its adherents. Spirituality, from my perspective, is a more comprehensive concept: it describes a way of being in the world rather than particular content. Thus, one may be spiritual without being religious, and vice versa. In order to get a better sense of the particular way of being in the world to which my construction of spirituality refers, let us consider several different perspectives.

The first view is in the form of a definition put forth by the California Psychological Task Force on Spirituality and Psychotherapy:

> It has been said that spirituality is the "courage to look within and trust." What is seen and what is trusted appears to be a deep sense of belonging, of wholeness, of connectedness, and of the openness to the infinite. (Krippner & Welch, 1992, p. 6)

Similar themes are expressed and expanded upon in the following discussion of spirituality:

> We have defined the spiritual dimension of life as that which deals with transcendent experiences or events, realms and processes that reach beyond ordinary limits, e.g., those evaluated as life's "highest" or "deepest" experiences, those marked by human nobility and magnificence, those associated with self-actualization and altruism,

those representing purported communion with spirits or deities, and/or those in which someone claims to encounter or merge with God, with the "ultimate organizing principal of existence," with the "pattern that connects," or with the "ground of all being." However, a person does not have to believe in God in order to acknowledge the importance of transcendent experiences. (Krippner & Welch, 1992, p. 232)

Given such a perspective, we find ourselves moving away from a notion of spirituality that is embedded only in specific religious institutions or belief systems. However, to reiterate, religion and spirituality are not mutually exclusive. While spirituality does not necessarily exclude those who don't espouse a religious belief system, one may be religious and also spiritual. The realm of spirituality, as I am using the term, is that of the soul and its process of growth and development, which may be facilitated both within and without the context of a specific religious perspective. As Zukav writes:

Spirituality has to do with the immortal process itself. . . . Your spirituality encompasses your whole soul's journey. It is the way that through your higher self you can ask and receive assistance from other souls and from your teachers and guides. (Zukav, 1990, p. 200)

A final, more elaborate delineation of spirituality has been provided by David Elkins (1990, p. 4), who says, "Spirituality is a way of being and experiencing that comes about through awareness of a transcendent dimension that is characterized by certain identifiable values in regard to self, others, nature, life, and whatever one considers to be the ultimate." In addition to a transcendental dimension, these values are defined by Elkins as meaning in life, mission in life, sacredness of life, ultimate satisfaction, altruism, idealism, realism, and consideration of the fruits of spirituality:

1: *A transcendent dimension.* This value may range from a belief in a personal god to a belief in a "greater self" or higher self. In either case, the spiritual person believes in "something more" and draws personal power from this realm.

2: *Meaning in life.* The spiritual person values a quest for meaning and is confident that his or her life has purpose. While the content of that "purpose" may vary, each spiritual individual has filled the "existential vacuum" with an authentic sense of meaning.

3: *Mission in life.* The spiritual person has a sense of purpose and vocation. It may be a "call" to answer, a "mission" to accomplish, or a "destiny" to fulfill.

4: *Sacredness of life.* The spiritual person does not divide living into the sacred and the secular; he or she is able to sacralize all personal experience, social experience and experience with nature, filling his or her days with awe and reverence.

5: *Ultimate satisfaction.* Spiritual individuals can appreciate material possessions and objects but do not seek fundamental satisfaction from them. They know that ultimate fulfillment is found in spiritual values, and that all else is illusory.

6: *Altruism.* Spiritual people are moved to respond to the needs of others. They know that "no person is an island" and that everyone partakes of a common humanity.

7: *Idealism.* Spiritual people are committed to the betterment of the world through prayer, meditation, acts of charity and/or social activism. They see the potential of people, of societies, and of the planet.

8: *Realism.* Spiritual individuals are aware of such tragic realities of human existence as suffering, pain, and death. This knowledge deepens their appreciation of life and stiffens their commitment to "make a difference" in the world.

9: *Fruits of spirituality.* Spiritual persons are those whose spiritual attitudes, beliefs, and activities have borne fruit. Their compassion, courage, joy, and devotion have a positive effect upon their relationships with other people, with nature, with themselves, and with whatever they consider to be the ultimate and transcendent reality. (Elkins, 1990, pp. 5–6)

Spirituality, construed consistent with these definitions, therefore directs our attention to some of the most basic existential issues: to the meaning and purpose of life and to creating a reality that is supportive of the best interests and highest good of the soul, both of the individual and of the world.

Given that a discussion of spirituality from my perspective thus inevitably includes consideration of the soul, I also must define what I mean when using this term. According to *Webster's New Collegiate Dictionary* (1959, p. 808), soul may be understood as:

1. An entity conceived as the essence, substance, animating principle, or actuating cause of life, or of the individual life, esp. of individual life

manifested in thinking, willing, and knowing. In many religions it is regarded as immortal and separable from the body at death. 2. The physical
or spiritual principle in general, esp. as informing the universe. 3. Man's
moral and emotional nature, esp. as manifested in or communicated by
what he writes, composes, etc. 4. The seat of real life, vitality or action.

Similarly, Sandra Ingerman, quoting from the *Oxford English Dictionary*, writes that the word *soul* refers to:

"the principle of life, commonly regarded as an entity distinct from the
body; the spiritual parts in contrast to the purely physical." According
to this authority, our language also regards the soul as the seat of the
emotions, feelings or sentiments. (1991, p. 11)

When I speak of the soul, therefore, I refer to our basic essence, the
ground of our being. Regardless of whether or not one espouses reincarnation, for those who believe in some form of life after death it is the
soul that endures. And the soul is that aspect of ourselves that speaks
to our connection with the divine, a connection that unites all that is.
Thus, attention to this dimension is a sacred enterprise. Consistent
with this perspective, Moore notes:

Psychology is a secular science while care of the soul is a sacred art. Although I am borrowing the terminology of Christianity, what I am
proposing is not specifically Christian, nor is it tied to any particular religious tradition. It does, however, imply a religious sensibility and a
recognition of an absolute need for a spiritual life. (1992, p. xv)

Moore also believes it is important to make a distinction between
religion and a more holistic spiritual orientation. In regard to caring for
the soul he writes:

The goal is a richly elaborated life connected to society and nature, wo-
ven into the culture of family, nation, and globe. The idea is not to be
superficially adjusted, but to be profoundly connected in the heart to
ancestors and to living brothers and sisters in all the many communities that claim our hearts. (1992, p. xviii)

Spirituality and soul thus are about connection and about acting
out of an awareness of that connection. Hence we come once again to

the overlap between spirituality and ecology as described by Bateson (1987). To emphasize this point, let us take a moment to consider the following excerpt from a conversation devoted to the relationship between spirituality and ecology from the perspective of a scientist, Frithjof Capra, as he talks with a Benedictine monk, David Steindl-Rast:

> What I've always heard about Christianity and what Gregory Bateson also emphasized is that Christianity, although monotheistic, is also dualistic in its basic outlook, because it separates God from the creation. It has a transcendent God who stands opposite creation, or dominates creation. He creates the world *ex nihilo* at the beginning, and then is always separate and always transcends the creation.
>
> I've also often heard that mystics talk about their experience of an immanent God, something like Spinoza's *Deus sive natura* (God = Nature). It seems that this would be more the position of the deep ecologist, of a deep ecological theology, if you can call it that. (Capra & Steindl-Rast, 1991, pp. 97–98)

Indeed, Capra was one of those who, early on, noted the commonalities between quantum physics and metaphysics. Accordingly, he saw the most crucial aspect of Eastern philosophy as:

> [T]he awareness of the unity and mutual interrelation of all things and events, the experience of all phenomena in the world as manifestations of a basic oneness. All things are seen as interdependent and inseparable parts of this cosmic whole; as different manifestations of the same ultimate reality. (1975, p. 117)

SPIRITUAL PERSPECTIVES ON HEALING

Whether intentionally or not, as we counselors and therapists have adopted a holistic perspective, we have incorporated spirituality, at least according to the above view, into our work with clients. Perhaps without realizing it, we have moved into the realm traditionally inhabited by the mystic, the realm, as noted earlier, which is also that of the shaman. Therefore, as we shift to a consideration of the ramifications of this move for our efforts to facilitate healing, it seems appropriate to look a little more closely at shamanism and the phenomenon to which this term refers:

Around the world and across many cultures, a person who deals with the spiritual aspects of illness is a Shaman. A Shaman diagnoses and treats illnesses, divines information, communicates and interacts with the spirit world and occasionally acts as a *psychopomp*, that is, a person who helps souls cross over to the other world. (Ingerman, 1991, p. 1)

Further, according to the same author:

In Shamanic cultures all things are thought to be permeated by spirit. Every earthly form is animated with its own soul or life force. The well-being of any particular life-form is dependent on its spiritual harmony with other forms. Imbalances or displacement in the spiritual essence of a living being can cause debilitation and disease.

For Shamans the world over, illness has always been seen as a spiritual predicament: A loss of soul or diminishment of a central spiritual energy. (Ingerman, 1991, p. 17)

To the extent that we include a focus on spirituality and the soul, therefore, we also may become a kind of shamanic counselor/therapist. Indeed, some of the ideas of the shamanic belief system have begun to emerge explicitly in more traditional discussions of illness and health. The psychologist Jean Achterberg, who began to explore imagery and the use of guided imagery in healing while working in a medical setting, is a case in point. She notes:

Soul loss is regarded as the gravest diagnosis in the Shamanic nomenclature, being seen as a cause of illness and death. Yet it is not referred to at all in modern, Western medical books. Nevertheless it is becoming increasingly clear that what the Shaman refers to as soul loss—that is, injury to the inviolate core that is the essence of the person's being—does manifest in despair, immunological damage, cancer, and a host of other very serious disorders. It seems to follow the demise of relationships with loved ones, career, or other significant attachments. (1988, p. 121)

Similarly, the Jungian analyst Marie Louise von Franz writes:

Both "loss of soul" and an "invading spirit" can also be observed today as a psychological phenomenon in the everyday lives of the human beings around us. "Loss of soul" appears in the form of a sudden onset of apathy and listlessness; the joy has gone out of life, initiative is crippled, one feels empty, everything seems pointless. (Franz, 1980, p. 30)

Further, as noted in the first chapter, there are a number of approaches to psychotherapy, most of them relatively new, which operate from the assumption that the client's spiritual concerns are vital for behavioral and attitudinal change. In addition to those approaches previously listed, there is also one that includes, in a predominant manner, the spiritual dimension, and it is not so very new: "Founded in 1935 by two alcoholics, a stockbroker and a surgeon, AA [Alcoholics Anonymous] relies on a spiritual approach, calling upon a 'Higher Power greater than ourselves'" (Krippner & Welch, 1992, p. 215). Certainly we know that AA has provided a highly effective means for healing relative to the challenging problem of alcoholism.

It is worthy of note that many of the more contemporary spiritual approaches have been influenced significantly by the Native American perspective, which is part of an ancient tradition. Spiritual healing, according to a Native American perspective,

> begins with respect for the Great Spirit, and the Great Spirit is the life that is in all things—all the creatures and the plants and even the rocks and the minerals. All things have their own will and their own way and their own purpose. This is what is to be respected. (Krippner & Welch, 1992, p. 54)

Also consistent with the Native American tradition, we are informed that:

> All forms of life are the children of Mother Earth and the Sky God. As sons and daughters of earth and sky, we are all related, not only to all races of people but to plants, animals, rocks, etc. Therefore, humanity must nurture all our relatives and find ways for the offspring of the earth and the sky to live harmoniously. (Krippner & Welch, 1992, p. 56)

While there is thus a wide variety of views regarding healing from a spiritual perspective, it may be apparent that regardless of the orientation there are also several common themes. Further examples may help to illustrate this point. According to one discussion of psychic healing, which in this case has evolved out of Eastern philosophy and metaphysics:

Each one is a beam in the whole light. No one can ever be more than that. It takes one person here, another there, each contributing his part to make up the whole. Every time healing is brought about, whether for yourself or for another, the world benefits. The world is that much closer to receiving the full spiritual light because of each individual healing that takes place. (Goldsmith, 1959, p. 19)

In other words, we are all connected. We all contribute to the well-being of one another and of the whole. Further, each time that there is a healing, we all are enriched.

Also building on Eastern philosophy, Delores Krieger, a nurse working in New York City, has incorporated into the nursing/healing paradigm an approach that she calls *therapeutic touch*. According to Krieger, who developed her approach with the help of her colleague Dora Kunz, healing

is a humanization of energy in the interest of helping or healing others or oneself.... [It is t]he conscious full engagement of your energies in the interest of helping another.... [T]his interest arises from a sense of compassion and a recognition that there is an underlying order in the universe. (Krieger, 1993, p. 16)

Therapeutic touch, which does not involve contact but does involve the transfer of energy between healer and patient, has been the subject of a number of rigorous scientific studies and apparently has achieved some degree of credibility in a variety of medical contexts. Indeed, it is interesting to note that, within traditional Western medicine and despite continuing controversy, nurses rather than doctors appear to be more willing to explore innovative and alternative therapies (Watson, 1995).

A final perspective on spirituality and healing, one which definitely lies outside the mainstream, is that coming from material that has been *channeled*. The story regarding channeling is that information is transmitted to someone who is alive and living in this dimension by someone who is no longer dwelling in physical reality but rather is living in a soul dimension. The entity in the soul dimension is referred to as a *discarnate*. Whether or not we believe this story regarding the origins of the information, I'm certainly willing to consider it and to incorporate what is meaningful and useful. I invite you to do likewise as we look in some depth at a summary of nine channeled perspectives termed by Young (1988) the basic laws of "cosmic healing." First, the principles:

1: There must be unconditional love for God, for His creation, and for each living being, including oneself.

2: There must be forgiveness of all those who have hurt or angered us, as well as the asking for forgiveness of those who have been hurt by us.

3: There must be acceptance of full responsibility for our own actions, thoughts, feelings and beliefs as well as for the physical symptoms that manifest as a result of these.

4: To be a healer necessitates surrender to God of one's own desires, ego and will, simply wishing to serve God in any way that He directs.

5: The healing power is available to all.

6: The cause of all disease is either *(a)* abuse of our body, *(b)* various negative emotions and thoughts creating an imbalance between mind, body, and spirit, *(c)* past lives' activity or experience needing to be balanced, or *(d)* possession by a discarnate entity.

7: Death is a rebirth, another step in the continuum that is Life. It is not a failure to heal.

8: If we know and understand that God is All There Is and that we, and all other forms of life, are part of that Wholeness, healing and illumination will follow.

9: Reincarnation and karma are part of the eternity of Life, giving us repeated opportunities to learn and grow.

10: It is important to live and heal in the present.

11: Some suffering will be experienced as we grow spiritually.

12: There is a great power in the word[s] "I Am" or "Aum." This is the name of God, and it can be used, with great reverence, in the healing process. (Young, 1988, pp. 153–154)

Now I'd like to share my view. That is, I wholeheartedly support the importance of loving, as expressed in the first principle, and of acting out of that love toward all that is. However, I prefer to think of the transcendent dimension in terms of the *universe* or of a *great spirit* as opposed to speaking of an anthropomorphic God and *His* creation. I believe we all are part of that which is the divine, however we construe it, and I would rather leave room and respect for each person's conception. Indeed, to do so is part of my loving.

In agreement with the second principle, I also believe in the power of forgiveness to facilitate healing both for the person who is forgiving and he or she who is forgiven. The act of forgiving, which for me is also an expression of love, enables one to let go of the anger or frustration that literally may be eating away at the person who is experiencing such emotions. And being forgiven allows for the release of such feelings as guilt and shame and thus for the enhancement of the well-being of the other. Even in the most hurtful situations, when faced with certain behaviors that are considered unforgivable, I believe it is possible to facilitate healing by at least being able to forgive another for not living up to one's expectations.

Given my systemic perspective, I struggle with the third principle and with the linear, causal notions of full responsibility being placed on any one person and with believing that certain "actions, thoughts, feelings, and beliefs" necessarily result in physical symptoms. Rather, although I believe that we must acknowledge our contribution, I also believe that the responsibility for and the creation of situations are shared by all participants. Similarly, I have a problem with the idea that we have conscious control of our feelings. At the same time, I see each person as having the ability to make choices about beliefs and behaviors. That is, I can tell myself a variety of stories about a situation and the feelings that arise spontaneously in response to it, and each of these stories offers me different behavioral alternatives. How I act, therefore, is up to me. While I do see symptoms as logical to context, a notion that will be discussed more fully later, this is very different from viewing them as being *caused* by thoughts, feelings, or beliefs.

In terms of surrender, as outlined in the fourth principle, I agree that it is important but prefer to think of myself as being guided by the universe in the interest of the highest good of the person I desire to help. That is, I am not the healer. My role is to facilitate the healing processes available from the universe in the way that is most appropriate for the client or person to be helped.

As for the fifth principle, which states that healing power is available to all, I couldn't agree more. I believe that we all have a great potential to facilitate healing, of ourselves as well as others. Rather than looking only to external sources, I prefer partnerships that share responsibility for the creation of contexts supportive of healing, in whatever manner healing may be defined.

The sixth principle presents me with the same dilemma as that posed by the third principle. While abuse of the body, negative emotions and thoughts, past life experiences, or even spirit possession, may all be possible contributors to a context supportive of illness, I reject the linear, cause–effect punctuation. This, to me, is not only too simplistic; it is problematic in that the victim winds up being blamed.

The seventh principle makes great sense to me, and I am particularly concerned that, in this society, we tend to see death as a failure and thus are unable to acknowledge the healing that may occur even though a person dies. By way of illustration I would like to tell you about my father, who at the age of 85 was diagnosed with cancer of the pancreas. My efforts on his behalf were for *healing that was meaningful for him*. Given that he was at peace relative to death but was extremely fearful of pain, I consider his dying process to have been a healing experience. That is, he died without either extreme discomfort or excessive medication from a disease that is generally very painful in its later stages. Indeed, it is my belief that how we die may be as important as how we live.

While I use different terminology, the assumption of interconnectedness expressed in the eighth principle is fundamental to my belief system. Accordingly, I am aware of and cautious about the impact of my behavior and its potential for harm or good relative to all creatures and things. As I act, out of this awareness, in a manner that is sensitive and respectful, I believe that I participate in a healing process.

Although I am a relative newcomer to the concept, in recent years I have found the story about reincarnation and karma noted in the ninth principle not only believable but also useful in resolving several issues. Thus I prefer to believe that we have more than one opportunity to experience both life and the people who are important to us. The notion of reincarnation also helps me create a story that makes sense of injustice. That is, for a long time I have wondered about the inequities in the world and how it could be appropriate for one person to experience relative affluence while so many others lack so much. While the "luck of the draw" story, among others, is an insufficient explanation for me, I can accept the notion that over many, many lifetimes we have a myriad of experiences and that we participate in choosing our situations, all of which provide opportunities for our continued growth.

Further, it is interesting to note that the belief in reincarnation is widely held throughout the world and that it perhaps was part of the early Christian belief system (Howe, 1974). As pointed out by a scholar on this subject:

> Since the dawn of history, reincarnation and a firm faith in life after death have occupied an essential place in nearly all the world's religions. Belief in rebirth existed amidst Christians in the early history of Christianity, and persisted in various forms well into the Middle Ages. Origen, one of the most influential of the church fathers, believed in the "pre-existence of souls" and wrote in the third century: "Each soul

comes to this world reinforced by the victories or enfeebled by the de-
feats of its previous lives." Although Christianity eventually rejected
the belief in reincarnation, traces of it can be found throughout Renais-
sance thought, in the writing of major romantic poets like Blake and
Shelley, and even in so unlikely a figure as the novelist Balzac. Since the
advent of interest in Eastern religions that began at the end of the last
century, a remarkable number of Westerners have come to accept the
Hindu and Buddhist knowledge of rebirth. (Sogyal, 1992, pp. 82–83)

However, while I may find it a plausible and useful story, I do not
believe one necessarily must accept the idea of reincarnation, or even
that life continues after death. Rather, for me, what is important is the
notion that each of us is connected to and is an expression of the divine
at a very deep, or soul, level.

The tenth principle speaks succinctly to a basic tenet of my systemic
perspective. Although information about the past may provide important clues about context, my focus is on the here and now. I can neither
change what already has occurred nor do I see past events as having
caused present problems. As I operate in the present, I believe that solutions may be found and lived into a more comfortable future.

The idea that spiritual development entails some suffering, as expressed in the eleventh principle, permeates the religious and metaphysical literature. Whether or not it is true, this principle may provide a
useful way to reframe experience as long as it is not overdone and suffering is not presented as a character-building growth experience completely outside of one's control. That is, it may be helpful to ask ourselves
and our clients to consider a situation, whether involving emotional or
physical symptoms, as though it had been chosen as an opportunity for
learning, and to then ask what the learning potential might be.

I translate the twelfth principle into an emphasis on the power of
sound in general and of language in particular, while at the same time
recognizing that the invocation of the name of a deity can also be extremely potent. That is, I am aware of the ability of sound to facilitate
altered states of consciousness (Campbell, 1989), healing (Tomatis,
1991), as well as self-discovery and personal transformation (Mathieu,
1991). And I am particularly sensitive to the way in which language
structures reality and thus participates in its creation, especially as it
relates to healing. In this regard, Chopra (1991, p. 25) writes, "One time
a man died because of something I said to him." He then recounts an
incident with a patient in which his seemingly benign message about a

possible heart attack was received with such fear and anger that the patient was dead within a few hours. As the recipient of many verbal messages that I have perceived as having the potential to influence the creation of a negative story, I am committed to helping my clients become more tuned in to the words they hear, particularly from professionals, that may or may not be supportive of healing.

In summary, I believe that each of us may facilitate healing as we are sensitive to our connectedness, as we acknowledge our ability to participate in the creation of realities, as we focus on the here and now, as we befriend illness, and as we strive for harmony and balance. The spiritual perspective on healing that I am describing thus takes us back to an awareness of the original meaning of the verb *to heal*. That is, noting that, "*Heal* comes from the same root as *whole* and *holiness*," Brooke Medicine Eagle (1989, p. 60) goes on to say:

> This holiness is the essence of healing, which means to manifest wholeness in spirit and bring it into our bodies, our families, our communities, our world. We heal by beginning to consciously embody . . . and manifest that wholeness of Spirit in such a way that . . . [we] can guide those who have fallen out of rhythm, who have stumbled into dis-ease, and help them to reestablish their balance and rhythm.

She adds that true healing "means coming into resonance with one law: *You shall be in good relationship with each other and with all things in the Great Circle of Life*" (Medicine Eagle, 1989, p. 62).

Accordingly, healing calls us to express wholeness not only relative to ourselves but also as we interact with others and our world (Moss, 1989). We are to honor our connectedness in the context of caring and concerned relationships (Remen, 1989). Our role is to help eliminate blocks to the innate capacity for self-healing and to help create a context that is supportive of this capacity (Rossman, 1989). Empathy, understanding, and the ability to resonate with another are important aspects of a healing context (Schwarz, 1989), as is the ability to encourage hope (Cousins, 1989) and communicate high expectations regarding what is possible (Solfvin, 1989). In sum:

> Healing is simply attempting to do more of those things that bring joy and fewer of those things that bring pain. . . . I believe that the attitudes and beliefs of the people we live with have a huge impact on what we do. For instance, in the case of illness, if my family believes that I'm

going to die and there is nothing that I can do about it, this makes the process of getting well incredibly difficult. On the other hand, if they believe that I can become healthy again, their beliefs strengthen my ability to achieve it. This is true in any significant relationship, including the one between patient and healer. (Simonton, 1989, pp. 50–51)

To all of this, a soul-healing perspective adds the awareness that illness, whether emotional or physical, is to be understood as providing information about an opportunity to learn and grow that is somehow appropriate. While the goal remains seeking solutions and thus dealing with the problem, the problem is not to be perceived as a crisis with which to do battle. Rather, we look for the meaning of the experience in terms of what it can teach us. Given this view, we understand that:

An illness is meaningful, although its meaning may never be translatable into entirely rational terms. The point is not to understand the cause of the disease and then solve the problem, but to get close enough to the disease to restore the particular religious connection with life at which it hints. . . . In a very real sense, we do not cure diseases, they cure us, by restoring our religious participation in life. (Moore, 1992, p. 168)

Adopting such a perspective, we imbue illness with a spirituality that allows us to be in touch with the core of our being. We look for the necessity and the value in the process as a means of enriching ourselves. We welcome and perhaps even embrace each crisis as an opportunity to gain further understanding of the complexity of life. That is:

The healing journey is surrender to the process of change. Sometimes the things that go wrong in our lives, including physical illness, may happen when we have refused change at the point it was most called for. . . .

Sometimes illness provides the terrible impetus toward an answer to our deepest existential questions—the ones which in normal life we are reluctant to pose. The story that disease tells, if we listen, may be as much one of the self as of the cells—a story we may have forgotten or perhaps never have really heard. (Barasch, 1993, p. 76)

Indeed the healing journey is the journey of life from the perspective of soul healing. And each of life's experiences offers the potential to realize more and more of ourselves as spiritual beings with a higher purpose. Further, as we explore the complexity of our sense of life we also may allow ourselves to explore our stories about death. In fact, all of our stories become the focus as we seek to create newer and more useful narratives by means of which to live.

It is this perspective which describes the larger context within which soul healing or counseling/therapy with a spiritual orientation takes place. And it is such a context that is assumed when I state that, for me, therapy is a spiritual process. Consistent with this view, the therapy room becomes a sacred space that reflects my orientation not only in the way in which I interact with clients but also in terms of the physical environment. Inasmuch as the specifics of this approach form the contents of the chapters in Part II, I will postpone further discussion of pragmatics. For now, I would like to consider briefly the aesthetic dimension of the soul-healing context.

That is, in addition to my beliefs and the behaviors that flow from them, I have attempted to translate the notion of sacred space into the way my office is designed. The setting, above all, speaks of warmth and of the possibility of closeness that is nevertheless safe and honors and respects appropriate boundaries. I have chosen colors that I experience as nurturing, and which are neutral enough that a wide variety of clients also will be comfortable with them. I have gone out of my way to avoid formality and to select and arrange the furniture in a manner that is friendly and welcoming. I have a variety of personal items in my office but have not included anything that someone might feel is offensive, e.g., symbols of a particular religious or spiritual belief system. I have a stereo system with speakers for those times when I wish to use tape-recorded music. I also have live plants as well as scented candles, which I may use if I think a client will find the aroma pleasing. My most recent addition is a small fountain that provides the soothing sound of running water as a background for the therapeutic conversation. I am fortunate in that my office is located in a building with other similarly furnished rooms, and that clients are able to enter through an inner doorway but may leave via a door that leads directly to the outside. Most important, however, is the fact that, upon first entering, my clients often comment on how nice the room is and how good it feels.

I have provided only a rather general description of my office because of my belief that it is not the specific way in which it is designed and furnished that is truly significant. Rather, what is more important is that my work environment, the room devoted to counseling/therapy, is a reflection of me and is an expression of my beliefs about important aspects of the soul-healing process. Thus there is consistency between what I say and what I do in the creation of sacred space, the spiritual context within which counseling/therapy takes place.

In addition to the larger spiritual context and its physical expression, there are other levels of context that I believe merit consideration if my spiritual orientation is to be sufficiently comprehensive. Such levels include that of the client and counselor/therapist as well the belief systems of each. In order to get a sense of the interaction of these various systemic levels, it may be helpful to have a visual model, described as follows.

BELIEF SYSTEMS

The systemic/spiritual context, as defined in the preceding sections and as illustrated in figure 2.1, forms the setting for soul healing. It may be thought of as providing the larger framework for counseling/therapy and thus may be embraced as a general orientation. However, this larger framework also is able, indeed must be able, to accommodate the specific belief systems of various individual counselors and therapists as well as each unique client system. It is important to note that while my focus at this point is on spirituality, the model I am describing is equally applicable to other belief systems.

In any case, in the ongoing cocreation of the relationship between counselor/therapist and client, there is an interaction between the spirituality of both, including awareness of its absence, or a story about unbelief. Further, what each expresses relative to spirituality is a function of the interaction between personal belief system and lived experience. That is, we all have our personal epistemologies, including assumptions about spirituality and what is or is not relevant in this regard. These assumptions have evolved over time, in response to a myriad of influences, and they form the basis of each individual's story about spirituality. This story may include adherence to the tenets of a particular religion and it also may be an agnostic or an atheistic story. Further, our clients may have embraced the secular, medical model concepts of psychology described earlier. Thus their stories also may include beliefs about the appropriateness or inappropriateness of talking about their spirituality in the context of counseling/therapy.

In my experience, discussions of spirituality, unless initiated by the client, rarely take place at the beginning of the first session. Rather, for me as for most other therapists, the first order of business is to hear the clients' stories about what prompted them to seek help. Having heard

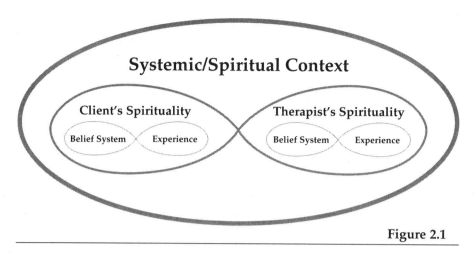

Figure 2.1

each person's perception of the problem, I then move to a search for so-lutions defined in terms of each person's goals. My method is to ask for a description of what would be going on if things were the way each person wanted them to be. Another way I might pose this question is, "If I were able to help you, what is it that we would have achieved at the end of our work together?" I encourage clients to phrase their re-sponses in concrete terms, which we then discuss. Having established some workable goals, I then like to spend some time exploring and get-ting a sense of the clients' context.

Like many other therapists, I have found it useful to have each per-son give me a brief history, starting at the beginning and continuing with an overview of major milestones up to the present. I am curious and may raise questions about families of origin, including relationships be-tween siblings, between parents, and between parents and children. I re-quest information about education, other significant relationships, and issues related to important life events. It is at this point that, in order to attempt to understand the role of the spiritual dimension in the life of a client, I often ask a general question such as, "Where are you in terms of spirituality or religion?" For me, inquiring about the relationship be-tween the client and a transcendent dimension is as important as finding out about any other significant relationship in his or her life.

Responses to my questions provide me with important information about the clients' world views, or the stories according to which they are operating. Given whatever information is provided to me regard-ing spirituality, I also am able to be more sensitive to what may or may not be experienced as appropriate or offensive in this realm. Further, client responses in this area help me to identify possible resources in terms of both the language I might use and potential support from rabbis, priests, ministers, spiritual directors, etc. However, my goal is to be respectful of the clients' belief systems and to obtain, in each instance, as full an understanding as possible.

I am quite willing to share my particular religious/spiritual orientation and the way in which it has evolved, if this seems appropriate. However, my intention in doing so is not to change the client's spirituality. Rather, it is to give permission for conversations related to this topic if such conversations seem to be useful in working toward the achievement of the client's goals. My desire is to communicate my respect for the client's belief system, enlisting assistance and asking for additional information if it is one with which I am unfamiliar.

If the client does not construe his or her world in terms of a particular religious or spiritual belief system, I change my language accordingly. However, the larger spiritual framework still forms the context of therapy. That is, at the level of interaction of belief systems, as expressed in specific words and interventions, my conversation continues to reflect acknowledgment of, respect for, and sensitivity to, the client's values and assumptions. In this case, however, it is done through exclusion of explicit references to religion or spirituality.

Similarly, the fact that the counselor/therapist does not story his or her world in terms of a specific spiritual or religious orientation does not preclude the possibility of working with clients who do. Given the larger spiritual context created by a soul-healing orientation, what becomes crucial is the way the counselor/therapist interacts with the client. Thus, for example, while she may be an atheist, she still can discuss with clients the problems with which they would like assistance and learn the degree to which religion or spirituality forms a part of their personal stories. Indeed, to omit such a discussion because it is not part of the counselor/therapist's world view may be to miss an extremely significant dimension in the life of the client. It also may be to miss important opportunities for facilitating healing. The following observation seems relevant in this regard:

> How can one remain silent on the place of spiritual issues, including prayer, in modern life? Skirting the spiritual has had a shattering effect on every dimension of contemporary existence. As England's great poet Kathleen Raine recently remarked, "Our society has lost the dimension of meaning and values—one could say the sacred—not only

in the arts but in life itself." Neglecting the sacred also bodes poorly, I am convinced, for the future. (Dossey, 1993, p. 10)

Regardless of the particular scenario, however, as the spirituality of the counselor/therapist and that of the client interact, each inevitably is affected by the other. And, as with all other aspects of belief systems, different experiences may influence the creation of different beliefs that are expressed in different behaviors. All of which undoubtedly affects the nature of the larger systemic/spiritual context. Thus there is mutual influence and interaction at all levels of the system, and changes reverberate throughout, moving both from micro to macro and vice versa.

COUNSELING/THERAPY WITH A SPIRITUAL ORIENTATION

Soul healing, from my perspective, thus involves being a counselor/therapist who operates with an awareness of a transcendent dimension that provides the context for all relationships, all interactions, all that is. And "all that is" is understood as interconnected and interdependent. Further, each aspect of the universe is considered to be an expression of the divine, to be infused with spirit, and thus to be sacred. Given this awareness, one recognizes that life has a larger meaning and purpose related to the growth and development not only of individual souls but also of the soul of the world. Indeed, in the words of one psychologist,

> Soul making, it seems to me, must be world-oriented rather than self-oriented; otherwise cultivation of soul is at the expense of world. The tremendous force that comes about through the cultivation of the inner life can produce radical changes in the outer world, if it is oriented in that direction always. (Sardello, 1992, p. 48)

Accordingly, one also recognizes the importance of respecting and valuing each person as well as each experience. For we all are involved in each other's destiny, and each of us is walking a path toward the self-realization both of our individual selves and of all. Along this path we have high ideals and at the same time we recognize the limits of what is possible. And we look for our efforts to make a difference in the world. As we work with clients, our function is to facilitate harmony and balance through support of each individual on his or her journey towards the attainment of the specific goals appropriate for him or her. Thus, it is understood that:

> Each of us has a divine mission or function. Each of us has a role to
> play in the Big Story, our natural role, the one we were born for. It is
> our part in the unity of consciousness, in all beingness. But we can only
> discover what our mission is by embracing the "I am," by reconnecting
> with our souls. (Warter, 1994, p. 229)

Hence, each individual is understood to have an urge toward wholeness, a wholeness which involves an alignment of the physical with the
spiritual. Such alignment allows the soul, through the individual personality, to manifest its destiny or purpose: "A condition of wholeness
can be described as one in which a person operates from a unified consciousness of body, mind, emotions and soul" (Raheem, 1991, p. 16).

Further, while the physical expression, or body, of the individual ultimately dies, soul is understood to exist both before and after physical
death. Thus at the deepest level, the level of the spirit, there is continuity,
just as at the physical level there is impermanence. And we become aware
that acknowledgment and acceptance of our impermanence, or death, can
transform our approach to life. For example, it has been found that a near-
death experience may have significant ramifications in this regard:

> Perhaps one of . . . [the near-death experience's] most important reve-
> lations is how it transforms the lives of those who have been through it.
> Researchers have noted a startling range of aftereffects and changes: a
> reduced fear and deeper acceptance of death; an increased concern for
> helping others; an enhanced vision of the importance of love; less inter-
> est in materialistic pursuits; a growing belief in a spiritual dimension
> and the spiritual meaning of life; and, of course, a greater openness to
> belief in the afterlife. (Sogyal, 1992, p. 29)

Indeed, through helping clients to accept death we may facilitate the
desired wholeness or balance. However, in our role as counselors/thera-
pists, we are not the healers. Rather, we become conduits for healing in a
process that is shared with our clients. As part of this process, we invite
clients to become the curators of their own souls (Moore, 1992), and to
understand the ability they have to influence their own healing. Further,
we encourage them to broaden their stories about whatever it is they are
experiencing. Thus we help them to consider different kinds of responses
to problems—including becoming quiet and going within to examine, focus and wonder—as well as to become aware that healing may take
many different forms. In his book *Healing Words*, Larry Dossey describes
such a process as follows:

During illness the quiet way of being . . . flows from one's true center. It is focused, authentic, genuine, and accepting of any outcome. It is not self-conscious and contains no pity for the "I" who is sick. It is not contaminated by fear of death, and contains no blame or guilt. It does not exclude any therapeutic approach, and may involve using drugs or surgery as naturally as contemplation, meditation, or prayer. It is unconcerned with tragic outcomes, even death, for it rests in the understanding that one's higher self is immortal and eternal, and cannot die. (1993, p. 23)

Dossey further notes that while an inquiring but calm attitude of acceptance is appropriate, it should not be equated with "doing nothing":

Beneath the tranquillity, equanimity, and acceptance lies a kind of action that bears little resemblance to the showy activity to which we are accustomed. This quiet, inner-directed action is acknowledged in many spiritual traditions as the highest form of activity in which humans can engage, and is almost identical with some forms of prayer. (1993, p. 24)

Thus, soul healing recognizes the significance of each problem and helps clients understand the potential for opportunity in each crisis. Similar to my own experience with cancer, which I now see as a gift (Becvar, 1995), we acknowledge the following possibility:

You may even come to feel mysteriously grateful toward your suffering, because it gives you such an opportunity of working through it and transforming it. Without it you would never have been able to discover that hidden in the nature and depths of suffering is a treasure of bliss. The times when you are suffering can be those when you are most open, and where you are extremely vulnerable can be where your greatest strength really lies. (Sogyal, 1992, p. 316)

Rather than offering sympathy to the sufferer, however, what we offer is a mirror that reflects support for the search for meaning and positive growth (Warter, 1994). This mirroring is possible because of the path that each counselor/therapist has walked in search of the ability to care for his or her own soul and that of his or her clients. It is this road to soul healing which is the subject of chapter 3.

In order to think meaningfully about religion today, it is not enough to remain within the boundaries of traditional religions. The search for spirituality and transcendence in our age cannot find its sole answer in intense private devotions or in escapist religious life. It has to grow and live in the market place; it has to be the source of meaning for all of life and relate to our daily problems, our family and our community, our science, our politics, the whole world as we scientifically explore and experience it today.

—URSULA KING

CHAPTER 3

The Road to Soul Healing

INTRODUCTION

I suspect that, having chosen to purchase this book and having read to this point, many of you already are on a road which, if not exactly the same, is at least parallel to that going in the direction of soul healing as I describe it. That is, my guess is that you are concerned about your own spirituality and that of your clients as well as with how religious/spiritual issues fit in the counseling/therapy context. In all likelihood, you have a sense of interconnectedness and perhaps yearn to facilitate exploration at the deepest level of your being. You undoubtedly hold all people and the world in high esteem and may be striving for moral/ethical behavior in your life and in your work. It is likely that you are open to and value each person's construction of reality, that you seek to enhance the strengths of your clients, and that your search is for solutions appropriate to each unique person/system. Thus, the information presented in this chapter probably will not be entirely new to you. Rather, my suspicion is that what I will be doing is integrating thoughts and concerns to which you already have given much thought. In doing so, therefore, my hope is to pull this information together and present it in a manner that is different enough to provide you with some meaningful and useful insights, perhaps adding a few new ideas along the way. Of particular concern will be the ways in which we as counselors/therapists take care of ourselves so that we may do the best job possible of nurturing and facilitating healing for our clients. I also will look at ways in which we can increase our knowledge and understanding in the areas of religion and spirituality. An additional focus will be the complex issues of assessment and diagnosis as well as the challenge involved in understanding different types of illness in a metaphoric sense. Finally, helping clients recognize and tap into their own potential to facilitate healing will be considered as will, by way of conclusion to Part I and introduction to Part II, the basic principles of soul healing.

SOUL HEALING FOR THE COUNSELOR/THERAPIST

Urie Bronfenbrenner (1979) raises an important question regarding who it is that cares for those who care for our children. I would like to pose a similar question about the care of those mental health professionals whose desire it is to care for others. My own answer to this question is that, to a great extent, we must care for ourselves. We must be concerned about our own healing/wholeness, which includes being open to receiving the care that others are willing to provide us. That is, ultimately, we must care for our own souls. And this, I believe, requires most of all that we love ourselves.

When I was an undergraduate student, I took a course entitled "American Ideals," which was taught by a professor who was also a rabbi. Although the majority of the course was focused on the more secular aspects of American ideology, the unit that left the most lasting impression on me was the one that dealt with the Biblical admonition to love one another as you love yourself. While the exact content of the lectures has long since been forgotten, I remember to this day, and clearly have taken to heart, the message we in the class received about how we cannot truly love others unless we love ourselves. What was encouraged was what I now refer to as a "healthy selfishness." This attitude honors and values our own needs, avoids self-demeaning, martyrlike behavior, and at the same time does not infringe on the rights or well-being of others. The point is that it is essential to be whole—"Physician, heal thyself"—if we wish to be effective facilitators of wholeness and healing for others. Further, the process of achieving the wholeness and healing that enable us to truly love ourselves encompasses all aspects of our lives, not just those which are lived inside the therapy room.

In an effort to encourage and support my clients in their ability to love themselves, I often suggest that they take time each day to do something that they would experience as fun or enjoyable, something that feels nurturing. This is advice I also take seriously for myself and recommend to other counselors/therapists as well. The story I tell myself, and others, is that there are 24 hours in each day and it is up to each of us to decide how to spend them. If we really love ourselves, then I believe it is not only appropriate but also essential to devote at least some time each day to things pleasurable. For me, such things include being with the people I love, walking, swimming, meditating, drumming, reading, and listening to music. Among other activities, my clients have chosen bubble baths (with and without candles), writing a journal, crafts, and playing a musical instrument. The list of possible enjoyable things to do is probably endless. More important than the activity, however, is the possibility that, as we are learning to love ourselves fully, taking time for ourselves may encourage a greater sense of worthiness and self-love. Indeed, it is my belief that feelings follow behavior rather than the other way around. Hence the need to behave, perhaps at first, *as if* we truly loved ourselves.

Other behaviors expressing self-love relate to our work environments. Accordingly, I attempt to choose professional contexts that I experience as nurturing and supportive. Although I am very good at being a workaholic and, in fact, enjoy putting in long hours when I am involved with tasks that are meaningful to me, I have high expectations when it comes to feeling valued and respected by those with whom I work. No matter how demanding a job may be, or how much pressure is associated with it, I think it is reasonable to expect our colleagues to observe the same standards of conduct that our clients expect us to follow. Further, I believe that as we give and receive respect and support, we participate in the creation of a context that allows the job to be completed in a more effective and efficient manner—even as we find more enjoyment and satisfaction in doing it. The reality is that we probably cannot reduce the workplace demands most of us experience. What we can do, however, is change the way in which we deal with such demands and with each other. In fact, what we expect from others and what we choose to live with makes an implicit statement about the degree to which we love, value, and respect ourselves.

What I am suggesting is that it is appropriate to give ourselves and our needs at least as high a priority as we do others and their needs. Thus, for example, I also am very choosy about how I use my discretionary time and with whom I spend it. I suspect that the reason I get so annoyed with the telephone, particularly with anonymous callers soliciting donations or trying to sell me something, is that it allows for an invasion of my space over which I have little control. (I also don't enjoy having to be rude in order to end such unwanted calls; nor do I want to have to spend the money to screen or block these calls.) Similarly, I choose not to watch TV, read the newspaper, or listen to the radio (except National Public Radio) because I experience much news, programming, and commercialism as negative input. My preference is to rent videotapes and listen to audio tapes, activities which enable me to be very selective about what I see and hear. While the particular behaviors I am describing may not be appropriate for anyone other than myself, I do recommend becoming aware of and sensitive to both the negative and the positive aspects of the contexts in which we live and work. I also recommend making choices that honor and express an attitude of self-love.

In addition, as counselors and therapists whose job it is to understand and facilitate meaningful relationships with and for our clients, I think it is crucial that we make time for and nurture the relationships we have with the significant others in our own lives. In the words of Elisabeth Kubler-Ross:

> The only thing that counts in life is love—not just how much love we can *give*, but we must learn how to receive it, because we can give only as much as we allow ourselves to receive. Everything has to be in balance. (Elliott, 1995, pp. 32–33)

Not only do we get back what we give in terms of love and support, but living according to what we believe is an expression of our integrity. Thus, I suggest it is important that we take our own advice regarding planning opportunities to enjoy our spouses/partners, children, friends, and other family members. We may need to build such time into our schedules, or even make appointments with friends and family members, in order to ensure that we will have time together. While such behavior certainly lacks the spontaneity we may prefer, it may be rewarded by the satisfaction of creating new rituals that foster identity and stability (Becvar & Becvar, 1987, 1994) at the same time that they acknowledge the sacredness of our daily lives (Carse, 1995). As Robert Fulghum notes:

> Patterns of repetition govern each day, week, year, and lifetime. "Personal habits" is one term we use to describe the most common of these repeated patterns. But I say these habits are sacred because they give

deliberate structure to our lives. Structure gives us a sense of security. And that sense of security is the ground of meaning. (1995, p. 21)

Acknowledging the sacredness of daily life, as well as being sensitive to the contexts in which we live and work, also are involved in the creation of the sacred space to which I briefly referred in Chapter 2. Although previously I described some of the physical aspects (i.e., furnishings) of sacred space, there are other dimensions that also may aid in its creation. For example, the Oriental practice of *feng shui* (Rossbach, 1987) considers space, time, and form in an effort to create balanced living environments supportive of comfort and well-being: "A household word in many parts of Asia, feng shui is a cross between an art and a science. Its goal is to arrange buildings, rooms, and furniture in the most beneficial way to achieve maximum harmony with nature" (p. 2). A fundamental goal of *feng shui* is to understand how our immediate environment may participate in the shaping of our lives and to make adjustments using such things as bright objects, sound, living objects, heavy objects, electrical power, flutes, colors, and other "personal cures" (Rossbach, 1987, p. 2). While you and I may not have the inclination to pursue an understanding of *feng shui* in great depth, we certainly can take time to reflect on the little touches or arrangements that will make our space a more pleasant one in which to work. And as we do so, it also may become a more welcoming and more comfortable one for our clients.

In addition, we might borrow from the Native American tradition the practice of *smudging*, or using the smoke from a smoldering bundle of sage, to purify our space. Perhaps a little less hazardous activity might be to burn a stick of incense or to light a scented candle. Negative ionizers or air purifiers also help to refresh an environment as do potpourri burners and aromatherapy dispensers. Regardless of the methods you choose, however, the goal is to honor and thoughtfully create your space, thereby emphasizing the sacredness of the activity in which you are engaged as you interact with clients in the process of soul healing—both theirs and yours.

PREPARATION FOR A SPIRITUAL/RELIGIOUS FOCUS

It also is essential to consider how to ready ourselves for client/therapist interactions that are focused explicitly on religion/spirituality. For, outside of seminary-based programs, preparation in this area is rarely part of the training of mental health professionals. Whatever knowledge we have acquired probably has derived from personal pursuits and in all likelihood does not provide us with in-depth understanding of traditions other than our own or those in which we have a special interest. This is not a total disadvantage, however. For as we admit our lack of knowledge, we truly may meet our clients from the not-knowing, non-expert stance advocated by postmodernist practitioners (e.g., Andersen, 1991; Anderson & Goolishian, 1988). Accordingly, as we are able to respect and learn from our clients, we may enhance our ability to foster a collaborative approach to the search for solutions.

Indeed, what may be more important than expert knowledge regarding specific content is an awareness of process, or the impact that religion and spirituality can have on the counseling/therapy experience (Benningfield, in press). For example, we may be vulnerable by virtue of being either insensitive or overzealous with regard to the role of religion/spirituality in the life of the client. We may believe neutrality is possible. However, a value-free position is not possible and the attempt to be neutral relative to spirituality implies a value in that regard. We may let our personal needs or interests inappropriately influence our behavior with clients. Or we may have a perspective that is too narrow to accommodate the beliefs of the people with whom we are working (Prest & Keller, 1993). We also may be vulnerable not only in terms of our inexperience but also as a function of our lack of education in this area (Bowman, 1989). It therefore behooves us to be sensitive to the variety of ways in which we may get "hooked," or lack awareness, and thus behave in a less than therapeutic manner.

In our efforts to become educated and knowledgeable relative to an awareness of process, however, we now have the opportunity to avail ourselves of a growing body of literature related to the inclusion of religion/spirituality in mental health practice. A variety of articles provide models for integration (Bergin, 1988; Georgia, 1994; Holmes, 1994; Miller, 1992; Peteet, 1994; Ross, 1994; Stewart & Gale, 1994; Worthington, 1994). There are also preliminary discussions of the incorporation of content on this topic in training programs for mental health professionals (Benningfield, in press; Stander, Piercy, MacKinnon, & Helmeke, 1994). Such discussions are certainly timely, given the increasing interest in religion and spirituality in the general public:

> Contrary to the predictions of the nineteenth-century prophets of modernity who saw only the decline of religion, recent research portrays a virtually unprecedented, if somewhat chaotic, swirl of religious

activity in the United States. Most of it occurs outside the walls of mainstream religious institutions. Thus a decline in church and synagogue membership has not meant a decline in religious interest. If anything, it has meant just the opposite. (Jones, 1995, p. 188)

However, I am not only an avid consumer of books and articles related to this topic; I believe it is equally important to strive for clarity about one's own spirituality. Thus I espouse taking time to focus on our inner lives in the way that is most appropriate for each of us. Certainly many mental health professionals are required to experience therapy or revisit their families of origin in order to come to terms with personal issues that may affect or be affected by the practice of therapy. Similarly, I believe that a spiritual orientation in counseling/therapy may be enhanced to the degree that the therapist is in touch with his or her own soul and its purpose. Along the same lines, the social worker and family therapist Harry Aponte writes,

> for us to address our clients about the spirit, we need to look first at ourselves. We need to recognize what gives meaning and purpose to life for us, just as we have in the past learned to explore our unconscious and our families of origin. We need to think about how our own views about life help or hinder our understanding and ability to relate to people and their struggles. How we think about values, morality, and spirituality may be primitive or elaborate, closed or open, harmonious with our lives or in conflict. Our philosophical and spiritual views can serve to connect or block us from others. There is work we must all do with ourselves to gain insight about the spiritual component of our lives and how it affects our views and relationships with others. (1994, p. 246)

The following addition to this admonition to the counselor/therapist also is worthy of note:

Work on himself, through spiritual attunement and practice, is essential. Vitality of Spirit requires nourishment at a soul level. The liberation of his own soul will help the therapist to bring the wisdom and vitality of living Spirit to his client. The awakened soul radiates a vital presence, out through the body and into the field around him, which stirs other souls. An alive soul is also more sensitive to soul signals from others. (Raheem, 1991, p. 189)

In attempting to portray the form that one's personal spiritual pursuits and reflections may take, once again I will use myself as an illustration. However, I am in no way suggesting that the particular behaviors I describe are appropriate for anyone other than myself. In fact, the impetus for much of my search during the years since my son's death and my bout with cancer has been my desire to understand the lessons it was appropriate for me to learn, and to become aware of my soul purpose in order to be able to live in a manner consistent with their achievement. Along the way, I have read, attended workshops, taken classes, meditated, consulted the runes and the *I Ching*, had astrological birth charts prepared, experienced past-life readings, added a practitioner of Chinese medicine to my medical support/surveillance system, and radically changed my diet and exercise routine. What is more, I have chosen to leave jobs that did not provide me with a supportive context even though such choices may be considered by some to have been bad career moves.

Some of my lessons include not only awareness of the power of the mind both to facilitate healing and create reality but also recognition of the importance of living and behaving in a manner consistent with this awareness. For example, I took a medication for four years following my surgery and chemotherapy even though I was convinced that I was well and really didn't need it. Not surprisingly, at least to me now, I developed side effects during the fourth year and finally recognized that continuing to take the medication was not appropriate for me given my particular beliefs. Against the advice of my oncologist, I went off the medication and went on a diet that took care of the side effects. Along the way, I developed eating habits with which my body apparently is much more comfortable: I no longer fight the "battle of the bulge" that had plagued me for most of my life.

Other lessons relate to my understanding of crisis in general, and of death in particular. Although I continue to long for my son's physical presence, part of me is grateful for the learning that has emerged from the crisis of his death. In addition, I have come to believe that, for those left behind, death represents a transition in the relationship with the one who has died rather than its termination. I also now believe that death may indicate that the person who dies has completed his or her life tasks, or soul purpose, and thus that, perhaps, we should celebrate this achievement. Such celebration is still hard for me, but then I obviously have many more lessons to learn!

In terms of my soul purpose, while the specifics are not clear to me, I am convinced that it has to do with morals, ethics, integrity, social justice—in a word, with spirituality as I define it. It seems to be important not only that I strive to live according to spiritual principles, but also that I be a voice for such principles. Indeed, I believe that writing this book and speaking out about my beliefs and behaviors, however far out of the mainstream they may seem, is a part of this process. It is clear to me that as I trust the universe and live each day with excitement, anticipation, and awareness of the deeper meanings in each moment, information about my purpose, as well as ways to fulfill it, is constantly being provided. Which brings us full circle to the recognition that, as a soul-healing orientation suggests, it is important that the counselor/therapist be engaged in a process of facilitating wholeness in his or her own body, mind, and spirit as well as for his or her clients. For soul healing is not a destination. Rather, it is a journey that encompasses every aspect of one's life:

> All the spiritual teachers of humanity have told us the same thing, that the purpose of life on earth is to achieve union with our fundamental, enlightened nature. The "task" . . . is to realize and embody our true being. There is only one way to do this, and that is to undertake the spiritual journey, with all the ardor and intelligence, courage and resolve for transformation that we can muster. (Sogyal, 1992, p. 127)

Such a spiritual journey requires that we have compassion, dedication, understanding, and love for ourselves. And inevitably, as we take this journey toward self-transformation we participate in the creation of a different reality, thus having a transformative influence upon all with whom we interact. That is, we model what we believe and therefore—consistent with a fundamental premise of systemic thinking—cannot help but influence one another by how we behave. And as we act in a manner consistent with what we believe and desire, we encourage its attainment, both for ourselves and for others.

ASSESSMENT AND DIAGNOSIS

The issue of consistency between beliefs and behaviors brings us to the topic of assessment and diagnosis. It also brings us to the section of the book most likely to give rise to controversy. For I am well aware that my views in this area are outside the mainstream and that to express them is risky. However, I believe that avoiding the issue would violate my own sense of integrity. Thus, I choose to tell my story. But I do so in full acknowledgment that it is entirely possible to have a spiritual orientation in therapy while taking very different positions relative to assessment and diagnosis. Indeed, I will attempt to describe such alternative positions.

Nevertheless, for me, the decision to engage in assessment and diagnosis consistent with criteria such as those defined by the *Diagnostic and Statistical Manual of Mental Disorders* (4th ed., 1994) presents an ethical and spiritual dilemma that challenges counselors/therapists in several ways. First, in order to survive economically, mental health practitioners currently must acknowledge and work within the constraints of a managed care environment. That is, if we are to be eligible to receive reimbursement from someone other than the client, we must assess, diagnose, and practice according to the guidelines and requirements of third-party payers. Second, diagnostic criteria are based primarily on an individual psychology model. However, systemic practitioners, who focus on relationship and context, at the very least, see problems as symptoms of system dysfunction. And if such practitioners operate according to the purest form of a postmodernist/second-order cybernetics perspective, they consider it inappropriate to participate in the creation of a reality shaped by the pathology-based diagnosis of a so-called expert. Some hard questions with which we thus are faced include the following:

- Is it ethical for family therapists to assign a diagnostic label to an individual, thereby defining him or her as dysfunctional, while operating out of a perspective that, even at the level of simple cybernetics, sees family rather than individual dysfunction?
- At the level of cybernetics of cybernetics, what are the consequences of the above action for our clients? What are the consequences for the larger society of our creating and maintaining a belief in pathology defined as individual rather than contextual?
- What is our ethical responsibility when we realize that we participate in a pathologizing discourse while at the same time recognizing that diagnostic categories and illness labels are our creation and do not exist outside of our constructions? (Becvar & Becvar, 1996, p. 120)

A third question raised by the standard diagnostic system is whether allowing the manner and form of therapy to be prescribed not only by a particular diagnosis but also by a person or persons other than the participants in the immediate therapist/client system is appropriate. Before considering this portion of the dilemma, however, I would like to examine further what happens when we assess and diagnose.

Assessment and diagnosis assume that the therapist can stand outside of and objectively observe what is going on with the client. Such behavior is consistent with the model of counselor/therapist as expert. And as we engage in such activities we participate in the construction of a reality that has serious implications for the way clients experience themselves. That is, to label a particular behavior as a problem is to become a creator rather than a discoverer. For example, when I was in elementary school, children who could not read were just that—children who could not read. Today we have learning disabled children: the same phenomenon but a very different reality for these children, their families, and the larger social context. And we mental health professionals have been instrumental in its creation by choosing to label a particular behavior or set of behaviors according to a diagnostic category. Indeed, we influence the power of a problem by the way we name it.

Further, there is an old adage that says, "Be careful what you call something because that is what you will wind up treating." That is, diagnosis at least implies, if it does not determine, what treatment will be and how others will regard the client. For example, we respond very differently to someone who is discouraged than we do to someone who is depressed. Each label, or metaphor, conjures up different images and logically provokes different responses. And the self-perceptions of the persons to whom particular labels are attached will reflect the labels. Writing about the process associated with assessment and diagnosis in the medical world, Ivan Illich describes some of the possible ramifications for the patient:

> His sickness is taken from him and turned into the raw material for an institutional enterprise. His condition is interpreted according to a set of abstract rules. . . . Diagnosis always intensifies stress, defines incapacity, imposes inactivity, and focuses apprehension on nonrecovery, on uncertainty, and on one's dependence upon future medical findings, all of which amounts to a loss of autonomy for self-definition. It also isolates a person in a special role, separates him from the normal and healthy, and requires submission to the authority of specialized personnel. (1976, pp. 159–160)

In the course of assessing and diagnosing, we are thus at risk of behaving in a manner that fails to acknowledge our connectedness or permit collaboration; that may neglect the uniqueness of each client or system as we lump people together into broad, general categories; and that may do a disservice in terms of the reality which we participate in cocreating. To do so also may assume knowledge that in all likelihood we do not have. For example:

> [A] modern diagnostic label treats key questions as foregone conclu-sions: Is disease a thing or a process? Is its "natural history" inexorable, or have there been instances of reversal? Does it reside only in a partic-ular organ, or is it merely the most visible evidence of a wider systemic disorder? Is it purely physical, or is it affected by interactions with the mind? Each of these usually unasked queries has enormous implica-tions, not only for diagnosis but for the treatment that will inevitably follow from it. (Barasch, 1993, p. 139)

Along similar lines, Bernie Siegel tells the following tale about Carl Jung, who noted,

> that a clinical diagnosis may be indispensable to the doctor, but only rarely helps the patient: "The crucial thing is the story. For it alone shows the human background and the human suffering. Only at that point can the doctor's therapy begin to operate." (Barasch, 1993, p. 11)

Having the time and opportunity to hear and work with the client's story returns us to the dilemma involved with practicing according to the prescription of the third-party payer. The challenge arises when, in following that prescription, the counselor/therapist loses the freedom to create the context most supportive of healing and wholeness for each unique client. Indeed, the findings of a survey aimed at learning whether or not therapy helps indicate that, "The longer people stayed in therapy, the more they improved. This suggests that limited mental-health insurance coverage, and the new trend in health plans—empha-sizing short-term therapy—may be misguided" ("Does Therapy Help?" 1995, p. 734).

Thus, if we choose to see or to use the labels of pathology, I believe it is important that we also understand that the Greek from which the term *pathology* derives, "implies a dialogue with what is wounded" (Barasch, 1993, p. 159). And as facilitators of soul healing, we must be able to respond in ethical ways, ways that acknowledge what we don't know and that allow for creative responses on the part of both clients and counselors/therapists: we must remember that we create the maps and that they are merely representations of territories. They are fictions, myths, stories that may have some truth but are not The Truth. Further, as we work in the realm of the soul, we must be aware that scientific responses aimed at explanation and delineation of causes may be less appropriate than constructions that are imaginative, creative, and which touch something deep within us, at the core of our being. As noted previously, in soul healing our focus is not on a single "univocal" interpretation of illness (Moore, 1992) but rather on a search for meaning. We consider a variety of interpretations, using such resources as poetry, mythology, and spirituality to explore the mystery of a problem. Among other things, we explore illness as a metaphor that can provide information which we may use to facilitate personal growth and development.

There is a good chance that by this point, even if you agree with what I am saying, you are keenly aware that the issue of economic survival still remains. So, how is this issue to be dealt with? Indeed, perhaps you may find yourself, as I do, on the horns of a moral/ethical dilemma, faced with having to make another of the tough choices with which life inevitably presents us. In the words of Kubler-Ross:

> Man was given the greatest, most difficult gift: free choice. Of all the beings I know, we are the only ones who have been given such a controversial gift. We have to choose. We're the master of our destiny. We can turn anything or everything into bad or good, into black or white, into evil or a blessing. (Elliott, 1995, p. 40)

Although I wish to emphasize that I cannot say what the right choice is for anyone else, I can tell you about my own choice. For me, working within the confines of the managed care system as currently structured would be inconsistent, for it would be to participate in the creation and maintenance of a context that I do not believe supports the best interests of either clients or mental health professionals. I therefore choose to do private practice on a self-pay basis. My clients pay me, and, if they request it, I submit the appropriate information to their insurance companies. However, I inform them of the requirement to make a diagnosis, and we have a conversation about the implications of doing so. Indeed, collaborating with clients on the issues of assessment and diagnosis is one of the ways in which many therapists offset the possible negative consequences.

I also let my clients know, from the outset, that I may not be reimbursable. That is, given my particular credentials and the fact that I am not on a panel of any managed care providers, there is no guarantee that therapy with me will be covered. As a function of this circumstance, I keep my standard fee relatively low, compared with the charges of other therapists in my area. In addition, I am willing to create payment schedules or to work on a pro bono basis with clients whose current inability to pay would prevent them from being able to come to therapy.

You may be wondering how I survive, especially in these tight economic times, given the choices I have just described. The answer to this question takes me not only back to my spiritual orientation but also to some other beliefs and behaviors that also may appear somewhat unusual. As I mentioned previously, I truly trust the universe. And when I need some help, I ask for it. I do not worry about where the money is going to come from because I believe that when I need it, it will be there. Although this attitude has proved to be a challenge for my husband (who is a child of the era of the Great Depression) to live with, even he will admit that it works. In fact, last Christmas he gave me a pad of Post-It notes printed with the following epigram: "I don't believe in miracles . . . I *rely* on them." And I do. Let me tell you a story by way of illustration.

During the last several months I purposely have tried to pare back my therapy schedule in order to have more time for my writing. However, a couple of weeks ago I noticed that my client load had gotten a little too low. So, during a meditation, I mentioned to the universe that I could use a few more clients. Within days I received several referrals. An even more wonderful occurrence followed a short time later. Ray and I, who own the building in which we do our therapy, had a conversation one evening about the fact that the income we were receiving from the therapists who rent space from us was not covering our expenses and that we are going into the hole each month. The next morning, a Friday, during my meditation, I requested that the universe provide us with some additional therapists who would like to rent space and who would fit in with the people who comprise our current group. A day later I received a call from a friend who said that she had a friend, a former student of mine, who was looking for space to rent. By Saturday afternoon we had signed a contract, and it looks like this new person also has a friend who wants to talk to us about renting space. As strange as all this may sound, I am thrilled but not surprised when I see evidence that confirms my belief in our ability literally to create reality.

Perhaps you're telling yourself that this was just a lucky coincidence. Certainly there is no scientific proof for my version of reality. And perhaps it was a coincidence. But according to my story, there are no accidents. Moreover, this sort of thing has happened to me often enough that I see a pattern, and I choose to give it a different meaning. What is more, scientific proof, at least in this instance, is not particularly important to me. Indeed, I agree with Carl Hammerschlag, a psychiatrist, who writes:

> We now look to science to provide us with the answers to the Great Questions. But the answers to questions about meaning usually lie within ourselves. If we are comfortable only with answers that can be proven, we'll never really get comfortable. Science is not something to worship. We worship to acknowledge and revere the things we *don't* understand. (1988, pp. 15–16)

In fact, there is much I don't understand, but my story works for me. My behaviors are consistent with my beliefs, and I feel a sense of moral, ethical, and spiritual integrity. It is this integrity, I believe, that is essential, not the particular choice to think or act as I do. And thus I also recognize that there are many ways to resolve the issues that surround assessment and diagnosis and to work within the current system that allow for a spiritual orientation. Perhaps the most notable way, as I have mentioned, is to work collaboratively with clients. Other ways include a heightened awareness of and sensitivity to the possible negative ramifications, awareness and sensitivity that evolve into more deliberate and conscious attempts to avoid harming clients in any way.

The choices I make afford me the opportunity to work with clients in the manner that I believe allows me to be most helpful to them. Further, I believe that in some small way I am acting to influence the creation of the reality that I desire on a larger scale. Among other things, such a reality would provide people with a metaphoric view, which I believe offers a potentially more useful perspective from which not only to understand problems but to search for solutions. In addition, this reality would be characterized by an awareness that every person has a tremendous, largely untapped ability to facilitate his or her own healing.

A METAPHORIC VIEW

Exploring the meaning of problems, or the opportunities for growth inherent in them, may include viewing them as metaphors that provide information about what is needed in order for healing to occur.

Such a view acknowledges that at some level we participate in the creation of reality, including the reality of problems. Thus we may find ourselves facing another interesting and challenging dilemma.

That is, there are many who would argue against a metaphoric view of problems (Sontag, 1977). But such arguments, which generally revolve around the issues of blame and guilt, emerge from a linear world view according to which it is understood that A causes B, or A does something to B and C happens. By contrast, from a systemic perspective we understand causality to be circular, so that A and B mutually influence each other and both participate in the creation of C. Thus, rather than cause or blame, we are talking about shared responsibility for any given situation. Further, responsibility may refer to something we either do or do not do and may well be something of which we are not consciously aware, or over which we have little or no conscious control.

For example, family therapists have been much criticized for their recursive perspective as applied particularly to the area of abuse. The questions that immediately arise concern how a child or a woman could participate in or share responsibility for his or her own abuse, particularly in the face of very real power differentials. The response is that for *purposes of understanding the larger pattern of interaction,* there is participation just by virtue of being present. To take such a view at the level of process, however, has nothing to do with condoning abusive behavior or blaming the person abused. Instead, it focuses on the dynamics of the situation as part of a contextual assessment of the problem, which also includes the larger social context.

From a systemic perspective, we understand that all behavior is logical, or somehow makes sense, in context. The goal is to help change the context so that problems or symptoms no longer fit. From this perspective, we do not search for causes. Indeed, the concepts of blame and guilt have no meaning when one thinks in terms of recursion, mutual influence, and shared responsibility. Rather than blaming ourselves for a problem, we search for the logic, we listen to and become partners with our problems, we explore potential avenues of learning, and we attempt to adjust our lives accordingly.

Questions that may facilitate understanding from this perspective might include, "How am I, or are we, participating, either inadvertently or not, in the creation of a context within which this problem fits?" or "What behaviors on my or our part might change the context in such a way that this problem would no longer be a logical response?" Thus, we acknowledge the possibility that "Symptoms—including pain—are just ways of saying something that, if you could find a way to say straighter, would make the symptoms go away" (Hammerschlag, 1988, p. 33). And from this perspective we welcome the awareness that we are not victims but rather have the power both to facilitate healing, wholeness, and balance and to influence the creation of the reality we desire. We are not looking for absolute Truth; we are searching for personal meanings, for our individual truths. And to do so returns us to the realm of spirituality:

> [C]ontemporary psychological research into the importance of meaning and purpose in life demonstrates that without a sense that life is meaningful, people are more prone to anxiety, depression, and a variety of physical ailments. Studies have found that hope too is essential to physical and mental well-being and is a major ingredient in a person's resiliency in the face of crisis, illness, and suffering.
>
> Hope, meaning, and purpose turn out to be critical for mental and physical health and for psychological strength and coping. . . . The quest for meaning and connection to the sacred is a fundamental part of human development and an essential resource for mental and physical wholeness. (Jones, 1995, p. 20)

As we pursue the search for meaning, we may move into the realm of metaphor and the imagination. In doing so, we honor problems and the pain associated with them (Dossey, 1993) and recognize that there may be mystery involved. The leader of the Sufi order in the West suggests that an appropriate question might then be: "What are the qualities that I am being tested in by the divine planning, that I must develop in order to meet this situation? . . . What are the qualities I'm supposed to develop now?" (Khan, 1982, p. 114).

We also may examine areas of possible imbalance (Ingerman, 1993). And, we may allow problems to lead toward wonder (Moore, 1992), particularly as we search for answers to some of the ultimate questions. Indeed, Jerome Miller suggests that wonder can open doors to many unexplored universes. He writes:

> Wonder is the hinge that turns my attention away from the immediately present toward what can only be known through questioning. In making that turn, one opens the door to another world—indeed, to all those worlds, all those universes of meaning that become accessible to us through inquiry. . . . Wonder is the hinge that opens up the absolute

future, not a future that is another now, but a future so different from the now that opening the door to it is quite literally the beginning of a new world. (1989, pp. 56–57)

Miller believes that by exploring the unknown mysteries of life we encounter the sacred. Such exploration also points us in the direction of the future in terms of what might be, to a search for solutions and the creation of the realities we desire. With a soul-healing orientation we thus encourage a conversation that may lead to healing at a deep level even—or perhaps especially—when we are confronted with some of life's biggest problems. For example,

> Tibetan Buddhists believe that illnesses like cancer can be a warning, to remind us that we have been neglecting deep aspects of our being, such as our spiritual needs. If we take this warning seriously and change fundamentally the direction of our lives, there is a very real hope for healing not only our bodies, but our whole being. (Sogyal, 1992, p. 31)

In all of this, however, it is important that counselors and therapists remember that we are but a catalyst for healing. Indeed, our efforts will be greatly aided, perhaps may succeed, only as we help clients realize their own vast potential for self-healing. Thus it is appropriate to turn our attention to a consideration of how we may create a context supportive of this awareness.

SELF-HEALING

First of all, however, I would like to make clear that when I talk about helping clients realize their potential for self-healing, I am not talking about my empowering them, which to me is almost a contradiction in terms. Indeed, to empower means "to give authority to" or "to authorize." Accordingly, I am sensitive to the possibility that from a place of greater power, I would be seen as giving to a person something which she or he previously did not have, an activity that still leaves me in a more powerful position. By contrast, what I am referring to is a recognition, on the part of both client and counselor/therapist, of the ability that all of us have to facilitate our own healing. And having such an awareness ourselves is of primary importance in helping another achieve it.

In fact, I am convinced that ultimately all healing is self-healing, and that mind and body are equally engaged in the process. This view may be summed up as follows:

> The brain, the immune system, the nervous system, all of our hormones, are a constantly moving interconnected informational network. It isn't just the brain and what we know that control our destiny. Every cell in the body can communicate with every other cell as long as you keep them moving. It turns out that becoming and remaining healthy has far less to do with what we know than what we feel. What fuels the human spirit turns out to be closer to things like hope, belief, love, or faith than to intellectual certainty. The body feels the things of our spirits that our minds never thought of. Our cellular selves know things that are invisible to the eye. (Hammerschlag, 1993, p. 62)

Thus, I believe that when we are ill, have an emotional problem, or have a relationship problem, all the things we do to take care of ourselves help to create a context which, ideally, is supportive of the body/mind's powers of rejuvenation. While I may choose to see a doctor or therapist, to take medicine, even to undergo surgery, I nevertheless do not believe that the doctor or therapist is healing me. Rather, I see us as partners in the cocreation of a healing context over which I, as well as the person(s) with whom I am working, have a great deal of control. For I also believe that the stories I tell myself about my ability to facilitate self-healing influence the course it will take. I therefore find a great deal of wisdom in the following excerpt from *The Pilgrimage* by Paulo Coelho (though I might state it a little less vehemently):

> "What's the world's greatest lie?" the boy asked, completely surprised.
> "It's this: that at a certain point in our lives, we lose control of what's happening to us, and our lives become controlled by fate. That's the world's greatest lie." (1993 p. 18)

Given my constructivist perspective, the story that I tell myself is that I am not at the mercy of fate. Instead, I believe that I can have a great deal of influence on my destiny and that as I follow this belief in a proactive manner, I participate in creating the health and healing I desire. Another way of understanding this behavior is to say that I construct a positive, self-fulfilling prophesy. If it is not working, or if I don't achieve my goal as quickly as I would like, is my story disproved? For me, it is not. My response is to rethink, and perhaps redefine, the nature of the healing that is appropriate for me.

As I interact with clients, I am comfortable sharing my beliefs about the usefulness of taking charge of one's own healing and of the need to make choices that are supportive of health and healing. I include in such discussions a sense of genuine optimism. Further, as I talk about what I believe, and relate to my clients in a manner that is consistent with my worldview, I also am aware that beliefs may have a powerful influence on the creation of a context that enables the client to experience his or her ability to facilitate self-healing. For, as Larry Dossey has noted in regard to physicians, the professional's belief system can be powerful indeed. He writes:

> The beliefs of the patient and the doctor ideally should coincide. The *best* possible situation is one in which both parties genuinely and honestly believe a therapy is going to be effective. The *worst* is one in which there is a collision or conflict between the two sets of beliefs, or in which neither the physician nor patient feels that the therapy is going to work. (1993, p. 139)

One of my favorite client stories illustrates this point. (I have changed details and omitted reference to sexual identities in order to protect the people involved.) Many years ago, Alex came to me seeking help with some relationship problems with a live-in partner, Lee. Because I had previously worked with one of Alex's parents, Andy, who had referred Alex to me, I was aware of a long psychiatric history in which Alex had been hospitalized repeatedly following psychotic breaks. After Alex and Lee had completed about six months of couples' therapy, Andy phoned me to say that Alex was once again exhibiting some very bizarre behavior and the other family members were considering hospitalizing Alex. I urged Andy to postpone this decision until Alex and I had had a chance to meet. I then arranged to have Lee bring Alex to my office later that day.

There is no question that Alex appeared distraught and had been doing some very strange things. However, since I see symptoms as logical in context and truly believed in Alex's ability also to behave in appropriate ways, I chose to relate to Alex as I always had, that is, as a normal, healthy person. Within 15 minutes, Alex had begun to laugh and to engage in a sane conversation with me; Alex even acknowledged an awareness of the strange behavior and distorted thinking. I encouraged Alex to arrange a psychiatric appointment in order to obtain medication but I recommended against hospitalization. Instead, I urged that all members of the family relate to Alex in as normal a manner as possible, thereby refusing to participate in the "Alex-is-crazy" story that had predominated for many years. I also supported Alex's choice to continue working.

Although healing did not come overnight, and Alex's employment eventually was terminated, Alex recovered without another hospitalization. Further, Alex found another job before long, and after several months was able to go off the medication. There has not been another psychotic break since that time. In the years since this episode, I have continued to work with Alex from time to time, as needed. In the process, Alex has recalled and subsequently resolved a childhood sexual abuse experience, and become aware of important lessons to be learned in terms of building satisfactory relationships, particularly with members of the opposite sex. Today, Alex leads a busy and productive life that no longer includes a story about mental illness.

Therapy with Alex, as with all of my clients, looks like a conversation in which we each share our stories. However, I am most interested in hearing the client's story and tell parts of mine only when it seems useful or to make a point. Often my self-disclosure is a way of expressing empathy or acknowledging our connection, or both, by describing the degree to which our journeys may be similar. With Hammerschlag, I recognize that:

> [T]he patient doesn't need a scientist who simply carries out instructions from the laboratory manual. Patients don't want to be cases—they want to be healed. They want to participate in their own wellness or their own death. Patients are the principal agents in their lives, and as much as they want to be well, they want peace and understanding. To find such a healing peace they need to feel that a connection exists between themselves and the healer and between themselves and something larger than self or science. (1988, p. 137)

As I participate in the creation of a context for soul healing, I thus see the client as the expert on his or her own life, and I make every effort to respect that expertise. As I have mentioned, I see this as a spiritual process and the client's trust in me as sacred. My goal is to let the client experience acceptance exactly as she or he is. In addition, I attempt to search for exceptions (de Shazer, 1988) that allow the client to have an awareness of times when he or she has been successful. In addition, I concur with Khan, who writes:

> In the person, there are many qualities that are on their way, that are not manifest; and that is the only way to understand a person. Most often, the person himself is unaware of all those qualities, but by seeing them we help him see them in himself; we can act like a midwife who is bringing these qualities into actuation. (1982, p. 70)

The questions I ask and the comments I make are focused on attempts to understand the client's story as well as how she or he would like things to be different. And from the outset, I attempt to tune in to the client and trust my intuition about possible directions in which to go as a way of helping the client achieve his or her desired solutions. Such intuition has been described as "an uncanny hunch we might have about things, which seems to be contradicted by our normal, rational thinking but is confirmed later on" (Khan, 1982, p. 8).

Further, as our conversation proceeds, I constantly am aware of the role of language and of perception-determining beliefs: "Looking at core beliefs is part of the process in all healing, whatever the form of healing. Once that limiting belief has been identified, the next step is to let it go" (Ingerman, 1993, p. 88). Thus I also attempt to explore with the client various ways in which she or he may story reality. Always, however, I believe that the client has the answers for which she or he is searching. Of course, I am not alone in this observation:

> I have been amazed again and again by how, if you just let people talk, giving them your complete and compassionate attention, they will say things of a surprising spiritual depth, even when they think they don't have any spiritual beliefs. Everyone has their own life wisdom, and when you let a person talk you allow this life wisdom to emerge. I have often been very moved by how you can help people *to help themselves* by helping them to discover their own truth, a truth whose richness, sweetness, and profundity they may never have suspected. The sources of healing and awareness are deep within each of us, and your task is never under any circumstances to impose your beliefs but to enable them to find these within themselves. (Sogyal, 1992, pp. 210–211)

Finally, for me the road to soul healing also requires that I continue my own spiritual pursuits. I think that all of us—counselors/therapists and clients—are in this together. And it is my belief that I cannot encourage or support another on a journey that I am not willing to take myself.

The ingredients that comprised the recipe for my work with Alex in particular, as well as for soul healing in general, may be summed up according to the following five principles: acknowledging connectedness, suspending judgment, trusting the universe, creating realities, and walking the path with heart. In Part II of this book, each of these principles is discussed in greater depth in a separate chapter. Before moving on, however, I would like to share a story that I think provides a fitting conclusion to Part I. Although it concerns the relationship between patient and medical doctor, I think it also speaks to those of us who are counselors and therapists.

The patient was Anatole Broyard, a literary journalist who worked for the *New York Times* first as the daily book reviewer for 15 years, and then as editor of the *Times Book Review*. When Broyard was diagnosed with prostate cancer at the age of 69, it had already spread throughout his body. A year after his diagnosis and seven weeks before his death, the following article, entitled "Doctor, Talk to Me," was published in the *New York Times Magazine* (August 26, 1990, pp. 33, 35):

[W]hat *do* I want in a doctor? I would say that I want one who is a close reader of illness and a good critic of medicine. . . . Also, I would like a doctor who is not only a talented physician but a bit of a metaphysician too, someone who can treat body and soul. I used to get restless when people talked about soul, but now I know better. Soul is the part of you that you summon up in emergencies. You don't need to be religious to believe in the soul or to have one. . . .

Just as he orders blood tests and bone scans of my body, I'd like my doctor to scan *me*, to grope for my spirit as well as my prostate. . . .

[A] doctor, like a writer, must have a voice of his own, something that conveys the timbre, the rhythm, the diction and the music of his humanity. . . .

Not every patient can be saved but his illness may be eased by the way the doctor responds to him—and in responding to him, the doctor may save himself. . . . It may be necessary to give up some of his authority in exchange for his humanity, but as the old family doctors knew, this is not a bad bargain. . . . He has little to lose and much to gain by letting the sick man into his heart. If he does, they can share, as few others can, the wonder, terror and exaltation of being on the edge of being between the natural and the supernatural.

PART II

Clinical Strategies

Here then for me is the golden thread: relationships. It is our capacity to merge, to become at one, however briefly, with ourselves, with each other, and with life in a larger sense. Healing, wherever and however it occurs, brings each person and humanity as a whole toward a more inclusive, more unobstructed relatedness to all that is emerging in this adventure of life. The relatedness is endless: to oneself, to one's sensations, thoughts, feelings, images, dreams; to other people in how we acknowledge and transcend the sense of separation. And it is relatedness to something more, however we conceptualize it: Self or God.

—RICHARD MOSS

CHAPTER 4

Acknowledging Connectedness

INTRODUCTION

I have long taken the position that family therapy is not about who is in the room but rather about how the counselor/therapist understands and behaves relative to who is in the room (Becvar & Becvar, 1982; Becvar & Becvar, 1988, 1993, 1996). Thus, as one thinks and operates systemically (e.g., in terms of recursion, pattern, process, and context), one is doing family therapy regardless of whether the client is an individual, a couple, a family, or a larger organization. The primary focus is on relationships, which are considered the appropriate unit of analysis in attempts to understand the system. Building upon this emphasis on the dynamics of interaction and mutual influence, a spiritual orientation—as I conceive of it—begins with the way in which one conceptualizes the nature of the relationship between the client and the counselor/therapist. That is, there is heightened awareness of the interdependence of all that is, as well as a recognition that together the parts, plus their interaction, create a larger unity that we think of as the whole. Indeed, we realize that wholes are subdivided into parts only as we choose to punctuate, or see them in such a manner. In this chapter, therefore, I begin with a brief discussion of the complementarity of separateness and connectedness. Following a summary of the ways others have facilitated an awareness of and the ability to acknowledge connectedness, a meditation exercise is presented. This exercise is designed to enable counselors and therapists to experience a sense of connectedness in general and, in particular, to develop greater sensitivity to the ways in which they and their clients are connected. For I believe it is in the context of such awareness that a therapeutic relationship infused with spirituality is cocreated, even when such a dimension is not explicitly acknowledged or named as spiritual. In this chapter, I also discuss learning how to hear, the use of self-disclosure and the sharing of one's own journey, a spiritual view of relationships, and when and how to introduce the topic of spirituality and how to proceed depending upon where the client is relative to spirituality and religion. I conclude with a consideration of the ramifications, for both the client and the counselor/therapist, of relationships in which connectedness is acknowledged.

SEPARATENESS/CONNECTEDNESS

As I have noted, when one thinks systemically, one thinks in terms of relationships and dwells in what may be described as a completely interconnected universe. It is important to be aware that if we were to carry this perspective to its extreme, we would think only in terms of the whole and could not conceive of parts. From such a position our total experience would be of a oneness with the universe. Thus, it is from this perspective that we also recognize that it is we who create components as we attempt to consciously analyze and make sense of our experience, or make the distinction that is necessary for any act of perception (Bateson, 1972; Flemons, 1991; Watts, 1963). We therefore "know" a phenomenon as we call attention to a difference we perceive between it and something else. Accordingly, we acknowledge that we need, for example, the darkness to understand light, evil to understand good, death to define life.

It is after drawing such distinctions, or defining components of a whole, that we create the concept of relationship, thereby attempting to reunite the parts that emerged as a function of the distinctions we made. Nevertheless, however we divide, count, sort, and classify the distinctions we make and the differences we note, the whole is never actually disjoined. Further, according to Watts, at some level we are aware of this phenomenon:

[W]hen consciousness is turned back upon its own organic basis, it gets some apprehension of that "omniscience" which is the body's total, organizing sensitivity. In the light of this deeper and more inclusive sensitivity, it becomes suddenly clear that things are joined together by the boundaries we ordinarily take to separate them, and are, indeed, definable as themselves only in terms of other things that differ from them. The cosmos is seen as a multi-dimensional network of crystals, each one containing the reflections of all the others, and the reflections of all the others *in* those reflections. . . . In the heart of each there shines, too, the single point of light that every one reflects from every other. (1963, pp. 212–213)

In a similar manner, we recognize that each individual member of a relationship gives meaning and existence to the other. Further, we become aware that the individuals also are one. From my perspective, it is a living in and an operating out of the awareness of this oneness that provides the spiritual dimension of counselors' and therapists' interaction with clients. The issue thus is not, "How do I create a relationship with my client?" Rather, the relationship is a given, it *is*. The issue, therefore, becomes one of participating in the creation of a particular kind of relationship, one that manifests an understanding of the depth of our connections, those which we may speak of as existing at a soul level.

I suspect that, at least in part and although perhaps not consciously, we already create spiritually-infused relationships as we accept, honor, respect, and behave in humane ways with our clients. Indeed, we all might benefit from a review of the work of Carl Rogers (1939, 1942, 1951, 1959, 1961), who emphasized a client-centered view of relationships and who articulated the necessity of such counselor/therapist behaviors as "genuineness or congruence," "empathic understanding," and "unconditional positive regard" (Meador & Rogers, 1984, p. 143). However, in contrast to Rogers, I am suggesting neither a formula for how to conduct therapy nor a description of its inevitable outcome were we to operate according to such a formula. Rather, I believe that the "how" of counseling/therapy is specific to each unique client-counselor/therapist configuration. But I also believe that, as we move to and become conscious in a more profound way of the source and meaning of our actions relative to the relationships between client and counselor/therapist, we may enhance the healing process.

That is, as we acknowledge our connectedness we may find that additional resources are available to us. For we may recognize that we share similar goals and that we walk paths that are headed in the same general direction. We also may realize that each is affected by the other, and that the growth or healing of one benefits all. And we may find different ways of understanding both the joy of successful relationships and the pain involved when a relationship ends. But perhaps most importantly, we may achieve the ability to access a deeper level of communication and energy transfer.

Such enhanced communication may occur as we succeed in moving beyond our usual mode of sensory perception to direct, mind-to-mind knowing. The latter is the mode most often associated with and described by mystics. While we may tend to think of accessing information as a unitary process, alternate ways of knowing have been defined and described:

> There are indeed fundamentally two categories of knowledge—Knowledge by Ideation and Knowledge by Being. All scientific knowledge, whether physical or super-physical, belongs to the first category. Such knowledge is based on the duality of the observer and observed. In spiritual perception, however, there is Knowledge by Being—it arises in that state where the duality of the observer and the observed has vanished. This is the very core of direct or what is otherwise called the Mystical Experience. (Mehta, 1967, p. 7)

In the view of some, Knowledge by Being allows the mystic to gain direct awareness of the nature of mind, or of consciousness. Consciousness from such a perspective is understood as the ultimate context of which everything is a part. Thus it has been noted that,

> Consciousness has enormous potential. It can—and unconsciously does—link up directly with other minds and material forms. It need not be bound by the five senses, by time, nor by space. As mystics have long held, consciousness is a unified totality; the divisive limits that we experience in everyday life are ultimately illusions. (Motoyama & Brown, 1978, p. 79)

Given the amount of information currently available on different states of consciousness, one need not be a mystic in order to achieve such direct mind-to-mind knowing. Relative to the client–counselor/ therapist relationship, I believe that what is required is acceptance of our oneness in the context of deep caring and concern. At the same time that the holiness as well as the wholeness of our connection is acknowledged, there also is a both/and awareness of the uniqueness of each individual. In such a relationship, both the unity/relationship and the components/people involved in its creation are valued.

Lawrence LeShan, a psychologist who has studied the phenomenon of knowledge by being in general as well as his own experience of connectedness between healer and what he calls the "healee" (i.e., the client), outlines the process he uses to achieve such an awareness for himself:

I . . . conceptualize this particular healee being in both realities [independent and interdependent] at the same time. I would attempt to reach a point of being in which I would *know* that he not only existed as a separate individual inside his skin and limited by it, but that he also—and in an equally "true" and "real" manner—existed in the furthest reaches of the cosmos in space and time. . . .

Often I would use various types of symbols to help myself reach this point of knowing. For example, I might use the symbol of two trees on opposite sides of a hill with the tops visible to each other. From one viewpoint, they looked like two separate trees, but inside the hill, the two root masses met and were one. The two trees were really one and inseparable. Further, their roots affected the earth and the earth the rocks until I could know that in the whole planet and cosmos there was nothing that was not affected by them and affecting them. (1974, pp. 119–120)

LeShan also cites Dr. Robert Laidlaw's approach, which illustrates another way to facilitate awareness of connectedness:

[According to Laidlaw] "If I can perfectly align myself with the harmonies of the universe, then their energies can flow through me toward the healee whom I hold in my consciousness." The effort here is not of will, but of awareness of and harmonizing oneself and one's consciousness to the total harmonies of the All. (1974, p. 151)

While I believe that each of us is capable of accessing such a deep sense of connectedness, I am not suggesting that it is necessary for the counselor/therapist to attempt to create the totality of this kind of experience in every encounter with clients. I do believe it is important, however, that the counselor/therapist has experiential information which she or he is able to draw upon in each encounter. Thus, while the descriptions just provided may be useful in giving you a sense of what it is I am talking about, firsthand knowledge is likely to be far more helpful. The following exercise is designed, therefore, to provide you with an opportunity to see for yourself. While the exercise probably would be most effective carried out literally, as a meditation, just reading it slowly and thoughtfully has the potential to facilitate greater understanding and awareness. In either case, the goal is to enhance your ability to acknowledge connectedness in the context of the client–counselor/therapist relationship.

A MEDITATION ON CONNECTEDNESS

Find a peaceful place where you know you will not be interrupted for at least 30 minutes. If you wear eyeglasses or contact lenses, remove them; take off your shoes and loosen any tight-fitting clothing. Either sitting or lying down, whatever is most comfortable for you, close your eyes and take two or three deep breaths. Fully expand and contract your lungs each time you breathe in and out. . . . Then, as you allow your breath to return to its normal rhythm, begin the process of becoming totally relaxed. Starting at the top of your head and moving carefully, easily, and deliberately down and throughout your entire body, imagine yourself breathing in energy each time you inhale and breathing out tension each time you exhale. Continue this process until you have released the tension in every part of your body, all the way down to your feet and toes. . . .

As you become more and more relaxed, feel yourself slowly and quietly moving inward. Allow yourself to move to the center of your being, to a place of calm, and balance, and harmony. . . . When you feel that you have become as centered as you can be at this time, take a few moments to experience fully the sounds, the feelings, the smells, and anything you might see in your mind's eye. Allow all of your senses to become attuned to and to receive whatever information is being offered to you, without needing to do anything. . . .

Now, from this place of quiet calm at the center of your being, imagine that you are going to take a journey. In your mind's eye, see yourself slowly drifting. And as you drift, imagine that you come to a beautiful garden, a garden where flowers of many different types and colors are blooming. Take several moments to carefully observe. Enjoy the way the colors of the flowers blend to create the beauty of the garden. Notice how the flowers sway together as a gentle breeze lightly dances through them. . . .

Now move closer so that, if you wanted to, you could touch the flowers, and so that you can smell their delicate fragrances. Notice the differences in the texture, and shape, and color of the leaves and petals of the flowers. Be aware of the uniqueness of each flower, separate and yet together in the creation of a harmonious whole. . . . After a few moments of quiet observation, imagine yourself lying down on the ground near the garden. Feel the earth under you, supporting you completely. Breathe in the rich, pungent odor of the soil. Feel nourished and supported by the earth even as the flowers find their nourishment and support there. . . .

Now, as you are lying near the garden, focus your attention on one of the flowers, one that you can see very clearly. Take in every detail of this flower. Then slowly allow your attention to drift inside the flower, to perhaps imagine yourself becoming the flower. Allow yourself to feel the warmth of the sun on your leaves and petals. Notice from your vantage point the other flowers that are nearest to you in the garden. . . . Begin to explore the whole of your flowerness, allowing yourself to slowly travel down your stem, moving below the ground into your roots. Notice that, despite the darkness, you can see. Notice particularly the way your roots are intertwined with the roots of all the other flowers in the garden. . . .

Now watch as you draw into your roots some of the water and minerals from the soil. Take a few moments to think about all the ways the soil has been enriched so that it may sustain you and your growth. Imagine the oceans that feed the clouds . . . which release the rainfall . . . which fills the rivers . . . whose waters traverse the land and seep into the soil, gathering minerals as they go . . . on their return back to the sea. Think about your participation in this neverending cycle.

And now, feel yourself being slowly pulled back up through your stem, moving up above the ground and into the light of the day. Feel yourself bending toward the sun, which also warms and sustains you. As you continue moving up and out, you may notice a sense of sparkling energy that hovers all around you like your personal, flower-shaped shimmering glove of light. Feel the way this energy invites you to expand into it, to grow to your fullest. Notice that each of the flowers around you has a similar aura of sparkling energy around it, each contributing to a larger pattern of energy hovering over the garden and as far as you can see. . . . As you look around, imagine that you can see yourself lying on the ground next to the garden. See that a similar aura of sparkling energy surrounds your body, connecting it with the energy of the garden. . . .

Now, slowly imagine your attention shifting from the consciousness of the flower to awareness of yourself, back once again in your own body. Notice the way you may continue to feel the sparkling energy around you as it also invites you to expand and grow. Take a few moments to experience and enjoy these sensations. . . . In a little while you become aware that it is almost time for your imaginary journey to end. Perhaps you may want to take another few moments to express your gratitude, appreciating whatever the experience has provided for you. Know that as you return to normal waking consciousness, you may take with you both a sense of relaxation and a feeling of being energized. . . .

Now, slowly allow your attention to return to your breath. Begin to notice also the sounds of the world around you as you wiggle your fingers and toes. Perhaps, as you become fully awake and alert, you may feel like standing and stretching. Be sure to give yourself a little time before returning to your usual routine. You may even want to spend a few moments reflecting on your experience, or writing about it in your journal.

LEARNING TO HEAR

As we acknowledge and operate out of a recognition of the kind of connectedness which, I hope, you have just experienced, I am reminded of the process described by the biologists Humberto Maturana and Francisco Varela (1992) as *structural coupling*. According to this concept, which also is used as a way to understand human interaction from the perspective of second-order cybernetics, organisms "survive by fitting with one another and with other aspects of their context and will die if that fit is insufficient" (Becvar & Becvar, 1996, p. 80). Of particular relevance for me is the notion of

> the recurrent coupling in which the participating cells can preserve their individual limits, at the same time as they establish, by their coupling, a special new coherence which we distinguish as a metacellular unity and which we see as their form. (Maturana & Varela, 1992, p. 88)

An image that comes to my mind, as I attempt to understand this concept, is of puzzle pieces fitting together and creating the totality that is the larger picture. It is equally useful for me to think in terms of people being tuned in to one another, or of both members of a relationship sending and receiving information on the same channel, achieving "a special new coherence." It is at this point that I believe information can be accessed at many levels, including, but also going beyond, the five senses. Accordingly, one's ability to hear one's clients is enormously enhanced, for "within the subconscious mind each individual has a mental connection with every other individual. Communication can be instantaneous for one who has learned to use this telephone of the mind" (Condron, 1991, p. 136).

Given this perspective and my desire to hear, as I sit with my clients I attempt always to remain conscious of our connection, regardless of the topic of our discussions. Acknowledging connectedness is an attitude for me, a way of being present. And while I doubt that an observer would be able to see any particular behaviors that would give evidence of my attitude, I believe that clients sense it, although most likely at a level outside of their conscious awareness. Nevertheless, it is for me an important aspect of the soul-healing context. At the same time, there are also many observable behaviors that are characteristic of the process of hearing, including focused attention, intuitive knowing, pacing on the part of the counselor/therapist, and expressions of feeling truly understood on the part of the client.

Giving *focused attention* requires that the counselor/therapist stay in the here and now and truly pay attention to the client. This is a skill which I learned early on as a function of my choice not to take notes during a session. Not only did I wish to give my complete attention to my clients, but I also realized that I needed to retain the information provided to me by clients for purposes of record keeping. However, it didn't take me long to recognize how significant it was for clients to know not only that I had heard them but that I remembered them—who they were and what they had told me. And I find that I can recall this information many months or even years later. Indeed, in Book 1, sutra 11 of *The Yogi Sutras of Patanjali*, a set of ancient spiritual teachings, it is noted that *"Memory is bringing to the attention mind images of past things perceived."* Daniel Condron explains this sutra, or verse, as follows:

> The quality of remembrance is dependent upon the degree of attention given to each experience, as that experience is occurring. Through initiating an excellent recording memory sequence, the information received from the experience is available to be drawn upon and reasoned with by the Thinker [person doing the remembering]. The greater the

degree of attention given to the situation, the greater the corresponding degree of memory. Likewise, a greater number of coded images are available for future consideration. (1993, p. 21)

Thus, the counselor/therapist gains from focused attention even as the client also benefits. Indeed, from my perspective, it is a spiritual activity that honors the client. Further, for clients, being the recipient of such attention may be very different from the behavior that they (and we) may have experienced at the hands of other professionals whose only knowledge or memory of a person comes from a quick scan of a chart or notes taken at the end of a previous visit. I know that when I have been treated by such professionals, I felt more like a nameless case than a unique individual who is valued and respected. I know also that the latter message is the one that I want to convey to my clients.

In the process of focusing on and hearing my clients, I am tuned in not only to what I hear, but also to what I see and to the totality of my experience with them. This tuning in involves trusting my *intuitive knowing*, or the ideas or images, or both, which seem to pop up from the center of my being in the course of my conversation with clients. At a workshop I attended recently, the family therapist Lynn Hoffman referred to a similar phenomenon, describing what she called the "deep well" of knowing and, as she spoke, pointing to an area in the center of her chest. I certainly could resonate with what she was saying inasmuch as that is also the place where my intuition expresses itself. What is more, I do not hesitate to act on the information that I receive in this way, sometimes discussing it explicitly as "just a hunch" or "a sixth sense" about what is going on. I have learned that I am most effective when I trust the knowing that comes to me intuitively. Indeed, it is my belief that it emerges as a function of the connectedness I experience with my clients. As Kahn describes it:

Intuition is based on affinity rather than otherness. It's the I–Thou relationship that Martin Buber speaks about, so that one can read into another being only because one discovers in oneself the same thing that is to be found in that being by resonance, you see, based upon affinity. (Elliott, 1995, p. 200)

Coelho (1993) adds another dimension to the experience of intuitive knowing, to which I also subscribe. He describes intuition as "a sudden immersion of the soul into the universal current of life, where the histories of all people are connected, and we are able to know every-thing, because it is written there" (p. 77). Regardless of how we define it, however, honoring our intuitive knowing also may be understood as a sacred act:

> Many indigenous cultures recognize that intuition is the source that sparks external seeing (perception); internal viewing (insight); and holistic seeing (vision). For these societies, paying attention to these modes of seeing is a way to honor the sacred. We extend respect to our own visionary processes when we give voice to what we see or sense. (Arrien, 1993, p. 84)

In addition to focused attention and intuitive knowing, and involved in both, learning to hear also involves *pacing*. By pacing I refer to a sense of appropriate timing that also emerges as a function of acknowledging connectedness and of being tuned in to clients. While this is a skill that any experienced clinician understands is essential, I believe it bears em-phasizing. For while we may have a sense of what we think would help our clients, real respect requires that we also acknowledge the clients' expertise. Accordingly, we must allow them to be wherever they are in terms of their thoughts and feelings and to take our cues regarding how and when to proceed from them. In the process, we may find that what we first thought might be a useful response is replaced by something better. Or if the initial idea still seems like a good one, we may find that later it is accepted more readily than it might have been had we inter-jected it in a premature or untimely manner.

Thus, learning to hear is a complex process involving far more than our ears. What is more, it is my belief that it is a clinical skill whose im-portance cannot be overestimated, despite the fact that not all of the as-pects of this process readily lend themselves to scientific study or measurement. The following appeal, made to the profession of social work by Dennis Saleebey, seems to sum up this issue and its importance:

> If we are to conduct inquiry into client situations; if we are to develop the kind of knowledge base we need in order to help a client, to reflect upon our practice, and to revise practice in response to changing situations; if we are to reflect and hypothesize as we act, then, as a profession, we should consider the importance of educating "right-hemispheric" func-tions—the capacity for holistic grasp, intuitive resonance, and immedi-ate comprehension. (1989, p. 562)

This statement seems to me to affirm that, in addition to the knowing of our linear, rational minds, it is important to pay attention to and value the knowing of our nonlinear, intuitive minds. It is my belief that as we do so, we facilitate total engagement with our clients and we participate in the creation of a context in which they feel understood and respected—they know that there has been a mutual connection at a deep level. Accordingly, as the counselor/therapist focuses his or her attention, values his or her intuitive knowing, and honors a sense of pacing appropriate for each unique client, he or she may truly touch the client, who then feels heard. The psychologist Jean Houston describes such an interaction as follows:

> When you touch people, you can be deeply present, witnessing, evoking, midwifing their entelechy [achievement of their potential]. Then you have to recognize when to stand back and not say, "Let me help you," and not get in the way while this natural process unfolds. (Elliott, 1995, p. 88)

Thus, the logical response to true hearing on the part of the counselor/therapist may be the facilitation of development or unfolding on the part of the client. In the process, the wisdom, or expertise, of the client also is respected, as are his or her inherent strengths.

As I think about therapists who have embodied the ability to connect and hear, I am invariably reminded of Virginia Satir. Regardless of whether or not one subscribes to her approach, I believe most would agree that she was able to touch people in deep and powerful ways. For me, she also was an important role model, one of the few female family therapists I could study when I was in graduate school. In addition to watching videotapes of Satir's work, I also had the opportunity, early in my career, to attend an all-day session with her and to observe her as she worked with a family. The most memorable part of this experience was my personal encounter with her.

As an eager new professional, I intentionally sat in the front row so that I could get the best view of everything that was going on. Although I knew that I would like to have the opportunity to meet and talk with Satir, I also knew that I would not be one of those who hurried up to talk with her during the break. That just was not my style. What I did do throughout the morning, however, was to make eye contact with her in a deliberate manner. Satir apparently "heard" me, for shortly before the first break was about to end, she made her way over to me and held out her hand. As I shook her hand and introduced myself, I told her that I really had wanted to meet her. Her smiling response was, "I know." We then proceeded to have a delightful conversation. In addition, when the workshop resumed and people were needed for role playing, she selected me, although, of course, there was no shortage of willing volunteers.

While the experience of being heard probably is not as dramatic for my clients, generally they comment on it when it occurs. For example, I recently worked with a single parent, a father, for whom the decision regarding greater contact with and visitation by the mother, the noncustodial parent, was the focus of our conversation. At issue was the well-being of their four children, ranging in age from 6 to 15, balanced by the children's need or right, or both, to have relationships with the two parents; whether the father or the children should decide what was in the best interests of the children; the tension between what was best for the father and what might be best for the children; the fact that, given the differences in age, the children could not necessarily be treated as a unit; and the ramifications for various legal decisions of whether or not to allow greater contact and visitation.

In the course of a lengthy dialogue, held in the presence of the children, we attempted to sort out and make sense of these concerns. At the end of the conversation, the father summed up by describing feelings of confusion and frustration despite having achieved greater clarity and some sense of direction. I replied by saying, "I understand." His response was, "I know you do. I have tried to explain my dilemma to others, but they haven't heard what I was trying to say, and I always come away feeling like I'm crazy. With you, I know that I'm not crazy." Indeed, learning to hear our clients, and in the process perhaps validating their sanity, may be one of the greatest services we can provide for them. Further, for me, learning to hear is an important acknowledgment of connectedness, which, in recursive fashion, is facilitated as a function of that acknowledgment.

SELF-DISCLOSURE AND SHARING ONE'S JOURNEY

Another way in which connectedness may be acknowledged is through self-disclosure and the sharing of one's journey. At the same time, while such therapist behaviors may facilitate a sense of connectedness, I believe that the client's experience of being heard is a prerequisite to the sharing of much personal information on the part of the counselor/therapist. So once again, timing is of crucial importance. I therefore may acknowledge early on in a conversation with a client, such as the single parent just mentioned, that I have been divorced. Indeed, for some clients this seems to give me greater credibility because I have firsthand knowledge of some of the things they are experiencing. However, I believe that telling parts of my story becomes appropriate only as a means of illustrating a point I would like to make, and then only after I have given the client an opportunity to tell me his or her story in its entirety.

I use similar guidelines regarding stories about religion and spirituality. However, when appropriate, and particularly when asked, I am willing to talk about my religious/spiritual belief system. In this case, I have found that an important part of the process seems to be emphasizing that my experience has been a journey, a quest for information that recognizes the limits of the answers we may find. That, of course, is part of the uniqueness of the religious/spiritual realm, the realm of faith and belief. And I believe that, as we discuss issues of faith with our clients, we may facilitate the opening up to and awareness of a sense of mystery, which may be an important part of the healing process. As Dossey writes:

> Acknowledging this mystery leads not to a forlorn but to a glorious conclusion—for the unknown is the approach to the sacred, the spiritual, the unnamable, the *numinous.* To honor this dimension *is* to be healed. As Jung described, "The approach to the numinous is the real therapy and inasmuch as you attain to the numinous experiences you are released from the curse of pathology. Even the very disease takes on a numinous character." (1993, p. 81)

For example, not long ago I had a conversation with a client who was feeling depressed about the fact that things were not working out as he would like. During the course of the conversation, the client expressed anger at God for this situation. Knowing the important role that prayer and faith have played in his life, I suggested to this client that perhaps it was time to go back to praying and having faith that things eventually would work out for the best. In making this suggestion, my intent was to help the client access a belief system that in the past has enabled him to create a reality in which depression was no longer a logical response. Not surprisingly, however, the client's response at this time was, "Do you really believe that?" My answer was, "Yes, I do, or I would never say it."

I then went on to explain my belief that while we may ask for the best outcome in a problem situation, it may not be useful to specify what the outcome should be. In my view, what may be missing is the faith that even while things are not going well in the short run, in the long run there is a good chance that they will evolve in a way more to the client's liking. Further, what looks negative now ultimately may be perceived as having been quite appropriate, part of the unfolding of a far more positive process.

In response to my explanation, it was not long before the client was remembering how well such an attitude has helped in other, similar situations. Although still lacking certainty, he was once again in touch with the sacred mystery that is part of life. While I didn't say much about my own belief system, what I did say was enough to validate something important for this client.

On the other hand, self-disclosure and the sharing of one's journey sometimes may be far more extensive than that described in the previous example. To illustrate, let me tell you about a client who has been coming to see me on a monthly basis for more than a year. The presenting problem was the threat of a serious physical illness. The client chose to contact me, aware that I had survived cancer but knowing little else about me. During the course of our time together, this client experienced the death of a dear loved one, so dealing with grief also became part of our focus. Over the many months we have worked together, I have considered it appropriate to talk not only about the things I have done to facilitate my own physical healing but also to discuss the way in which the death of my son propelled me into an exploration of the mysteries of life. As it turns out, although our religious backgrounds are somewhat different, our spiritual beliefs are similar, and somewhat nontraditional. My sharing the varieties of my explorations has provided what is perceived as both validation and permission for the client's story about spirituality.

In addition to acknowledging connectedness, then, self-disclosure and sharing one's journey may facilitate a storytelling process and the creation of expanded narratives that clients may experience as more useful. While such a narrative approach is certainly consistent with a postmodernist, second-order family therapy perspective (Hoffman, 1985), we also may define ourselves as making recourse once again to the spiritual realm, or, as described in the following passage from *The Four-fold Way* by Angeles Arrien, to the way of the shaman:

Indigenous cultures recognize that storytelling can reshape an individual's experience or life story. Many shamans and medicine people are
gifted storytellers. Such people are called "shape-shifters," because
they have the capacity to shift the shape of an individual's story, or
even to shift the shape of their own physical appearance. A shaman
who has this ability is considered a healing catalyst and change agent.
(Arrien, 1993, p. 56)

Similarly, in recent years, the mental health field has witnessed the
development of several family therapy approaches that acknowledge
the power of stories and storytelling (Andersen, 1991; Anderson &
Goolishian, 1988; de Shazer, 1991; O'Hanlon & Wiener-Davis, 1989;
White & Epston, 1990). Fundamental to these approaches is the assumption that there are many ways to understand, or story, reality,
rather than one right way. Further, it also is understood that there is no
one right way to live or be. Counseling/therapy becomes a context that
enables the search for new meanings, and thus new understandings,
and language is understood as the vehicle for change. Included in this
process may be the search for exceptions, or times when the presenting
problem was not experienced, as well as for an understanding of the
solutions desired by the client. It is assumed that the client and the
counselor/therapist both have their respective expertise, and the coun-
seling/therapy process often resembles a conversation between colleagues. During such conversations, the clients' experiences are valued
and validated, the attempt is made to help clients see themselves as
separate from their problems, and clients are encouraged both to become aware of the influence of prevailing cultural stories and to create
new, more useful personal stories by means of which to live their lives.

Self-disclosure and the sharing of one's journey thus provide ways
for the counselor/therapist to emphasize that reality is made up of stories as well as to suggest possible new ways for the client to view a particular situation. In addition, as the client experiences respect and
validation for his or her story and simultaneously learns that the coun-
selor/therapist operates on the basis of a different belief system, or
story, the client also may recognize that there is more than one "right"
way to live or be. Fundamental to this process, however, from a soul-
healing perspective, is an acknowledgment of connectedness as a function of which client and counselor/therapist participate in the creation
of a therapy context infused with a spiritual orientation. While often
remaining implicit, there also may be times when it is appropriate and

useful to make explicit the acknowledgment of connectedness, or the inclusion of a spiritual view of relationships.

A SPIRITUAL VIEW OF RELATIONSHIPS

In addition to the counselor/therapist's acknowledging and acting out of an awareness of connection with his or her clients, then, it also may be helpful to discuss such a perspective relative to other relationships in the lives of clients. Indeed, clients may derive important information from a story about the ways in which people are connected and what such connections may mean. For example:

> If I *know* that in a real and profound sense you and I are one and are both integral parts of the total One, I treat you in the same way I treat myself. In addition, I treat myself with love and respect because I am part of the total harmony of the universe (or "a part of God" or "contain the indwelling light" or "an expression of Brahma"). (LeShan, 1974, p. 53)

Conversations describing such a perspective may be relevant in the counseling/therapy context both for the facilitation of closeness and intimacy in ongoing relationships and for achieving resolution when a relationship is terminated. The challenge in this, however, is to present ideas in a way that makes sense to the clients. Thus, it becomes important once again to truly hear clients and to speak in a manner that is meaningful for them.

I have found, for example, that parents in particular most often describe or can resonate with stories about connectedness with their children. Indeed, it is a fairly common occurrence for a parent to talk about "knowing" when something has transpired with a child before direct communication has taken place. Similarly, parents may describe waking in the middle of the night just before a baby begins to cry. And most of us also have had the experience of knowing who was at the other end of the line before picking up the phone. Or we notice that we get a surprise phone call from a person we were just thinking about. Although we may tend to pass off such events as coincidence, it is possible to see them as evidence of the connectedness between ourselves and others and to talk about these incidents as such with our clients.

Accordingly, and with the help of similar examples, I have found it useful to offer clients the possibility not only that they mutually influence and are influenced by other people at a behavioral level, but that there may be a deeper connection at a soul level. That is, they may have intuitive knowledge and information that would enable them to create more mutually satisfying relationships. However, I am careful to distinguish such knowing from attempts at mind reading, since such attempts, in my experience, are invariably disastrous. In addition to encouraging awareness of connectedness, I note the deep level at which pain may be experienced when disconnection occurs in the context of a significant relationship.

Sometimes the possibility of a soul connection is framed in explicitly spiritual terms. For instance, I have worked with a couple from another country who were struggling to make an arranged marriage work. During the course of therapy I borrowed some ideas from a religious group that espouses arranged marriages in the belief that all of the matches are "made in heaven." In the course of conversation, I asked my client couple, who were deeply religious, to consider that theirs might also be a match made in heaven. I then suggested that they search for the divine purposes for which they might have been brought together. This perspective provided a useful window for them to look through and united them in a joint effort that led eventually to mutual satisfaction.

A spiritual perspective that acknowledges connectedness, as I have mentioned, also may help clients make sense of the pain involved with the termination of a relationship. Certainly I know first-hand that such pain may be physical as well as emotional, and I have heard similar stories from my clients often enough to confirm that my experience is not unique. As I attempt to help clients understand and accept the need to be patient with their pain, I may describe it as a function of the severing of a very real connection. I affirm that feeling as though one has a "broken heart," or has been "kicked in the chest," or that one's "guts have been ripped apart" (expressions I have heard my clients use), may be closer to the truth than generally is recognized.

Finally, acknowledging what may be going on at a soul level as the members of a relationship struggle to complete its dissolution also may help individuals treat each other in a kinder, gentler fashion. Particularly in the case of unwanted divorce, I have found it beneficial to encourage clients to become aware that the pain they inflict on others may be more hurtful to themselves in the long run. In addition, if they are open to the idea that there are no accidents, they may find it useful to consider how what is going on may make sense in some way, perhaps at a soul level.

Indeed, all of us, clients as well as counselors and therapists, may benefit from a view of relationships as providing both the challenge and the opportunity to bring out the best in ourselves and in the other. That is, "people tend to see in themselves what we see in them. The grander our vision, the grander their willingness to access and display the part of them *we have shown them*" (Walsch, 1995, p. 142). Further, consistent with this view, one might also think of relationships according to the following story:

> If you both agree at a conscious level that the purpose of your relationship is to create an opportunity, not an obligation—an opportunity for growth, for full Self expression, for lifting your lives to their highest potential, for healing every false thought or small idea you ever had about you, and for ultimate reunion with God through the communion of your two souls—if you take that vow . . . the relationship has begun on a very good note. (Walsch, 1995, p. 141)

THE RELIGIOUS/SPIRITUAL CONVERSATION

Obviously, as I have reframed situations, I also often have found myself engaged in some very explicit conversations about religion and spirituality. That is, in the course of acknowledging connectedness, or in a context in which I have offered a spiritual view of relationships, conversations either about religion/spirituality, or of which religion/spirituality is a part certainly may evolve. For example, I once had a client ask me, "So where is God in all of this?" Since this was not the first time that religion had been discussed, I had a good sense of the client's belief system, which was quite a bit more conservative than mine. However, the question emerged in the midst of a dialogue about the unwanted breakup of a relationship, about which my client was experiencing a great deal of grief and confusion. I knew that the way I answered the question was extremely important.

My response was, "All I can tell you is *my* story about where God is." I then explained my belief that what we have been given by God is free will. That is, I don't believe that God causes the problems we experience. Rather, I believe that, out of the free will we have been given, we all make choices, some of which inevitably are experienced by others as painful. It is "man's inhumanity to man" rather than God's cruelty to humanity that is the source of our pain. This was an explanation that my client could accept, saying, "That makes sense. I also believe that we have free will."

This example illustrates how clients may themselves introduce religion/spirituality into the therapy process. Indeed, I find that people of faith often experience the doubts that emerge when life does not seem fair or just. In this regard, I am reminded particularly of a client family that was torn between religious beliefs according to which homosexuality is a sin, and love for and attempts to understand a child who acknowledged being homosexual. Not surprisingly, many of the conversations in therapy were focused on attempts to resolve this situation without the clients having to abandon their faith in God, a choice they clearly did not want to make.

In addition to conversations initiated by clients, as I have said, I do not hesitate to make inquiries about clients' religious or spiritual orientation when this seems appropriate. I do so both because I believe it is important to learn of the significance of this dimension in the life of my clients and also to let clients know that this is certainly a permissible topic of discussion should they desire to pursue it. Further, for those for whom religion/spirituality is an important dimension, it is an opportunity to acknowledge that this is an area of interest we have in common.

I tend to be very matter of fact but interested, for what I most want to communicate is an openness to hearing and learning about where my clients are in whatever ways seem most useful to them. Responses to my questions, of course, run the gamut in terms of the role that religion/spirituality plays. Moreover, I have found that it is not possible to predict, even for those who describe an active religious/spiritual orientation, its relevance either to the problem or to the related search for solutions that for me is the focus of therapy.

For example, I am currently working with Tony, who initially came for help with grief that followed the death of a spouse. Having attained relative peace, Tony now is feeling a great deal of stress related to the attempt to reconcile religious beliefs with the normal pulls of a new relationship. On the one hand, religion is an extremely important part of Tony's life. However, according to Tony's belief system, a sexual relationship outside of marriage, or at least a committed relationship, is sinful. On the other hand, Tony is in love and would like to be sexual with this new partner. Although Tony experiences being appreciated and respected in this relationship, there is no sense of a long-term commitment. While my own belief system may be different, I believe it is important that I explore with Tony—and help Tony understand—the ramifications, for Tony, of whatever decision Tony makes. Thus Tony's religious beliefs are a frequent and important part of our conversations together.

I have another client who is about the same age and who also has an active religious affiliation and observes all of that religion's traditions and holidays. This client is coping with a serious illness, the second in not very many years, and this time the illness is more life threatening. However, we rarely talk about religious/spiritual issues and generally only when this client initiates such a discussion. If in the course of such a discussion the client explicitly rejects a specific religious/spiritual interpretation or connection, however tentatively I offer it, I readily acknowledge that I have misunderstood or misspoken. I see my question or comment as a perturbation, the response to which influences how I proceed, and I never push beyond what the client deems appropriate. I believe that to do otherwise would be disrespectful. Further, I am aware primarily of the client's goals for therapy, and this client is most interested, at least for the short term, in handling the treatment process and facilitating physical healing. For the long term, the focus is on how to do a better job of self-care and how to reorient priorities in order to maintain health and wellness.

Thus, in spite of what you might perceive as great differences in the magnitude of the problems of these two clients, religious issues are far more salient for the first than they are for the second. Indeed, another client with whom I am working is quite a bit younger and has a far more serious health problem than the one just described. While we do talk about the meaning and purpose of life, as well as the possibility of death, we have never done so explicitly in terms of a religious or spiritual perspective. To do so would not be appropriate given that this client does not make recourse to such a belief system.

To reiterate, I believe that it is essential for the counselor/therapist to take his or her cues from the client. If the topic of religion/spirituality is not relevant for the client, then the counselor/therapist does not explicitly refer to it, regardless of how important it may be to him or her. If it is relevant for the client, then different kinds of conversation may ensue. However, the counselor/therapist still may be faced with other challenges, for the client may ask questions that the counselor/therapist does not feel equipped to answer. I believe that if this happens it is appropriate for the counselor/therapist to acknowledge his or her igno-rance. In such situations, or in those in which the client has expressed a belief or concept that is foreign to the counselor/therapist, she or he might ask the client to say more, to describe the context of the question or concept. Doing so may help to facilitate greater understanding. And despite differences in belief systems, taking such a position still may help to create a context in which connectedness is acknowledged. Which brings us, finally, to a consideration of the ramifications for relationships of acknowledging connectedness and the attitude by means of which it is expressed.

RAMIFICATIONS

Acknowledging connectedness—one of five principles that character-ize my version of counseling/therapy with a spiritual orientation, the process I have termed soul healing—primarily describes the client–counselor/therapist relationship. Frances Vaughan offers what I consider to be an important perspective on this relationship:

> The psychotherapeutic relationship provides a safe space for telling the truth about our experience. We learn to listen better to ourselves and to others. As we do that, we enhance our capacity for learning, for seeing things as they are, for loving, and for making a more significant contribu-tion to the well-being of the world. The quality of life does change as we do these practices, both in terms of increased inner peace and in terms of our capacity to deepen our relatedness to each other. (Elliott, 1995, p. 239)

It is my belief that the "safe space" to which Vaughan refers is also sacred space, and its sacredness is honored to the degree that we recog-nize our mutual interdependence and connectedness at a soul level. In the process we may facilitate an opening up that allows for more meaningful experiences for everyone involved. For as we become aware of our relatedness, we may recognize that we truly are involved in each other's destinies. We also may realize that there is much more information that is available and that may be accessed as we tune in to one another and to the universal mind, or consciousness, within which we all exist. Although our clients may not be able to name what they have experienced with us, they will know that something significant has happened. And they may take this information with them as they interact with others in their lives.

Indeed, acknowledging connectedness may have very important ramifications for other relationships in the lives of both clients and counselors/therapists. In the words of Albert Einstein:

A human being is part of a whole, called by us the "Universe," a part limited in time and space. He experiences himself, his thoughts and feelings, as something separated from the rest—a kind of optical delusion of his consciousness. This delusion is a kind of prison for us, restricting us to our personal desires and to affection for a few persons nearest us. Our task must be to free ourselves from this prison by widening our circles of compassion to embrace all living creatures and the whole of nature in its beauty. (Sogyal, 1992, p. 98)

What is to be gained is a greater sense of compassion, or an enhanced ability to love unconditionally on a much larger scale. As Taggart has written:

[I]t seems to me that one reason why the great commandments in most religious traditions have to do with love, rather than with understanding and knowledge, is that when we love, we appreciate the unique other unconditionally, and we make room for that other to grow, whether the other is a person or a culture or a belief system. And we somehow incorporate the other into ourselves, thereby enriching both heaven and earth. (1994, p. 174)

All of which brings me to an issue of great importance: the family. Currently the subject of much political debate, the family has been the focus of my interests, thought and attention for many years. The matters I have pondered relative to the family include the following:

- the fact that the meaning of the family has changed over time;
- the fact of loyalty to, often despite lack of connection with, family members;
- the fact that our most meaningful relationships are not necessarily with family members;
- the fact that it is friends who often become our consciously chosen families;
- the degree of love we are capable of feeling and expressing toward some family members, particularly spouses or partners and children; and

- the reality that might be created if we felt toward all members of the family of man/woman the degree of love we are capable of feeling and expressing toward some family members, particularly spouses/ partners and children.

The phenomenon of the family as an entity with a distinct consciousness about itself is fairly recent. During the 1700s, the boundaries between family and community were still quite blurred (Morgan, 1944). However, over time families became more private and much more inwardly focused as individuals sought to have their needs met within the context of the family (Demos, 1979). While the current movement may be toward a more individualistic focus (Lasch, 1979a), many still yearn for the family as a "haven in a heartless world" (Lasch, 1979b). Therefore, the degree of loyalty we often experience toward family members makes a great deal of sense, as does our disappointment when family members don't live up to our expectations.

The fact is, however, that many times our relationships with family members are less than satisfactory. And we may continue—to an unreasonable extent—to have unrealistic expectations of our relationships with family members rather than accepting what is realistic and moving on. At the same time, however, we also generally search for and create relationships with others. And it is often within the context of these other relationships that we feel truly known, heard, loved, and respected. We experience with friends what we have been looking for in our families. Hence the not uncommon choice to think of these friends as our chosen families.

Nevertheless, our family, as we conceive it, tends to comprise a small and circumscribed circle of people. Further, it is within the family that most of us experience our most intense and intimate relationships, and it is here that the ability to love unconditionally is expressed most frequently.

Perhaps the best examples of unconditional love are to be found in the relationships between parents and children, between the members of a loving and committed couple or among people who have an enduring friendship. My purpose here is not to reflect on why this is. Rather, my goal is to point out the kind of love and compassion each of us is capable of expressing in the context of relationships such as these. And, for me, the questions that emerge include: What would happen if we chose not to limit our expressions of love in such a manner? What would happen if we were able to see everyone in our world as a family member worthy of the same kind of compassion we currently save only for our personal families?

Certainly, I believe that the degree of emotional attachment would have to continue to differ in different relationships. The goal in all relationships, however, would be to reach out to help others, knowing that as we did so our capacity to receive from others would increase. Further, our friendship, or our reaching out, would not be conditional, requiring a particular response in order to maintain the friendship. Rather, our efforts would be toward sharing our whole self with others in acknowledgment that our separation, at least at a spiritual level, is an illusion.

While all of this may seem idealistic, I believe we are capable of this kind of awareness and of the behaviors that might logically flow from it. I believe further that this is what many of us already do when we connect with our clients. And as more and more of our clients experience such an acknowledgment of connectedness in their relationships with counselors and therapists, the impact will ripple out to an ever-expanding circle within our society and our world. Just as acknowledging connectedness is only one principle of a spiritual orientation, however, so is it only one aspect of what might be required to bring about the kind of reality in which the scenario I have just described might be brought to life. Thus, the time has come to consider the second principle of soul healing, that of suspending judgment.

I think that whenever soul is present, it's because what you're doing, whom you're with, where you are, evokes love without your thinking about it. You are totally absorbed in the place or person or event, without ego and without judgment.

—Jean Shinoda Bolen

CHAPTER 5

Suspending Judgment

INTRODUCTION

As we begin the discussion of the second soul-healing principle, suspending judgment, it is appropriate to point out that the enterprise we think of as counseling/therapy probably would not exist if we as a society did not operate according to values that define good and bad, right and wrong, health and illness. Indeed, to paraphrase Paul Dell (1983), we really do not treat problems or pathology. Rather, what we treat are our values, or our beliefs about the behaviors we decide are dysfunctional or sick. Further, as Aponte notes:

> Values frame the entire process of therapy. Values are the social standards by which therapists define reality, identify problems, formalize evaluations, select interventions, and determine therapeutic goals. All transactions between therapists and clients involve negotiations about the respective value systems that each party brings into the therapeutic process. (1994, p. 170)

In this context, the idea of suspending judgment may seem challenging, if not impossible. However, a postmodern perspective affords us a way to do just that, even as we recognize our own and our society's values about which behaviors are considered appropriate, acceptable, and functional, and which are not. Therefore, this chapter opens with a consideration of the systemic/cybernetic notion that all behavior makes sense, or is logical, in context. This discussion also includes the constructivist and social-constructionist views that problems exist in the eye of the beholder and that they are considered problems on a larger scale as a function of the dominant discourses characterizing a particular society.

Having assumed such a postmodern perspective on problems, I then propose that the ability to suspend judgment is further facilitated when counselors and therapists are able to detach themselves from outcomes and accept clients as they are; to operate according to a belief that each person is doing the best he or she can; and to maintain a focus on the here and now. Each of these modes of behavior is also a topic of discussion. Finally, given that the ability to help clients suspend judgment may be of importance in the process of cocreating a soul healing context, the chapter concludes with reflections on the role of expectations, on dealing with the question "Why?" and on thinking relatively. Throughout the chapter the relationship of each of these issues to a spiritual orientation in counseling and therapy also is considered.

A POSTMODERN PERSPECTIVE ON PROBLEMS

As we have learned, or been socialized into, theories consistent with a modernist, or neo-positivist, worldview, most of us have internalized a belief in the power of science and the possibility of understanding reality in an objective way. We have trusted that, through "systematic observation and rigorous reasoning" (Gergen, 1991, p. 29), we were progressing toward possession of the truth. Such a view is consistent with the prevailing paradigm in our society and thus also is pervasive in the mental health professions. Given this perspective, the role of counselor/therapist traditionally has been more consistent with that of social engineer, particularly as it entailed helping people fit such cultural ideals as that of the mature, autonomous individual. As a part of this process we have sought to understand problems and pathology, which we have assumed exist as phenomena separate from our observations of them.

From a cybernetic perspective, however, problems do not exist "out there." Rather, problems exist in the eye of the beholder as she or he observes and labels certain phenomena as problematic. That is, if the universe is understood as an interdependent whole, everything fits, or is coherent, and thus, at least at some level, makes sense. It therefore is assumed that all behavior in a system is normal when understood in context and that problems emerge only as a function of the way we story, or give meaning to events. It is only relative to a particular frame of reference that we punctuate, or describe, experience as either problematic or satisfactory.

To explain this perspective a bit further, second-order cybernetics, consistent with quantum physics, suggests that the observer is part of the observed. Thus, we must include ourselves—our inevitable subjectivity in the form of our personal worldviews—in whatever we are observing. Further, we must recognize that the act of observing influences the objects of our observation, a notion that has been validated empirically in the field of quantum physics (Briggs & Peat, 1984; Capra, 1983; Hayward, 1984). From this perspective, we create behavior rather than discover it as we look at reality through the lenses of our individual perspectives. In other words, believing is seeing.

Such cybernetic thinking is quite consistent with a constructivist perspective (von Glasersfeld, 1984), according to which we understand that we create reality as a function of our perceptions. For, "Constructivism holds that the structure of our nervous systems dictates that we can never know what is 'really' out there" (Hoffman, 1993, p. 34). Further, "The two basic principles of radical constructivism are (1) knowledge is actively constructed by the individual and not passively received; and (2) the function of cognition organizes the experiential world rather than seeks to discover ontological reality" (Gale & Long, 1995, p. 13). Thus, we cannot know the truth about people or things in our world in any objective way. Rather, all that we can know with any certainty are our constructions of people or things.

What is more, consistent with the assumptions of social constructionism, that which we tend to believe, and thus see, is what the worldview of our society promotes as being real, or "out there." In other words, the ecology of ideas created by a particular society guides our values and beliefs, and it is as a function of these values and beliefs that we view and give meaning to various events and situations. Indeed, "Social constructionist inquiry is principally concerned with explicating the processes by which people come to describe, explain, or otherwise account for the world (including themselves) in which they live" (Gergen, 1985, p. 266).

What we learn from such inquiry is that problems and pathology, like other aspects of "reality," are socially constructed. We become aware that it is in the process of defining and utilizing diagnostic categories that we create pathology, or behavior which is viewed as maladaptive rather than adaptive. Thus, we recognize that there are no "objectively treatable structures" in individuals, couples, or families.

Rather, the choice of a diagnostic label or category by means of which to describe individual, couple, or family "dysfunction" says as much or more about the one doing the diagnosing as it does about what is "really" going on in the individual, couple, or family.

In addition, we have learned from our inquiry that the totalizing discourses that characterize our society tend to have a deficit focus, and that both the social sciences and mental health practice are inclined to be pathology based. However, this is not an indictment; it is merely a way of describing reality. Indeed, the description too is a social construction, one, however, which may be very liberating. For, if we are able to acknowledge our participation in the construction of pathology, we also may see the potential for deconstructing problems through a process of examining assumptions and shifting perceptions. And as we become aware of what it is we must value and believe in order for a phenomenon to gain the status of problem, other ways to view that phenomenon also may be revealed. Further, if we recognize that the so-called experts do not necessarily have sole possession of the truth, we may pay greater attention to the truths, or the expertise, of all. And finally, if we become conscious of the discourses that are privileged in our society, we also may become more sensitive to those conversations which are excluded by such privileged discourses.

All of this takes us to a caution to counselors and therapists "to be wary of an expert posture, to operate out of a more respectful, ethical stance, and to acknowledge the limits of what can be known" (Becvar & Becvar, 1996, p. 96). For, in the words of Maturana and Varela:

> Every human act takes place in language. Every act in language brings forth a world created with others in the act of coexistence which gives rise to what is human. Thus every human act has an ethical meaning because it is an act of constitution of the human world. This linkage of human to human is, in the final analysis, the groundwork of all ethics as a reflection of the legitimacy of the presence of others. (1992, p. 247)

Thus, a postmodern perspective suggests that we view people in all of their contextual complexity and attempt to understand the logic of their situation. Our goal is not to make them fit in with society's beliefs and our related theories about how they should be. Pursuing such a goal would be disrespectful and perhaps unethical. Moreover, given a soul-healing orientation, we recognize the possibility of an additional dilemma:

Often the goal of psychotherapy is to make small shifts in the personality so that it may function more successfully within society's structure of values. But this strategy may not be successful for the person whose soul is striving for a different kind of expression or for people who live in a predominantly neurotic or destructive society. (Raheem, 1991, p. 13)

While I would not label our society either predominantly neurotic or destructive, I do recognize that we have some potentially crazy-making culture tales (Becvar & Becvar, 1995). For example, let's look more closely at the idea of the mature, autonomous individual, the type of person so highly valued in our society. The contradiction inherent in such an ideal, at least according to the systemic/cybernetic story, is that we all exist in relationship and cannot know ourselves or each other separate from our interactions with one another, that "Our definitions of people necessarily define the nature of the relationship between us and thus define us as well" (Becvar & Becvar, 1996, p. 358). Therefore, to try to help a client fit the ideal of the autonomous individual may be to participate in maintaining a problem rather than in achieving its solution. In a similar manner, if in our work we do not take into consideration what is appropriate for growth at a soul level for each individual, consistent with his or her own goals, we may do him or her a great disservice.

It also is important to note that, just as trying to help clients conform to a general theory or a cultural ideal is likely to be problematic, such a stance may have negative consequences for the groups to which these individuals belong. Indeed, promotion of the ideals of the counselor/therapist about how people should be may constitute a spiritual violation at various other levels of the system. For example, "Service providers who try to substitute their personal political and social views for a community's views about moral behavior and family relationships stifle the souls of communities" (Aponte, 1994, p. 11).

Rather than promoting a particular way to be, counseling/therapy consistent with both a postmodern/constructivist/social constructionist perspective and a spiritual orientation is concerned with helping clients achieve the solutions which they have defined as appropriate and desirable and which are consistent at all levels of their being. Further, in the course of the counseling/therapy process, the attempt is made to hold in abeyance judgments about particular behaviors. Regardless of our beliefs about these behaviors (e.g., that they are wrong or bad), the focus shifts to an attempt to understand the larger pattern of which they are a part and within which they make sense and thus are being maintained (Watzlawick et al., 1974).

In order to better illustrate the perspective I am describing, I offer the following description of the "Knudsen" family. Although I will be moving back and forth between theory and practice, I will return to a consideration of my work with this family throughout the remainder of the chapter as I describe how the various aspects of suspending judgment may be implemented. I have chosen this particular family, which is a composite created from aspects of therapy with several families, because I suspect that their story is not unlike that of many of the clients with whom you have worked or who you will see in the future.

The Knudsen family is comprised of Mom, Dad, and five children who have the following birth order: The oldest is Alan, followed by Bonnie, Carl, Debbie, and Elaine. They are a white, Protestant, rather traditional, very close-knit, middle-class family. Dad has a college degree, earned at nights and over many years while also working to support his growing family. Mom is a high school graduate who currently is attending a local college where Bonnie also is a student. Alan has a college degree and is following in Dad's footsteps professionally. Everyone is living at home except Carl, who has just begun college in another part of the state. Debbie (eleventh grade) and Elaine (ninth grade) are students at the same high school.

The Knudsens were referred for family therapy following both inpatient treatment for Debbie's alcohol abuse and the completion of a related aftercare program attended by all members of the family. Debbie's truancy and failing grades were the symptoms that first triggered awareness of a problem. Upon the advice of the school counselor, Debbie volunteered to be hospitalized. It was during the course of the inpatient treatment that Debbie revealed that as a small child she had been sexually abused by her Dad's oldest brother, now deceased. Subsequent to Debbie's disclosure, Elaine revealed that she also had been abused by the same uncle.

At the time of our first meeting, everyone expressed distress about the uncle's abusive behavior. The problem was exacerbated by the fact that the uncle had been a much-admired, even revered, family member. As a young man he had taken over the responsibility for rearing Dad, who was 15 years his junior, upon the death of their parents. After successfully discharging his responsibility for his brother, the uncle had worked his way through seminary and had become a clergyman. Although he eventually married, he never had children of his own. He became the pastor of a church in the very remote, rural area of the state in which he had grown up and was totally devoted to his work among the people there. He was loved and respected not only by his extended family, with whom he maintained close ties, but also by the members of his church and his community. When he died five years ago at the age of 65, there were many who mourned his passing.

It was Mom who called to make the appointment and who expressed most vocally the pain being experienced by all the family members. Her story was one of betrayal, a theme that was reiterated to some degree by both Debbie and Elaine. Mom continually spoke of how much the uncle had been trusted and how wrong they all had been in their opinion of him. For it was now her view that in reality he had been nothing more than a dirty old man.

Much of Mom's anger spilled over onto, and often was directed at, her husband, a rather quiet, soft-spoken man. Indeed, Dad was torn by conflicting emotions and loyalties. On the one hand, he was outraged by what had happened to his daughters. But, on the other hand, he did not want to completely vilify the uncle, his brother, whom he knew also to have been a good person in many ways. While certainly upset about the uncle's behavior, all of the siblings were more concerned with helping Debbie and Elaine come to terms with what they had experienced and with helping them to find ways to go on and live happy, productive lives.

From my perspective, Debbie's alcoholic behavior and school-related problems truly made sense given the secret shame with which she had lived for many years. Inasmuch as Debbie is the fourth child, I also could make recourse to the story of the "family trouble-shooter" (Hoopes & Harper, 1987) being the logical family member to experience the symptoms that signaled distress in the larger context. Mom's anger and Dad's ambivalence also were logical to me. That is, Mom was understandably outraged not only because her daughters had been abused but also because the perpetrator had been someone whom she felt should have been eminently trustworthy. And it was clear that Dad had experienced the uncle not only at his worst, but also at his best. Similarly, the desire on the part of the children to focus at a more pragmatic level fit, relative to their ages and developmental stages.

Upon learning something about the uncle and his life circumstances, I was able to understand how his incestuous behavior was logical to context, despite the fact that, like my clients, I find it abhorrent. My position was therefore similar to that described by another group of family therapists:

Sometimes, in the beginning, you get a negative feeling about a family, but when you begin to see the connections in the system, your feelings change. Neutrality is to accept the whole system; it's not to be outside or to be cold. It's to feel a sense of compassion, interest, and curiosity about a family's dilemma: How did they get there? How did they organize themselves that way? We try to see the logic even in situations that are repugnant from a moral point of view. (Boscolo, Cecchin, Hoffman & Penn, 1987, p. 152)

While I was certain that the family members could easily hear and accept my stories about their behaviors, my real concern was to cocreate with them, and particularly with Mom, a new story about the uncle. It was my belief that this new story would facilitate the achievement of the goals of each in such a way that the integrity of the family in the long run was maintained.

Accordingly, my focus was on the larger patterns, or context, and the ways in which the problems experienced made sense in context. And my hope was to work with the family in order to achieve "story repair" (Howard, 1991), or the cocreation of a new context within which such problems were no longer a logical response. However, from my perspective, such a stance requires, first of all, not only that we accept the limits of what we as counselors and therapists may be able to accomplish, but also that we accept our clients where they are.

ACCEPTANCE

Indeed, one of the hardest lessons that we professionals may have to learn is how to care deeply about our clients and their lives and at the same time be able to detach ourselves from outcomes. This, in turn, requires a commitment to do one's best while at the same time trusting the process. Such a commitment is facilitated by a systemic perspective according to which we recognize that responsibility is shared. And it is further facilitated by a spiritual perspective according to which we recognize that in fulfilling our portion of responsibility, we have done all that we can do. In other words:

[T]he successful healer is the peaceful healer! For she or he totally understands the process that is going on spiritually. When . . . there has been no healing, the healer can still be peaceful. For the healer has done one hundred percent of his part, and he does not take responsibility for the one who has just left the office. . . . [T]he pain is not your responsibility. Your responsibility is in your passion and your science. We say to use it to one hundred percent. . . . Let the humans who come to you do the rest, and then be peaceful with your own process. Love them fully, but do not take responsibility for their process. This peace will result in increased power for you. No healer can be at one hundred percent and be in unrest. (Carroll, 1995, p. 154)

It is my belief that if we are able to achieve such acceptance of the process and of the limits of what we may be able to accomplish, we may help ourselves avoid the problem of burnout. We also may learn another valuable lesson, namely that we cannot always know what ultimately is the best, either for our clients or ourselves. The following story, related by Alan Watts (1968), illustrates this point:

Once upon a time there was a Chinese farmer who had a horse. One day the farmer's horse ran away. In the evening, all of the farmer's neighbors gathered and they said to the farmer, "That's too bad."

And the farmer said, "Perhaps."

The next day, the farmer's horse returned and brought with it seven wild horses. And when the neighbors gathered that evening they said to the farmer, "How lucky you are!"

And the farmer said, "Perhaps."

The next day the farmer's son was grappling with one of the wild horses, trying to break it in. The horse threw the farmer's son and the son broke his leg. When the neighbors heard what had happened they said to the farmer, "Oh, that is too bad that your son has broken his leg!"

And the farmer said, "Perhaps."

The next day the conscription officers came to the village in which the farmer lived, gathering young men for the army. They rejected the farmer's son because he had a broken leg. And upon hearing this, the neighbors said, "Isn't it wonderful that your son does not have to leave to join the army!"

And the farmer said, "Perhaps."

When, like the farmer, one is detached from outcomes it is not that one does not care. Rather, one attempts to act wisely, to trust, and to be open to whatever may evolve in the knowledge that there may be a greater wisdom to which we may have access only with the passage of time. Indeed, according to the anthropologist Angeles Arrien:

The majority of spiritual traditions address the theme of detachment. Harrison Owen, in his book *Leadership Is*, has consolidated these themes into four principles, which he calls the immutable laws of the spirit: "Whoever is present are the right people to be there; whenever we start, it's always the right time; what happens is the only thing that could have happened; when it's over, it's over." Underlying each of these premises, whether we agree with them or not, is the principle of acceptance rather than resignation. Can we accept the experience as it is and then be creative with it, rather than be resigned or fatalistic about it? Acceptance is an important part of detachment. (1993, p. 112)

And I would add that detachment is an important part of acceptance. Thus, as I sat with my client family, the Knudsens, I was able to understand not only how the problems they had experienced were logical to their context, but also that I was only one of many people who would have an influence on the outcome of therapy. I also knew it was not for me to judge either what the outcome of therapy should be or the behaviors of individual members during our work together to facilitate achievement of their goals. Therefore, I wished neither to judge the uncle for his abusive behavior, nor to judge Mom for her belief in a story that had the potential to destroy the family as well as its history, nor to judge Dad for his ambivalence, nor to judge the younger generation for wanting to get on with life.

Rather, each of these factors was understood as interesting and perhaps important information. Period. For I believe that one of the greatest gifts we can give to another person is total acceptance, regardless of behavior of which neither we nor the larger society may approve. For me, this is a deeply spiritual commitment, emerging in part from my belief that each of us is at the deepest level a manifestation of the divine. And perhaps nowhere is this attitude more crucial than in the context of counseling and therapy. As described by psychiatrist Arthur Kleinman:

> Whatever else it is, psychotherapy is a deeply moral relationship. The practitioner attempts to be with the patient in the ambit of suffering. The patient actively opens his life world to their conjoint exploration. Practitioner becomes a moral witness, neither a judge nor a manipulator. Patient becomes an active colleague, not a passive recipient. Both learn and change from the experience. (1988, p. 246)

Further, according to a similar perspective provided by the medical doctor and transpersonal psychotherapist Carlos Warter:

One cannot think about why the patient is not well, whether the healing techniques being used will work, why the patient is reacting a certain way or anything else that would get in the way of focusing on the person as a whole and sacred being. (1994, pp. 40–41)

Indeed, from a soul-healing, spiritual orientation, the focus on the sacredness of the clients with whom the counselor/therapist has the privilege of working is of great importance. Such an attitude certainly facilitates acceptance, which, in turn, is a part of the process of suspending judgment. In addition, given this attitude, it also is possible to assume the best, to assume that no one is inherently bad. This, for me, is another important aspect of suspending judgment.

ASSUMING GOOD INTENTIONS

I prefer to think that people are fundamentally good. Accordingly, I assume that while people behave in ways we may evaluate negatively, ultimately they are doing the best they can, given their circumstances and beliefs. Thus I would concur with the view of human nature subscribed to by Virginia Satir:

Over the years I have developed a picture of what the human being living humanly is like. He is a person who understands, values, and develops his body, finding it beautiful and useful; a person who is real and honest to and about himself and others; a person who is willing to take risks, to be creative, to manifest competence, to change when the situation calls for it, and to find ways to accommodate to what is new and different, keeping that part of the old that is still useful and discarding what is not. (1972, p. 2)

From my perspective, while human beings may do things we would label as negative, such behavior is inconsistent with their basic nature. Our responsibility, therefore, is to participate in the cocreation of contexts within which behaviors we would label as positive on the part of all involved are chosen or evoked, or both. To do so is to acknowledge "that we were created to be companions and cocreators with God . . . spiritual beings who happen to be having a physical experience" (Todeschi, 1996, p. 10). I also subscribe, then, to the following admonition:

To do things beautifully, to handle ugly problems beautifully, with a deep regard for the sacredness of the human status—that is the Divinity in each of us. That means, for example, loving people whom one dislikes, which is unconditional love. That's how one is able to overcome the limitations of one's judgmentalism. It means having the courage to stand by one's ideal, particularly of truth, when one is being threatened or frightened or cast upon by people; building a beautiful world, of beautiful people, even when circumstances around one are ugly. I don't say that one will have immediate success, but doing things beautifully has the ultimate value, and so eventually it will carry success with it. (Khan, in Elliott, 1995, p. 199)

Thus, one of the first things I attempted to do with my clients the Knudsens was to gather information about the uncle. What I learned, and what I helped the family members to understand, was how it was that the uncle could have sexually abused his young nieces and at the same time still be considered to have been a moral person, at least in other areas of his life. This seemed to be a particularly salient issue given that he was a clergyman, which further confounded the ability of the family members to understand his behavior. However, clergyman or not, his story, unfortunately, is not especially unusual. That is, he was socialized into a culture in which behavior such as his was fairly commonplace and, even if disliked, often was tolerated. Indeed, the women in such cultures traditionally have kept silent in the belief, however mistaken, that this was the way men were or that there was nothing they could do about it.

What the Knudsens were doing, of course, was judging past behavior by present standards. However, as we know, such standards have changed radically in recent years. While abusive behavior is far older than our country, in many of its forms it not only was condoned but also mandated by law during the early years of American society. For example, wives were subject to their husband's authority and fathers were expected to beat the "sin nature" out of their children when necessary (Morgan, 1944). What has changed, therefore, are not the behaviors but our perceptions, or values, about these behaviors, as well as our willingness to speak out about those now considered unacceptable. Although we certainly must acknowledge that the incest taboo is hardly new, it is worth seriously considering that

when we look at the behavior of human beings before our time, there can be no evaluation of right and wrong. It is so important not to view the past from a place of judgment but to acknowledge that this is what the collective was working on at the time. This nonjudgmental way of looking at the past gives us the freedom to change. (Ingerman, 1993, p. 50)

While there is no question that the uncle's incestuous behavior was wrong, not only in the past but by today's standards, it is possible that he may not have believed it to be so. Or at least he may have been able to tell himself a story that enabled him to rationalize his behavior. Indeed, if I were working with him today, one of the questions that I might want to ask is, "How was it that you came to believe that it was OK to be sexual with your nieces?" A question such as this is aimed at understanding rather than judging. Similarly, if, as the family suspects, the uncle's wife knew what was going on, her silence was at least understandable if not what we might have preferred. And it is such understanding that I would want to communicate to her in an effort to facilitate the trust that I believe is essential to an effective therapeutic relationship. Another message that I would like to send is that participation in behaviors, even those we label as morally reprehensible, does not automatically make the total person bad or negate the good things which she or he also has done. Such was the focus of my story as I worked with the Knudsens to help them create a new, more comfortable story for themselves.

While the sexual abuse probably never will be either forgotten or condoned, and I do not believe that it should be, the ability of the Knudsen family members to expand their story about the uncle allowed them to hold on to and continue to feel pride in parts of who they were in terms of their history. It also enabled a shift to dealing with the problems they were currently experiencing. This was an important turning point given my belief that a here-and-now focus is also part of what is involved with suspending judgment.

HERE-AND-NOW FOCUS

As we all certainly are aware, past events cannot be changed. However, as we change our responses to, or our way of storying, events, in a sense we recreate the past. And as we participate with our clients in such re-storying, the hope is that they will be able both to live more comfortably in the present and to create the potential for a more satisfying future. Such a stance is consistent with a cybernetic perspective according to which one views history as providing information about the larger context and sees the system, in the present, as offering its own best explanation of itself (Becvar & Becvar, 1996).

A here-and-now focus is also consistent with a spiritual orientation, according to which the point of power is always in the present moment

(Roberts, 1974). That is, the present moment is all there ever really is. Or in the words of Jon Kabat-Zinn:

> [T]he only time you ever have in which to learn anything or see anything or feel anything, or express any feeling or emotion, or respond to an event, or grow, or heal, is this moment, because this is the only moment any of us ever gets. . . .
>
> The past is gone, and I don't know what's coming in the future. It's obvious that if I want my life to be whole, to resonate with feeling and integrity and value and health, there's only one way I can influence the future: by owning the present. If I can relate to *this moment* with integrity, wakefully, then the sum of that is going to be very different over time, over mind moments that stretch out into what we call a life, than a life that is lived mostly on automatic pilot, where we are reacting and being mechanical and are therefore somewhat numb. (1995, p. 112)

Keeping such a here-and-now focus in mind, let's return to the Knudsen family, whose members stated at the beginning of therapy that our work together would be deemed successful when Debbie was once again succeeding in school and feeling good about herself and when Mom and Dad had reconciled their differences. A significant first step in this process involved rewriting, in the present, the family story, as just described. Such a re-storying enabled them not only to achieve a more acceptable perspective on an undeniably negative past situation but to shift their focus to a consideration of the present.

Indeed, I viewed the Knudsen family, as I would most clients when they enter therapy, as stuck in repetitive patterns of behavior and in need of new information, or a new story, that would help them become unstuck, or create a new context. In this instance, the stuckness largely revolved around patterns that reflected their inability to come to terms with behaviors which, in their judgment and that of society, are wrong. I suspect that if I had chosen to stay with this judgmental focus, however, the course of therapy would have been very different and perhaps not as satisfactory. That is, I believe that to do so would have been to participate in their stuckness by helping to maintain the old patterns of behavior. However, having achieved a sense of resolution with which everyone was at least somewhat comfortable, we then were able to move on to conversations about current and desired behaviors.

Specifically, the focus turned to a consideration of how each family member could participate in creating the reality he or she wanted. In doing so, I also recognized that judgment merely had been suspended, not eliminated, in an effort to discuss ways in which the *incestuous behavior* might have been logical to context, and that it might be possible to consider avoiding total condemnation of the *person* involved with its perpetration. We therefore discussed, within the context of the family's religious belief system, the possibility of forgiving the uncle. Certainly there is precedent for, as there are many examples of, the importance of forgiveness within most religious traditions. I asked my clients where they stood relative to this topic, and learned that it was indeed an important part of their faith story. Thus, this proved to be a fruitful conversation.

However, such an outcome is not always so easily achieved. Therefore, when forgiveness of specific behaviors has seemed impossible for clients, I often have suggested that they focus on forgiving others for not living up to their expectations. The process for facilitating forgiveness on these terms is explained more fully in the last section of this chapter. For now, I would like to note that according to my story, the person who forgives has as much to gain as does the person forgiven. Indeed, it may be understood as an important aspect of the spiritual journey. For example, according to the psychologist John Gray,

[F]orgiveness is one of the attributes of soul growth. And each time we are called upon to forgive, we nourish our souls and learn more about who we are and what we have to share in this world. This is also an example of unconditional love. (1995, p. 57)

The psychologist Joan Borysenko offers a similar commentary:

The process of making sense of our wounds is a very personal one. But a common theme in wound healing is the universal need to forgive. If we don't forgive ourselves for our mistakes, and others for the wounds they have inflicted upon us, we end up crippled with guilt. And the soul cannot grow under a blanket of guilt, because guilt is isolating, while growth is a gradual process of reconnection to ourselves, to other people, and to a larger whole. (1995, p. 47)

Thus it is not surprising that I have found that many of my clients have felt freed up to create a more comfortable reality by a story that enables them to offer forgiveness.

In addition to forgiving her uncle, for Debbie Knudsen creating the reality she desired also involved choosing to make new friends who would support her desire both to maintain sobriety and to succeed academically. As anyone who has worked with adolescents knows, this can be a daunting challenge for a young woman in the middle of her junior year in high school. However, we plotted a variety of strategies, including keeping a journal, having the family give her permission to be as moody as she needed to be around home, attending AA meetings, and working with the school counselor so that academic assistance was available when needed. We also planned ways in which she, as well as her siblings, could have some meaningful and enjoyable private time with each of their parents on a regular basis. As things with Debbie began to improve, we then moved to a focus on the relationship between the parents, at their request.

As I mentioned, Mom expressed a great deal of anger towards Dad, who rarely showed much emotion and tended to say very little. Indeed, exploration of their marriage revealed a long-standing complementary pattern of nagging and withdrawal, which predated any knowledge of the uncle's behavior. While things certainly had become more heated after Debbie began experiencing symptoms, entered treatment, and revealed that she had been abused, all was not immediately well with the couple once their daughter started to feel better. Thus, Mom was particularly anxious to address her concerns about the marital relationship.

Once again, part of the focus was on understanding how the behaviors of each toward the other made sense, or were logical complements. The couple was involved in a classic dance in which the more she nagged him about being close, the more he withdrew, the more she resented and nagged, the more he got angry and withdrew, etc. However, as Mom and Dad were able to understand how both were participating in this pattern, they also were able to stop blaming each other and to consider different ways to create the kind of marriage they desired. Not surprisingly, both were worried that it probably would not be long before the children moved out of the home, leaving them to face each other as a couple once again. Indeed, they also were aware of the possibility that the children, out of concern for their parents, might choose to stay at home longer than might be appropriate.

A here-and-now focus in the couple's therapy evolved into conversations about ways that Dad could be more responsive and attentive to Mom; Mom could give Dad the space he needed; and each could find ways to express affection that were meaningful to the other. This search for solutions led to consideration of what happened when things were going well and to an articulation of what it was that each loved about the other. It also culminated in a commitment on the part of both not only to forgive the other for past hurts but to agree to cease discussing them. Although success did not come overnight, the couple eventually felt their goals had been achieved and initiated termination of their therapy.

As I reflect on this family and my work with them, I believe that, at least at an implicit level, they learned a great deal about the power of stories and the importance of perception in creating reality. I am also aware that my ability to suspend judgment encouraged them to do likewise. This process of suspending judgment was aided, I believe, by my sincere acceptance of each person and of the limits of what was possible, by my assumption of good intentions on the part of all, and by a here-and-now focus. Further, consistent with my soul-healing orientation, I often was quite explicit in my use of stories with a more general application in which judgment is suspended, stories relating to the role of expectations, dealing with the question "Why?" and thinking relatively.

HELPING CLIENTS TO SUSPEND JUDGMENT

The role of expectations is significant for most of us and indeed may be the source of some of our greatest pain. We all have stories in our heads about how we and others are supposed to be. For example, mothers *should* be nurturing and selfless. Fathers *should* be protective and reliable. We daughters and sons *should* live up to our parents' expectations of us. Friends *should* be loyal. Tragedies *should* not happen.

However, each "should" involves general assumptions that may or may not be appropriate for specific individuals or particular contexts, or both. For nowhere is it written that life is created according to these or any other shoulds. Nevertheless, we tend to live by them and then to be disappointed when events evolve in a different manner. And we also tend to hold the person who has not lived up to our expectations responsible for our pain when this may be neither fair nor realistic. Hence my suggestion, as described in the preceding section, to encourage clients to forgive others for not living up to their expectations.

Certainly we encounter many instances, particularly in families, in which the behavior of one person does not meet the expectations of others. While I am not for one minute condoning or excusing behaviors such as incest or any other form of violence or abuse, I am attempting to encourage the search for the logic of such behaviors within a given context in our efforts to help all those involved. In the process, I am sensitive to the fact that while by today's standards our expectations may make sense, by the standards of another time or place we cannot be so sure. Indeed, as we attempt to view a particular behavior, however negative, within the larger social context of a given era, it is possible to see not only how its emergence and continuation fit but also how our own ideas regarding how things should be perhaps do not—all of which may help clients to suspend their judgments even as counselors and therapists are able to suspend theirs, so that new and more satisfying stories, and thus, realities, may evolve.

Another way in which the process of helping clients to suspend judgment may be facilitated is through our answers to the question I am most often asked: the question "Why?" It is not surprising to me that clients inevitably want to know why something has occurred. Certainly the question is logical, given its utility in the natural sciences and the fact that most of us have been socialized to believe that if we can understand the cause of a problem, we can find its solution. However, this has not proved to be the case in the behavioral sciences, nor is it likely that it ever will. That is, given the degree to which each of us has the ability to think, to make choices, to decide how we will respond, the goal of predicting human behavior seems quite unrealistic. As Hammerschlag notes:

> When it comes to understanding the mind, we are like children. Even if we someday know the brain and its chemistry, the mind will always have a mind of its own. The mind is a multifaceted jewel that snatches at whatever light comes in from many angles and creates a myriad of hues and colors. There are as many ways to see the light as there are ways to create it. (1988, p. 112)

What is perhaps more important from my perspective, however, is that asking why is not consistent with a systemic/cybernetic epistemology. Rather, it implies linear causality. And it also implies that it is possible to know answers with a sense of confidence in and certainty about the truth they supposedly express. But, as we have discussed, when operating in a manner that is consistent with the assumptions of cybernetics as well as of constructivism and social constructionism, we understand that all we can know are our stories. And there are probably several stories that may provide equally plausible responses to any "Why?" question a client poses.

Therefore, this is the story I share with my clients when they ask, "Why?" I also may add, when appropriate, that I have a T-shirt, made for me by a former student, on which are printed the words: "Systems Theory Means Never Having to Ask Why." If clients persist in their desire for an answer to the question "Why?" I may oblige, although I always add that the answer is just my story. In doing so I also am aware that providing such a story can be useful in helping clients gain a different perspective on their situation and perhaps help them be less judgmental in the process.

Not surprisingly, my stories, or my answers to the "Why?" question, typically have a spiritual orientation. In addition, I generally see such answers as an opportunity to talk about purpose rather than cause. Thus they may be consistent with the following view:

> The purpose behind the programming of the universe—the objective or motivation—is not that things will run smoothly, so we can discount that possibility. The purpose is that people should progress and gain realization. In order to make that possible, people have to be tested.
>
> There are two factors by which we can account for things: cause and purpose. The causal chain can be traced back in time, perhaps, but the purpose is like the horizon; we can never see it because as soon as we approach the horizon, we find that behind it is a still further horizon. But we can have some inkling that we are going in the right direction; we can understand that when a person seemed to be doing us harm, it was a test, so we need not blame that person anymore. (Khan, 1982, p. 53)

For example, I may talk about the fact that any crisis presents both challenge and opportunity and that each of us has the response-ability for deciding which it shall be. While not negating our very real and valid feelings, we may respond either by diving further into the depths of despair or we may use the crisis as a springboard for creativity. Regarding the latter option, I also may suggest that perhaps it is we who, however unconsciously, create crisis situations, which then provide us with opportunities to facilitate growth or allow for the achievement of our soul purpose. To expand on this, I may share a version of the following Buddhist perspective on crisis:

> The word "bardo" is commonly used to denote the intermediate state between death and rebirth, but in reality bardos *are occurring continuously throughout both life and death,* and are junctures when the possibility of liberation, or enlightenment, is heightened.
>
> The bardos are particularly powerful opportunities for liberation because there are, the teachings show us, certain moments that are much

more powerful than others and much more charged with potential, when whatever you do has a crucial and far-reaching effect. (Sogyal, 1992, p. 11)

Accordingly, the current crisis being experienced by a client may be likened to a "bardo" experience. Similarly, from such a perspective it is also possible to talk about karma. This is the idea that the pain being felt indicates resolution of an unfinished situation from the past.

While the notion of karma does not fit with the Judeo-Christian tradition that is predominant in our society, the idea of pain and suffering as an opportunity for growth certainly does:

> In the whole biblical tradition, both Hebrew and Christian, wherever there is talk about suffering (and there's a lot of talk about suffering), the image used is always that of birth pains. Positive suffering is birth-giving. It gives birth to the child within us. It gives our life for the world, as a mother gives her life for the child. It's always life-giving. (Steindl-Rast, in Elliott, 1995, p. 254)

In addition to such purpose-oriented responses to the question "Why?" there also are some stories, reflecting both spiritual and non-spiritual perspectives, which focus more on cause and which I may share. For example, there is the story about imbalance and its role in creating a context within which disease or problems are a logical response. Thus I may describe the belief that we carry the potential for disease within us at all times (Weil, 1995). When our immune systems are strong, disease is not manifest. However, when our immune systems are depleted, disease may emerge. What is required in the latter instance is rebuilding the immune system so that the body may heal itself.

Another causal story may be found in the shamanic perspective:

> From a shamanic point of view, illnesses usually are power intrusions. They are not natural to the body, but are brought in. If you are power-full, you will resist them. Thus possession of a guardian spirit is fundamental to health. Serious illness is usually only possible when a person is dis-spirited, has lost this energizing force, the guardian spirit. When a person becomes depressed, weak, prone to illness, it is a symptom that he has lost his power animal and thus can no longer resist, or ward off the unwanted power "infections" or intrusions. (Harner, 1990, p. 69)

And finally, there is the story about the power of thought to create whatever it is that one is experiencing in his or her life:

> Nothing occurs in your life—nothing—which is not first a thought. Thoughts are like magnets, drawing effects to you. The thought may not always be obvious, and thus clearly causative, as in, "I'm going to contract a terrible disease." The thought may be (and usually is) far more subtle than that. ("I am not worthy to live.") ("My life is a mess.") ("I'm a loser.") ("God is going to punish me.") ("I am sick and tired of my life!") (Walsch, 1995, p. 188)

However, as the counselor/therapist shares stories such as these with clients, I believe it is crucial to be wary of the issues of guilt and blame, as discussed in chapters 2 and 3. My preference, therefore, is to emphasize that the role we play in the creation of reality is participatory rather than causal, and that however we may have influenced the emergence of a crisis, the choice was neither conscious nor is it bad. It is at this point that I may move into a discussion of relative thinking, or the importance of perception and the role of values, in understanding problems. This discussion returns us to an explicit focus on the issue with which the chapter began.

When we think relatively we recognize that nothing is *intrinsically* either right or wrong. Rather, right and wrong are understood to be subjective judgments that are made relative to personal and societal value systems. Thus, for example, although we may experience pain, we also may recognize that it is not bad unless we label it as such. From such a perspective we may see that, above all, what pain provides is information:

> There is no suffering, no evil. If there is a cause for suffering and evil, it is ignorance. Out of ignorance, we call it suffering or evil, but in reality they are helpers. Pain, yes. My master used to say, "Pain is my friend. If the pain is not there, you will not know where the problem is." (Satchidananda, in Elliott, 1995, p. 230)

According to this view, pain indicates the presence of a situation in need of attention. It is like a fever that signals the body's attempt to deal with disease. That is, it is neither the fever nor the pain that is bad. However, by judging and labeling painful situations in a negative manner, it is likely that we make them more difficult to deal with and change. Further, while we may not like a situation and therefore acknowledge the need for change, each circumstance offers the potential to make a choice that becomes a statement about ourselves and the kind of reality we wish to create. Thus we might heed the dictum: "Seek then to create change not because a thing is wrong, but because it no longer makes an accurate statement of Who You Are" (Walsch, 1995, p. 36).

Consistent with this perspective, if we participate in the creation of our reality, such participation includes not only those things that we label in a positive manner but also those things we judge to be negative. Thus, as cocreators of our reality, to call an aspect of that reality bad is to judge ourselves negatively as well. Similarly, as we do or do not choose to evaluate others for the choices they are making, it is important to be aware that we also make a statement about who we are and how we want to be with these others. Therefore, we may wish to consider the following advice:

> Be watchful, therefore, of the choices of others, but not judgmental. Know that their choice is perfect for them in this moment now—yet stand ready to assist them should the moment come when they seek a newer choice, a different choice—a higher choice. (Walsch, 1995, p. 47)

If we also believe in a divine power that has a hand in the creation of reality, we may recognize as well that our judgments have far-reaching implications. As Rabbi Harold Kushner writes,

> We must remember that everything in this world has God's fingerprints on it—and that alone makes it special. Our inability to see beauty doesn't suggest in the slightest that beauty is not there. Rather, it suggests that we are not looking carefully enough or with broad enough perspective to see the beauty. (1995, p. 19)

Therefore, the problem is neither in participating in the creation of crisis situations, nor in the fact that we have such situations in our lives. Rather, what is problematic is that we create additional challenges by choosing to call a crisis situation bad. It follows then that the way to reduce the pain associated with these situations is to change our perceptions of them. From such a relative perspective we would attempt to look at the unique circumstances and see that what is happening is happening. It just *is*. Whether or not we suffer, or the degree to which we suffer, depends on our reactions to this situation. In addition, we might recognize that every situation is temporary. It is occurring in this moment only. What occurs in the next moment is a function of how we respond now. And finally, we might remember the story of the farmer, and realize that it probably will take time to understand the full ramifications of a particular situation:

> Often, when a traumatic or catastrophic event occurs, we don't understand the significance. But with time and understanding, we see how that event caused our soul to grow. When we view the event with a different perspective, we see that it was necessary for our spiritual growth, even though it was painful at the time. (Weiss, 1995, p. 65)

However, while relative thinking such as this may seem perfectly plausible in the calm of an intellectual discussion, as I'm sure you are aware, it is a perspective that must be shared with great respect and sensitivity. That is, in the turbulence which generally accompanies crisis, the counselor/therapist certainly cannot expect ready reception of such a message. Rather, it is a view I find appropriate to bring into the conversation only during the period after the storm has subsided. Even then, I believe it may be most useful when offered within the frame of *temporarily* suspending judgment and only for purposes of reflection. Thus, the ideas become something to be considered, perhaps to be tried out, but never to be insisted upon. If such ideas are rejected, so be it. If accepted, the ability on the part of the client to suspend judgment may aid in the process of achieving his or her goals. Indeed, I believe that to the extent that the counselor/therapist is able to suspend judgment, not only will therapy be enhanced but the creation of a soul-healing context also will be facilitated. And we further participate in the creation of such a context as we learn how to trust the universe, which is the subject of chapter 6.

There is a desire deep within the soul which drives man from the seen to the unseen, to philosophy and to the divine.

—KAHLIL GIBRAN

Trusting the Universe

INTRODUCTION

In this chapter we will be focusing on the third principle of soul healing, trusting the universe. This process, to which I have alluded several times, is the ability to make recourse to nonlinear ways of knowing. It also involves having faith both that information is ever accessible and that the information received is valid and therefore may be trusted. Tuning in to and operating on the basis of knowledge obtained from the universe is consistent with what has been termed a mystical approach to reality (LeShan, 1974), or as described in chapter 4, knowledge by being. While it is the opposite of the analytic mode of the scientist, it is truly its logical complement inasmuch as history reveals that the scientific community has reaped the benefits of such an approach in many important ways. For example,

> Rudolph Otto has suggested that from the mystical intuition of a oneness behind the various phenomena of the world arose the beginning of the search for the underlying substance that made up the cosmos, and that it was this search that started the development of science. (LeShan, 1974, p. 77)

Several other significant benefits that science has derived from the mystical approach to knowing have been described as follows:

John Dee, the great flower of Elizabethan science, actually had com-
merce with angels and all sorts of entities of this type over decades. No
less a founder of modern scientific rationalism than René Descartes
was set on the path toward the ideals of modern science by an angel
who appeared to him in a dream and told him that the conquest of nature was to be achieved through measure and number. . . .

There is also the well-known example of Kekule, the discoverer of
the benzene ring, who dreamed of the uroboric symbol—the snake
taking its tail in its mouth, the ancient symbol of eternity—and understood that it was the solution to a molecular structure problem
that he'd been searching for. (Abraham, McKenna, & Sheldrake,
1992, p. 95)

In order to understand fully what is involved in learning to obtain
and believe information derived from mystical ways of knowing, our
explorations begin with a consideration of the concept of nonlocal
mind. This discussion is followed by a look at several ways in which
the process of trusting the universe can become operational as a means
of guidance for both clients and professionals in the context of counseling and therapy. A section on the education of intuition examines how
to learn to tune in to and respect such phenomena as feelings and
hunches. Both dream work and ways to help clients perceive the various levels of meaning that may be ascribed to a situation are the focus
of the subsequent discussion. The implementation of several shamanic
practices as well as the use of oracles, for example the runes, the tarot,
and the *I Ching* are then described. Throughout these discussions, emphasis is on the importance of balance as one moves between worlds,
with their related ways of knowing. And it is an exploration of such
balance that concludes the chapter.

NONLOCAL MIND

Fundamental to my view of the process of trusting the universe is the
concept of nonlocal mind, or of a universal consciousness. According
to this view, mind is understood as

the means through which the Absolute . . . manifests Itself. It is the infinite ocean of vibrations from the most rarefied highest levels all the
way down to the gross material. So gross matter is Mind and Mind is
not God but the manifestation of God. The Absolute, or God, is in

everything, in every single particle of Mind, but everything is not God. The Absolute God is beyond all manifestation, it is Absolute and pure Spirit. (Markides, 1995, p. 39)

The concept of nonlocal mind thus assumes both the individual soul as a manifestation of the universal spirit as well as the notion of total interconnectedness, of mind in nature, rather than of minds bounded by the skin or as located in individual bodies. Therefore, non-local mind "implies *infinitude* in space and time, because a limited non-locality is a contradiction in terms. In the West this infinite aspect of the psyche has been referred to as the soul" (Dossey, 1993, p. 6). All human consciousness, then, is understood as a unity that operates outside of such spatial limitations as brains and bodies or such a temporal limita-tion as the present moment. Further, it is understood as being equally accessible to all.

While certainly there is widespread skepticism regarding the notion of nonlocal mind, as well as of intuitive ways of knowing, there does seem to be consensus regarding descriptions of such phenomena. In-deed, according to LeShan:

Bertrand Russell did not think very much of the mystical approach to reality, although he confessed himself to be puzzled by the very high quality of the people who believed in it. He did, however, turn that su-perb analytical brain of his to the problem of exactly what it was that the mystics believed in. He reported that in the moments when they be-lieved that they were really comprehending "reality," really perceiving and being at home in it, they all agreed on four of its characteristics. These, said Russell, are:

1: That there is a better way of gaining information than through the senses.
2: That there is a fundamental unity to all things.
3: That time is an illusion.
4: That all evil is mere appearance. (1974, pp. 43–44)

Russell was not alone in his skepticism, for the assumptions he de-scribed as fundamental to a mystical approach to reality are inconsis-tent with traditional Western, scientific ways of thinking. By contrast, however, such assumptions are fundamental to Eastern views of the world:

The experience of the Tao or of a unifying principle in the universe to which everything in the world relates, underlies the major Eastern religions—Hinduism, Buddhism, Confucianism, Taoism, and Zen. Although each religion may call the experience by a different name, the essence of all varieties of Eastern mysticism is the same. Each holds that all phenomena—people, animals, plants, and objects from atomic particles to galaxies are aspects of the One. (Bolen, 1979, p. 4)

Similarly, in his introduction to the Richard Wilhelm (1962) translation of the ancient Chinese text *The Secret of the Golden Flower*, Carl Jung describes the idea of a fundamental unity as basic to the Chinese worldview. Referring to Chinese philosophy, he writes:

It is built on the premise that the cosmos and man, in the last analysis, obey the same law; that man is a microcosm and is not separated from the macrocosm by any fixed barriers. The very same laws rule for the one as for the other, and from the one a way leads into the other. The psyche and the cosmos are to each other like the inner world and the outer world. Therefore man participates by nature in all cosmic events, and is inwardly as well as outwardly interwoven with them. (Wilhelm, 1962, pp. 10–11)

It was to such a perspective that Jung had recourse in his creation of the concept of synchronicity, which for him was "an acausal [sic] connecting principle that manifests itself through meaningful coincidences" (Bolen, 1979, p. 6). That is, according to Jung, when an individual finds meaning in the coincidence between an event and either a thought or feeling, a dream or vision, or a precognitive experience, for none of which there are "rational" explanations, synchronicity has occurred. Further, such coincidences defy our normal, rational perceptions of space and time. Although not labeled as such in its original context, the following story provides a dramatic illustration of synchronicity:

When my wife and I were traveling in India some years ago, she had a very painful vision of one of her brothers dying. . . . About one week later a telegram arrived at the ashram where we were staying on Mount Abu in Rajisthan. Sadly, it told my wife that her brother had in fact died in the fashion that she had seen in her vision. The telegram was dated the day she had her vision. How could she see her brother's death halfway around the world? She could because we are all connected. (Kornfield, 1993, pp. 280–281)

Thus it is through the story of synchronicity that we may understand ourselves to be interrelated and all of life to have meaning. As in the example just cited, the limits of space and time do not operate as we normally understand them, and information is perceived/received by means of a so-called sixth sense. Further, as discussed in chapter 5 and consistent with the fourth characteristic of mystical knowing described by Bertrand Russell, all evil is understood as "mere appearance." In other words, an event in and of itself is neither good nor bad; it is our experience of that event to which we give meaning and value and to which we ascribe the labels good or bad. Or, as Huston Smith, a student of what has been referred to as the perennial philosophy, argues with regard to this tradition:

[E]vil is only a relative reality nonexistent at the highest levels of consciousness and awareness—that evil is the dialectical mechanism and provocation for the very evolution of human consciousness toward God. Therefore, evil as such is playing a central, functional role within the totality of the divine symphony of creation. To Huston Smith and every other "perennialist," therefore, evil, although it must be fought at all levels, is only apparently real. At unity consciousness, at the highest levels of awareness, evil is transcended, and only the Absolute Love of God remains. (Markides, 1995, p. 87)

It is to "unity consciousness" that we refer when speaking of nonlocal mind. Thus, for Dossey (1993), it is nonlocal mind that also explains the power of prayer as well as the mechanism of extrasensory perception (ESP) as manifested in such practices as diagnosis or healing at a distance, shamanic healing, noncontact therapeutic touch, transpersonal imagery, remote sensing, and telesomatic events. Dossey characterizes such forms of therapy as falling into what he calls "Era III" approaches to healing. The key to inclusion in such a category is that in each case there is a recognition that the effects of consciousness form a bridge between individuals.

There is thus at least a beginning awareness of our basic interconnectedness and a recognition of mind as a nonlocal phenomenon, though these are certainly not mainstream views. However, while many of us may begin to acknowledge that we truly are interdepen-

dent, few of us have been schooled in techniques to access nonlinear
ways of knowing. Rather, we have learned to rely almost exclusively
on and to trust only the more traditional analytical style, leaving the
nonlinear processes for generating knowledge both underdeveloped
and generally mistrusted. Further, we typically have not been educated in the esoteric knowledge of the perennial tradition. The ramifications of this situation are significant indeed:

> All modes of knowing outside analysis, be it intuition, tacit knowing,
> reflective practice, or sudden realization, . . . are tied to sensual aware-
> ness. The abstractness of modern theorizing and intellection leaves us
> prey to the rationales and schemes of scientists, technologists, and ex-
> perts. Because we are not privy to such esoterica and are not taught to
> trust knowledge sprung from sensual awareness, we have become ig-
> norant of and vulnerable in our world. Ultimately, however, we are
> vulnerable not because we can't fathom the words of the theorist, but
> because we cannot open ourselves to the promptings and urges of our
> bodies. (Saleeby, 1989, p. 560)

Participation in Era III approaches to healing, the category in which
I would also place soul healing, therefore requires additional knowledge and different kinds of practice. Accordingly, seeking to open ourselves to "sensual awareness," to the experience of nonlocal mind,
brings us to a focus on the education of intuition. Given its lack of fit
with traditional Western ways of thinking, this discussion begins with
an overview of the challenges and dilemmas associated with such an
undertaking.

THE EDUCATION OF INTUITION

In his book *Zen and the Art of Motorcycle Maintenance* (1975), Robert
Pirsig discusses the dilemma of teaching rhetoric, a subject that is
"undoubtedly the most unprecise, unanalytic, amorphous area in the
entire church of reason" (p. 170). The problem, according to Pirsig,
arises from the attempt to use a left-brain, linear modality to impart
knowledge about what is essentially a right-brain, nonlinear activity.
From my perspective a further complication is that as a result of repeated requests for creativity, students of rhetoric find themselves in
the midst of a "Be spontaneous!" paradox. Such a paradox has been
defined as "the demand for behavior which by its very nature can

only be spontaneous, but cannot be spontaneous as a result of hav-ing been requested" (Watzlawick et al., 1974). I see this situation, along with its inherent dilemmas, as analogous to the process of ed-ucating the intuition, at least in the context of mainstream practices in our society.

The Western educational tradition, the epitome of rational, linear thinking, provides a stark contrast to the nonrational, nonlinear mode of knowing associated with intuition. What is more, the impact of this tradition is cumulative inasmuch as the more time the student spends in school, with its goals of increasing knowledge and strengthening judgment, the more the imaginative, creative aspects of the mind tend to be subdued. Indeed,

> University students are highly verbal (they are admitted to school that way) and are relatively less competent visually. They are not used to re-lying on taste, smell, or feel for problem-solving. They have mostly been posed problems that can be solved (they think) verbally or mathe-matically. (Adams, 1976, pp. 28–29)

Robert Ornstein (1975) addresses this issue relative to the psychol-ogy of consciousness when he writes of the concentration of Western educational systems upon verbal and intellectual abilities almost to the exclusion of other styles of learning. As an alternative, he points to the esoteric psychologies whose traditions are the embodiment of the re-ceptive, intuitive mode:

> In the Chinese *I Ching*, this mode is even named *k'un*—the receptive. In Sufism it is variously called "deep understanding," intuition, or direct perception. Don Juan apparently calls it "seeing." In Zen, the word *ken-sho*, a word for the enlightenment experience, also means "to enter in-side," the same meaning as intuition, which is *in* and *tuir* in Latin. Satori in Zen is often pictured as a flash of intuition illuminating a dark area. (Ornstein, 1975, p. 162)

Thus the Zen master answers questions by telling stories and teaches by posing *koans*, puzzles that seem unanswerable. Koans are "designed to force the mind out of the trap of assertion and denial and into that quantum jump to the next higher logical level called satori" (Watzlawick et al., 1974, p. 91). The Sufi teacher also works to produce "higher states of mind" in pupils by means of:

1. Auditory, visual and other sense impacts.
2. Verbalized materials, including legends and parables, intended to establish in the mind not a belief but a pattern, a blueprint which helps it to operate in "another manner."
3. Working, worshipping, exercising in unison for the purpose of engendering, liberating and making flow a certain dynamic (not an emotional or indoctrinational one) which furthers the "work." (Shah, 1970, p. 113)

The Eastern psychologies, whose goal is the education of intuition and the expansion of awareness, make use of a wide variety of techniques, including geometric forms, such as mandalas and "magic carpets"; crafts, such as weaving and calligraphy; dreaming and meditation; body movement, music, and sounds, such as the mantra or the dervish call; as well as stories and oral literature (Ornstein, 1975). Given that an experiential approach seems to be required for the honing of intuitive skills, attempts either to write or learn about such an education in our usual linear fashion are likely to have limited success. In an ideal situation we would learn by becoming fully immersed in the process. Indeed, throughout this discussion it is important to remember that experience is the best teacher when it comes to the education of intuition.

For intuition refers to an instinctive knowing that has been described as "the inner voice, the flow of the universe, energy, the Oversoul, the Higher Self, the I Am presence . . . in short, it's the sum total of all that we know, all that we can become" (Winter, 1988, p. 46). While such a definition may describe the phenomenon more broadly than we typically do, it points to the way that our intuition may give us access to soul knowledge and to the most far-reaching levels of consciousness. However, learning how to achieve such mystical knowing, or knowledge by being, may require that we focus our awareness in new ways.

That is, intuitive information may be received in a variety of modes, including physically, emotionally, or mentally. For example, we may become aware of bodily sensations such as a chill, or "the hair standing up on the back of our necks." Some people pick up on and may even experience the feelings of others. Some may see images or hear sounds or voices. Others may notice that ideas just pop into their heads. Information also may be provided through hunches, dreams, artistic creations, or imaging.

Given the level and kind of knowing that are possible, intuitive information can be very helpful to counselors and therapists. Indeed, as we operate from a soul-healing, spiritual orientation with awareness of our connectedness in the context of a universal consciousness or nonlocal mind, we may find our work enhanced to a surprising degree. Or, as one therapist has noted, "To help other people, what is really needed is intuition" (Khan, 1982, p. 7). Elaborating on this point, he observes that:

> When we are very sensitized in our spirit, we react to the presence of a person in a very clear way. We will always feel in ourselves what that person is, because everything is in us; if that person is insincere, we are aware of those aspects of ourselves that are insincere when we say, "Oh, how nice to see you," and do not really mean it. If that person is violent, we feel the violence in ourselves. This is the elementary school of intuition. (Khan, 1982, p. 108)

My experience of intuitive knowing, however, is somewhat different, and my guess is that it also will vary for each of you. For me, as I have mentioned, hunches and feelings seem to arise from the center of my chest, near my heart. I also sometimes get an image that seems to float through my awareness when I pause and tune in to myself. While I suspect that I always have been somewhat intuitive, my consciousness of this way of knowing and my willingness to seek it out and to trust it as providing valid information are now heightened. And in recent years I have participated in new behaviors which, I believe, have enhanced my skill and influenced my beliefs in this regard.

While I was not deliberately focusing on such an outcome when I began to meditate, I noticed at some point after beginning this practice on a daily basis that my intuitive ability had increased enormously. Having become more aware of my intuition, I then began consciously to test my ability. In reading the "Seth" books, I learned that their author, Jane Roberts (1974), was advised to start each morning by trying to predict some things that might happen during that day. So I decided to do likewise, noticing my thoughts. By this practice I found that, for example, in the morning I might suddenly think of something I had ordered from a catalogue quite a while ago only to have it arrive in the mail that afternoon. I also have attempted to mentally "call" a member of my family or a close friend and been "heard": within a short period of time the desired call came in response, without my having used the phone.

I also have found that the more I express trust in the universe by acting on my intuition, the stronger it gets. In therapy this means that I pay attention to and often act on the hunches, images, and other reactions I experience in the course of conversation. Thus, I might say something like, "What I'm about to say may seem strange, but I just got the image of X, and I wondered if it has any meaning for you?" Generally I find that such statements are right on target. Similarly, in supervision, I have noticed that if I listen with my heart and my intuition as well as with my ears, I tend to get a much better grasp of the client system being described and am therefore better able to help those with whom I am consulting. I actively encourage this process in both clients and other therapists, asking, for example, "What is your gut telling you?" about a particular situation and suggesting that they might do well to pay attention.

I also would suggest that anyone interested in the education of intuition participate in activities that engage the creative, nonlinear portions of the brain. Whether we use painting, dancing, meditating, making music, or dream analysis, for example, we may learn to tap into our higher awareness, or our souls. And this opportunity to receive new information can be enormously exciting and rewarding in terms of our development. For example, when asked what she does to enhance her own spiritual growth, Elisabeth Kubler-Ross replied:

> That depends on when you ask me. Right now, I'm trying to get in touch with my soul by many means. I'm trying to meditate, trying to recall my dreams. I'm trying to do this fabulous thing where one writes the question with one's right hand and the answer with the left. Boy, does it work! I can't believe my eyes. I ask questions of my soul, and—BOOM! BOOM! BOOM!—the most poetic language comes. Fantastic language comes out, stuff I could never write or think of. I use any means and tools to get in touch and grow. (Elliott, 1995, p. 43)

As we "get in touch and grow," the hope is that we may become better facilitators of the process of soul healing, both for ourselves and for our clients. From my perspective, as I have indicated, healing is not just about physical awareness and analytic modes of analysis. Rather, healing also may be understood as a spiritual process, or one which, according to Warter:

> occurs as we tap into our own inner resources instead of looking for external intervention. Meditation and a quiet mind; prayer and a

hopeful mind: these change human physiology. With intention, attention and practice we can learn to control our minds. With this control we can find the deepest kind of healing, which is victory over suffering. By opening the intuitive heart to soul awareness humankind can recover the sacred and go beyond the search for the meaning of disease or healing, to the search for meaning and purpose in life. (1994, p. 225)

As we seek to facilitate healing through the search for meaning and purpose, we also have readily available another source of information that we may tap into at an intuitive level—namely, dreams. This source, you may have noticed, has been mentioned at several points in this consideration of the education of intuition. Described by Bolen (1979) as a form of synchronicity, dreams and their exploration provide one way in which the process of trusting the universe may be operationalized or put into practice.

EXPLORING DREAMS

I am not suggesting that working with dreams is an approach that is appropriate for all clients or that we should force fit clients' dreams into preconceived interpretations. Instead, I have found that some clients recall their dreams in great detail and wish to discuss them. Further, when searching for a meaningful topic of conversation, I also sometimes ask clients whether they remember their dreams and would like to talk about them. I see such discussions as useful inasmuch as I believe that dreams may offer messages or provide important information. Consistent with my own experience, I also believe that they may be healing. Indeed, in earlier times, dreams not only were considered to be messages from either the soul or the gods but also were employed in a deliberate manner to facilitate healing:

In ancient healing temples throughout the Mediterranean, dreams were used by those who sought to diagnose diseases. The dreams were used as part of the cure as well. A patient would go to the temple and spend some time in preparation—praying, meditating and fasting. He would then go to sleep, usually in front of a statue of the god. His dream would be carefully analyzed by the priests in hope that it would contain information about the patient's illness leading to a cure. This use of dreams presupposed that they came from divine sources and sometimes elaborate preparations were used to insure that the gods spoke clearly. (Jacob, 1988, pp. 28–29)

While we may no longer utilize dreams in so formal a manner, I believe that they may still be an important resource. They can help us solve puzzles with which our conscious minds have been wrestling unsuccessfully, as in the case of Kekule, which is described at the beginning of this chapter. They also may be used to locate lost items or to answer personal questions. In addition, according to Arrien:

> Recurring dreams or favorite images are often our psyche's way of showing what is important within our own nature. For example, if we dream repeatedly of going to school and taking exams, this may be an important message for us to pay attention to the repeated challenges or tests we are facing in our current life situations. (1993, p. 59)

However, from my perspective, the meaning of the dream is in the eye of the beholder, and thus, "Dreams and their interpretations are as individualistic as the dreamer himself" (Winter, 1988, pp. 53–54). Accordingly, the role of the counselor/therapist is to help clients interpret their dreams in ways that make sense to them. Moreover, dreams are understood to provide clues that may be used in various ways in the search for problem solution and healing. For example, the therapist/counselor may use the process of amplification, asking clients to magnify and describe particular details of a dream. Clients also may be encouraged to consider how different parts of the dream might relate to various symbols, real life events, or potential meanings. Another way of exploring dreams, one that is often used by Jungian analysts, is active imagination:

> In an active imagination, the person starts with an image of a person or place, animal, object, or symbol, often from a dream, and in a relaxed state "sees" or imagines what happens next. The image elaborates itself as a person observes. It can be like a waking dream. (Bolen, 1979, p. 27)

Regardless of the technique, my goal is to help clients focus on and make sense of their dreams by asking questions about such things as the emotional context, or the feelings that were being experienced. Indeed, "running out" all the emotion has been called the second rule for working with dreams, the first being to record them (Jacob, 1988). I also am interested in possible dream interpretations that clients already have considered. Some questions that might be asked include, "Is it 'commenting' on an inner situation? Is it a metaphor for something going on in my life?" (Bolen, 1979, p. 30), or "What was troublesome? What was the problem in need of solution? What was the state of affairs, or inner mood and outer circumstance?" (Bolen, 1979, pp. 40–41).

Sometimes no questions are needed and it is sufficient just to listen or validate the meaning already ascribed to a dream by the client. For example, one of my clients is aware of having several dreams every night and recalls most of them vividly. She also is very interested in the messages they may be providing. I would like to share with you a sequence of dreams and events related to her illness that she reported and that have proved to be both meaningful and helpful to her in the process of healing.

The first significant dream in this series occurred shortly before the diagnosis of and surgery for ovarian cancer. In this dream a large horse appeared. Although the horse was friendly, it had a bull's-eye on the side of it body. The bull's-eye was formed by concentric circles of gold, red, and green. The emotions my client associated with this dream were a mixture of fear and a larger sense that there was no need to be afraid. The second dream occurred following surgery but prior to receiving the pathology report, and thus during a time of great anxiety regarding the extent of the cancer. In this dream my client was attending the symphony with her fiancé and although extremely thin, was dressed in a beautiful velvet cloak. The sleeves of the cloak were decorated with sequined designs of gold, red, and green. The emotions associated with this dream were happiness and a sense of serenity. This dream was followed by a visit to the surgeon during which my client had expected to receive the pathology report. After learning that the report was not yet ready, and despite otherwise good reports on her checkup, my client left the doctor's office, accompanied by her fiancé, her mother and her sister, feeling very depressed. However, as they arrived home and were about to get out of the car, a beautiful golden butterfly flew in the window and perched for several minutes on my client's arm. The butterfly then flew out of the window and went immediately to a cluster of tall plants with long, green leaves and large red flowers. My client was so excited by this event that she called me to share her story and to seek validation that this was indeed a positive sign.

In retrospect, her interpretation was that the bull's-eye on the horse in the first dream pinpointed the illness and suggested that, although the illness was serious and thus something to fear, she would regain her health. In the second dream, she saw her thinness as an indication of the impact of chemotherapy. At the same time, her happiness and the beautiful designs on her sleeve represented the movement of the cancer out of her body. The real-life experience with the butterfly, not only as a symbol of transformation but also as part of a configuration of colors that were now all external to her, implied that total healing was in process and that the pathology report would be as favorable as possible under the circumstances. This indeed proved to be the case.

My role in all of this was to listen, and it was easy for me to agree that these dreams and events appeared to be very positive signs. In subsequent meetings, when fear and the impact of chemotherapy have threatened to overwhelm my client's efforts at equanimity, I have reminded her that she has received some important information in which she might place her trust. In addition, we both are very much aware of similar recurring patterns and themes in the dreams she continues to have.

For clients who don't remember their dreams but who would like to do so, the recommended strategy (Jacob, 1988) is to get a notebook whose only purpose is recording dreams. Along with the notebook, it is important to put a pencil or pen as well as a light or flashlight next to the bed. Before retiring, it may be useful to make a self-suggestion in the form of an affirmative statement such as, "I will awake in the morning with easy and clear recall of my dreams." Perhaps the statement might also be written in the notebook. Upon awakening, no matter what the hour, it is essential to write down a description of the dream(s) in as much detail as possible. The counselor/therapist also may plant the idea that the process of recording dreams in this way is likely to increase the dreamer's ability to recall them. Such an indirect hypnotic suggestion may encourage the creation of the reality desired by the client.

For those who are successful at recall, exploring dreams provides an excellent way to allow clients to learn how to trust the universe. As we and they recognize that we all are constantly receiving potentially useful information, we may get a different view of consciousness. In addition to the enhancement of such awareness, clients also may learn to employ their dreams in a pragmatic way. That is, they may be encouraged to focus on a question to which they would like to have an answer. Before going to bed, they might explicitly ask for a dream that provides the information for which they are searching. For example, I have a friend who successfully used such a technique to locate a lost but prized piece of jewelry. In a more important instance, I have another friend who related the experience of being absolutely devastated upon receiving the news that a close relative had been a victim of sexual abuse. Before going to sleep, this friend requested a dream that would help to make sense of this situation. The dream that was received was filled with reassurance and hope, both for the victim and for the larger society, and has enabled my friend to go forward and be of assistance in a positive manner.

Because dreaming is essential to our well-being, because we all dream every night, and because apparently we all have the ability to learn to recall our dreams, we have constant access to a potentially useful resource. The key to realizing this potential is to give conscious attention to the dreaming process. Having done so, we may then learn to work with our dreams, to recognize instances when we have received useful information and thereby to enhance our ability to trust the universe. Certainly this is one of the most accessible and acceptable routes to intuitive knowledge that we have at our disposal. Less well-known but perhaps equally useful are practices derived from the shamanic tradition.

SHAMANIC PRACTICES

As I have explained, in the shamanic tradition healing is understood as a process of restoring balance and of regaining the personal power lost as a function of an intrusion at a physical or at a spiritual level. Such a perspective is consistent with a worldview in which interconnectedness with the universe as a whole is a given, and disturbances of the spirit are taken very seriously. As Achterberg writes:

> The function of any society's health system is ultimately tied to the philosophical convictions that the members hold regarding the purpose of life itself. For the shamanic cultures, that purpose is spiritual development. Health is being in harmony with the world view. Health is an intuitive perception of the universe and all its inhabitants as being of one fabric. Health is maintaining communication with the animals and plants and minerals and stars. It is knowing death and life and seeing no difference. It is blending and melding, seeking solitude and seeking companionship to understand one's many selves. Unlike the

more "modern" notions, in shamanic society health is not the absence of pain. Health is seeking out all of the experiences of Creation and turning them over and over, feeling their texture and multiple meanings. Health is expanding beyond one's singular state of consciousness to experience the ripples and waves of the universe. (1985, p. 19)

In order to facilitate the restoration of balance and harmony when illness occurs, ritual and ceremony are common practices within the shamanic tradition. Indeed, it is through rituals and ceremonies that the shaman maintains an ongoing relationship with the higher spiritual powers and receives messages from the universe in order to facilitate healing (Deloria, 1994). However, that which is revealed is not intended as a universal revelation but rather is understood as specific to the time, place, and circumstances of the person for whom it is received. Thus, of primary importance are the sites of such revelations, places that represent the sacredness of all life. They are reminders of the responsibility, shared by all, to the larger world, a responsibility that transcends individual wishes and desires. As Deloria describes the Native American view of religion,

> Context is therefore all-important for both practice and the understanding of reality. The places where revelations were experienced were remembered and set aside as locations where, through ritual and ceremonials, the people could once again communicate with the spirits. Thousands of years of occupancy on their lands taught tribal peoples the sacred landscapes for which they were responsible and gradually the structure of ceremonial reality became clear. It was not what people believed to be true that was important but what they experienced as true. Hence revelation was seen as a continuous process of adjustment to the natural surroundings and not as a specific message valid for all times and places. (1994, p. 67)

Although the sacred places mentioned here generally refer to those found in natural settings, the emphasis on the importance of context is certainly systemically consistent, and there is no reason we cannot transpose the sacred space to our counseling/therapy rooms. Further, by means of ritual and ceremony adapted to the individual needs and goals of our clients we, too, may facilitate healing, obtaining information at an intuitive level, and trusting the universe to guide us in the process. Indeed, the use of ritual—although generally without the spiritual overtones—as a therapeutic intervention has been advocated widely in the family therapy field (e.g., Imber-Black & Roberts, 1989; Selvini Palazzoli, Boscolo, Cecchin, & Prata, 1978).

Like the shamanic practitioner Sandra Ingerman (1993), I have suggested ritual with fire in my practice and found it to be an extremely useful way to help clients release old beliefs. For example, when working with couples who are ready to let go of and move past their grudges and resentments, I have asked that each person write down, using 3" x 5" cards, every issue which they have been holding on to— one issue per card. After discussing and ascertaining that they are indeed ready to release these issues, I suggest that they create a ceremony in which they are to take turns reading their cards, prefacing the reading of each with the words, "I release my anger or my belief about . . . ." They are then to drop their cards into a fire built either in a fireplace or in a safe place out of doors. Following this ritual burning and releasing ceremony, they are to do something together that both would enjoy. According to Ingerman,

> By itself, ritual creates change. In order to use ritual, one's body, mind, and spirit must get involved. The mind develops the ritual, the body actually performs it, and the spirit acts as a guide and witness at the ritual. This process alerts our psyche that a change is about to occur. So much of our energy goes into preparing and performing the ritual that the psyche takes this act very seriously and follows up by making the appropriate change. (1993, p. 88)

A simpler version may be to have a client write a word on a piece of paper and burn it in a trash basket or over a candle in a safe place. In any case, there is something very transforming about fire, and when used appropriately it may help to externalize and to release a problem or story that is no longer useful. Obviously there are many other types of rituals that may be employed, but in all instances what is important is the creation of a process that supports the ability of the client to trust that change is occurring.

Another technique that the counselor/therapist may use to help clients access information from the universe has been derived from the Maori culture (adapted by Angeles Arrien and described in a workshop given by shamanic practitioner Myron Eschowsky). This exercise is to be done once a year, preferably on one's birthday, and is intended to provide information about the healing that the individual soul needs to work on in the coming year. You might want to try this exercise yourself, right now.

· In order to do the exercise, you will need a large piece of paper, a pencil, and some crayons or colored pens. I would suggest that if you are going to do it, you not read ahead before beginning. The experience may be more meaningful for you if you follow the instructions step by step.

Once you have gathered your supplies, imagine that your best friend is sitting at your left witnessing what you are doing. Imagine also that someone who cares about you, or someone to whom you might go for help, is sitting at your right sending you healing energy. Once you have taken a few moments to create a healing context through the use of your imagination, you are ready to proceed to the next part of the exercise.

On your piece of paper, use your pencil to draw a large circle that fills the entire page. Then, using your crayons or colored pens, create a drawing within the circle that includes all of the following elements: a snake, a flower, a bird, shelter, a tree, a mountain, a path or track, a butterfly. When you have completed the drawing, give your finished picture a title.

The next step requires that you fold your paper in half twice, into four equal parts. Now you may unfold it and look to see into which of the four quadrants the elements in your picture fall or cross. As you proceed, you may want to reflect on the way specific elements relate to the general theme of the drawing as revealed by its title.

The upper left quadrant refers to the mental sphere and is known as the valley of the bird. This quadrant contains all that you need to maintain mental health and well-being. You might check to see whether there is a lot of activity here or whether it is empty. If the bird is here, the message is that you have no mental issues requiring attention. The lower left quadrant refers to the emotional sphere and is known as the valley of the flower. It is the heart quadrant. If you have drawn the flower in this quadrant then the information you are receiving is that you do not have an emotional or heart issue of concern. The upper right quadrant refers to the spiritual sphere and is known as the valley of the mountain. If the mountain is here, you are to understand that you do not have a spiritual issue that needs to be recognized. The lower right quadrant refers to the physical sphere and is known as the valley of the tree. It is the quadrant of health, finances, creativity, and relationship. If the tree is here, you are being given information which indicates that you do not have a physical issue about which to be concerned.

Each of the elements in this picture also has a symbolic meaning that may help you to further understand your drawing. The snake symbolizes healing, regeneration, something that you are releasing. You may want to look again at the quadrant in which it is located. If you added eyes to the snake, perhaps it would be helpful for you to give voice to what you see. If you added a tongue, it may be important to communicate your feelings about the way in which you are transforming. If the snake is striped, it may be useful to bring more beauty into your life. A moving snake indicates that movement may be significant for you. A coiled snake ready to strike is a message about honoring and respecting boundaries or about allowing leadership abilities to emerge, or both.

The flower symbolizes opening up or unfolding, and the butterfly indicates transformation and the completion of a cycle. If the butterfly is decorated, it may be sending a message about beauty, while the inclusion of antennae indicate that you are clear, that you see what is happening. The path symbolizes your goals, so you may wish to consider where it originates and where it ends. The location of the path indicates where it is appropriate for you to initiate activity. Its design also provides information about structure and discipline. The mountain symbolizes your quest or dream as well as your spiritual journey and connection. It also reveals spiritual resources. For example, the drawing of a volcano may indicate spiritual fire in need of expression. The shelter symbolizes identity and the ego as well as your capacity to work intensely. Its location indicates the sphere in which you have a strong identification. The tree is a symbol of natural organic growth, or the subconscious level. It indicates what and who you are. Roots refer to your ancestors and the past. The absence of roots may indicate that you desire them to unfold according to your own timing. Tree branches point to the future, while blossoms or fruit may indicate that harvest time is at hand.

Finally, you may want to ponder some additional considerations. Did you add anything? Everything you need was given. Did you amplify anything? Doing so may indicate something your psyche wishes to explore. Is there a symbol you fussed over? This may indicate where your healing is coming from. What is the overall pattern, and how is everything connected? What colors did you use? Relative to this exercise, green represents creativity, fertility, abundance; white represents integration and purification; blue represents, in equal amounts, wisdom and emotionality; brown represents cultivation, productivity, and the ability to manifest that which you desire; purple represents leadership and royalty; orange represents fire, light, energy, and vitality; yellow represents spirit; red represents love, desire, and passion; and black represents strength, the unknown, and letting go.

Such an exercise may be very surprising in terms of what it reveals. I never cease to be amazed at the apparent validity of the stories that emerge as I utilize practices such as the Maori drawing, and thus my ability to trust the universe certainly is enhanced by them. However, I believe that we need to be very sensitive to our clients and to how they would perceive such an exercise before proceeding. As with any therapeutic intervention, its utility can be determined only relative to context, and thus you may find it sufficient to try this kind of exercise as an experiment for your own edification. I would make a similar admonition relative to oracles, which are the subject of the next discussion. That is, while I don't often employ them in my work with clients, I have found them to be very helpful in my personal life as a means of accessing information from and reinforcing my ability to trust the universe.

ORACLES

I use the term oracles to refer to such out-of-the-ordinary sources of information as the tarot, the runes, or the *I Ching*. I see them as tools that have the potential to aid in understanding ourselves at a soul level. The idea is to pose a question and to receive appropriate counsel for action or attitude based, respectively, on the card or rune drawn at random or by the hexagram created through the random throw of coins. According to Bolen (1979), synchronicity is the mechanism underlying such oracles inasmuch as intuitive knowing and meaning are connected to provide guidance for the search to live in harmony with the universe. She writes further that:

> The *I Ching* is probably one of the most important books in the literature of the world, because the two branches of Chinese philosophy, Confucianism and Taoism, have common roots in the *I Ching*. It emphasizes eternal values in the middle of a continually changing universe, assumes a cosmos that has a discernible underlying pattern, and strongly advises holding to inner values yet counsels about action and attitudes appropriate to the outer situation. The *I Ching* teaches principles through which it may be possible to learn to live in harmony with

the Tao, the invisible meaning-giving matrix of the universe. (Bolen, 1979, p. 63)

When using an oracle, we are told that it is not appropriate to look for answers to yes or no questions. Instead, the goal is to seek a different perspective on a situation as well as suggestions regarding appropriate behaviors to be implemented. The effectiveness of this process seems to be enhanced if we first take time to center ourselves and then to approach the oracle with a meditative state of mind. Indeed, it may well be that an attitude of trust and our mental focus create a context of expectancy that allows the outcome to be positive. Certainly this holds regarding experimental attempts to validate ESP (Bolen, 1979). Similarly,

> The person who sincerely approaches the *I Ching* needing an answer or some direction about something about which he or she is highly concerned and focused, hoping for some help to resolve a decision, also is in a similar state of focused expectancy. In this state, the *I Ching* reading that results is likely to be highly relevant. (Bolen, 1979, p. 80)

The reading that emerges is based on the manual that accompanies the particular oracle one is consulting. When using the *I Ching*, a coin is thrown six times in order to create a hexagram. Use of the runes requires drawing a stone on which a symbol has been traced. The tarot takes the form of a deck of cards. With the latter two oracles, a variety of spreads may be employed, depending upon the information for which one is searching.

It may not surprise you to learn that, as I mentally prepared to write this section, I had a certain amount of trepidation. That is, I am aware that inclusion of a discussion of oracles, particularly as they relate to the process of counseling/therapy, might lead you to conclude I have gone off the deep end. It therefore also might interest you to know that I decided to pull a rune relative to this issue. What I received was Othila reversed: ⋉. The message for this rune reads as follows:

> This is not a time to be bound by old conditioning, old authority. Consider not only what will benefit you but what will benefit others, and act according to the Light you possess now in your life. Because you may be called upon to undertake a radical departure from old ways,

total honesty is required. Otherwise, through negligence or refusal to see clearly, you may cause pain to others and damage to yourself.

Adaptability and skillful means are the methods to cultivate at this time. Yet you must wait for the universe to act. Upon receiving this Rune, remember: We do without doing and everything gets done. (Blum, 1987, p. 93)

Obviously, I interpreted this message as permission to proceed. Indeed, the messages are always open to our interpretation. In this case, I felt I was being urged, according to the first paragraph, to spread the word about a tool that I consider very useful, regardless of how nontraditional this may be. The second paragraph is less clear to me, but I believe it indicates that even though the way I am perceived may be affected, I need to trust that, as long as I proceed with integrity, the universe will take care of whatever fallout there may be.

Perhaps you may question my interpretation. Certainly if you never have consulted an oracle, you may have difficulty believing that it could have any validity. All I can suggest is that you try it for yourself and see. Indeed, there are many other oracles you may wish to consider as well, selecting the one that feels right for you. For example, the Medicine Cards (Sams & Carson, 1988) have been designed consistent with Native American belief systems. There is also the Gaia Matrix Oracle, created by the visionary artist Rowena Pattee Kryder (1990) and aimed at a healing and re-creation of the earth. Regardless of which you choose, however, the following seems to be an important proviso:

> You should not attempt to equate the archetypes and symbols from one of these oracle systems with another, for they each are self-contained integral wholes. These oracle systems are not fortune telling devices. They offer a vantage, in much the same way as a person able to predict the arrival of a friend by climbing a hill or tower. Oracles do not present opinions, judgments or infallible truths but form an alliance with mythic patterns which are deep underlying "ley lines" [energy channels] of our psyches and spirits. (Kryder, 1990, p. 1)

While you may remain skeptical, and while I think your skepticism is healthy and certainly respect it, I also invite you into the world in which trust in the universe is second nature and your experience testifies to what is possible. Although I am fully aware that "believing is seeing" may be the rule with the use of oracles, if what I am doing seems useful to me or helpful for my clients, then I am open to the possibility. At the same time, I do recommend balance in this as in all other activities.

BALANCE

That is, while I may well have recourse to such measures, I would be vehemently opposed to running my life solely according to psychic readings or to feeling that I had to consult an oracle before doing anything. Rather, for me such tools are an adjunct, one way to get additional information regarding a specific situation, particularly in times of crisis or of great uncertainty. Similarly, while I advocate expanding our ability to access a mystical approach to reality, I see it as the logical complement to the analytic mode of knowing rather than as its replacement. Thus, while I certainly trust the universe, I am ever aware that "God helps him who helps himself," and I see all of life as a cocreative process.

The problem, from my perspective, is that we arbitrarily have divided our world into the material and the spiritual and, as a society, have chosen to invest most heavily in the former. In a similar manner, we previously have been limited to the extent that spirituality has been omitted from the practice of counseling and therapy. The following poem, entitled "Two Worlds," written by Nancy Wood, seems to speak most eloquently to this issue:

> *For us, there are Two Worlds of Being.*
> *The First World is the outer world we live in,*
> *A shell that encases the body, an attitude*
> *That stifles the mind and pretends*
> *That money is the measure of worth.*
>
> *The First World is harsh, though comfortable,*
> *Alluring, though vain. It is the popular world*
> *Where everyone longs to be, yet once they arrive,*
> *They dream of a new direction. In this world,*
> *Everything costs something and what is free costs more.*
>
> *The First world is one of wheels and destinations,*
> *Membership dues and limitations. It is a sanctuary*
> *For those who desire conformity in all things.*

Here duplicate people wearing duplicate clothes
Speak a language without meaning, and think thoughts
Without substance to their form.

The First World is where everyone lives, yet
No one actually survives. It is an acceptable address
Where you forfeit all that you are for what
You will never become and what you are not
Is what you want those around you to remember.

The First World has power, but no strength.
It is one of mirrors, but no reflection.
In this world, there is success, but no mystery.
Goals, but no journey. In this world,
Boundaries keep ideas from colliding.

The Second World is the inner world of harmony,
Where you can go anytime your spirit aches for company.
Here you can listen to the songs of rocks and leaves and
Embrace the wisdom of rivers and essential things contained in
Raindrops or a flower's belly or the earth's warm breath of spring,
In this world, beauty is companion to mystery.

The Second World is one of joy and curiosity,
A connecting thread to birds and oceans, plants and animals.
The Second World is one of children's laughter, women's songs,
Men's stories, the essence that remains long after the experience
Has passed on. In this world, all circles return.

The Second World is where you can travel
On the wings of dreams or the tails of newborn stars.
This world is revealed through a rainbow's colored eyes,
Or in a spider's silver road between two leaves,
Or even in silence, the kind that follows ecstasy.
The Second World is able to survive without the First,
But the First World cannot last long without the Second.
The Second World offers meaning to existence
While the First World offers existence only.
Between these two Worlds
Lies reason, the seam that connects one World to another.

The Second World is yours for no money.
The First World is yours for no effort.
  Which one will you choose? (1993, pp. 54–55)

While for me the obvious choice is the second world, such a choice seems valid only to the extent that it encompasses and includes the best of the first world. Indeed, I believe that a spiritual orientation focuses on transcending dichotomies, on bringing our worlds together, on acknowledging that such divisions are spurious and unhelpful. In addition to learning in traditional ways, we thus may learn to access the wisdom of the universe, thereby participating in the creation of a reality in which matter and spirit are integrated in a manner that best facilitates healing not only for ourselves but also for our clients.

Accordingly, soul healing involves sensitivity to the whole person, to body, mind, and spirit. Indeed, long before reading Nancy Wood's poem, I experienced myself as being faced with the challenge of reconciling and living comfortably in two worlds, or, as I referred to them, two different levels of reality. Certainly this is similar to the story often told by my clients. That is, while there are beliefs that may make sense in one realm, they may be problematic, at best, in another. What is more, we may find ourselves on the horns of a dilemma as we experience a tension between "the soul's push to fulfill its destiny and the pull of the physical word, that is, the environmental and material forms that life takes" (Raheem, 1991, p. 22). However, as we seek to heal divisions and transcend dichotomies, we may find that we are aided to the extent that we learn not only to access but also to trust the universe. Further, in doing so, we also may find that we have devised a new, more satisfying story according to which we may live.

We will save further discussion of the issue of living in two worlds for chapter 8. For now, we turn our attention to the fourth principle of soul healing: creating realities.

The soul looketh steadily forwards, creating a world before her, leaving worlds behind her.

—Ralph Waldo Emerson

CHAPTER 7

Creating Realities

INTRODUCTION

From a postmodern, second-order cybernetics perspective (Becvar & Becvar, 1996), to live is to participate in the construction of our reality. We cannot do otherwise. We are continually involved with others in a mutual process of perturbation, feedback, and response, and the system is recreated in each moment through our perceptions and interactions. The world, thus, is not a fixed entity but rather is open to constant change and transformation. Similarly, we may understand from a spiritual perspective that it is we who are the creators of reality. As we are told poetically in the book *Illusions: The Adventures of a Reluctant Messiah*:

> *The world*
> *is your exercise-book, the pages*
> *on which you do your sums.*
> *It is not reality,*
> *although you can express reality*
> *there if you wish.*
> *You are also*
> *free to write nonsense,*
> *or lies, or to tear*
> *the pages.* (Bach, 1977, p. 127)

Given such a perspective, we inevitably are challenged to focus on the nature of the reality we wish to participate in creating. In chapters 4, 5, and 6 we have considered the realities that may evolve in counseling/therapy as a function of acknowledging connectedness, suspending judgment, and trusting the universe. Assuming these principles as fundamental to the creation of a soul-healing context, we will be examining in this chapter some ways in which the unique issues of client systems may be addressed in order to cocreate realities within which healing is facilitated. Our discussion begins with a look at various sources of the random, or of new information, including some of those previously mentioned and especially as related to a spiritual orientation. Particular attention is given to meaning and purpose and to the encouragement of a deeper understanding of what is possible through the use of bibliotherapy, or the use of books, of writing journals and of meditation. A consideration of how to frame questions and offer reflections that provide a variety of windows through which problems may be viewed and understood follows. This exploration of perceptual expansion leads to the consideration of a focus on solutions, particularly those which emerge from a spiritual orientation. The role played by the therapist's beliefs in the creation of realities as well as ways to facilitate and support clients' awareness of the process of creating reality are then explored. The chapter closes with a discussion of the crucial issue of ethics in general as well as of moral and ethical behavior on the part of the counselor/therapist in particular.

SOURCES OF THE RANDOM

According to Bateson (1979, p. 147), "Without the random there can be no new thing." This notion is basic to my story that when clients come to therapy, rather than being mad or bad, they are in a stuck place. Consistent with this view is my belief that, in their attempts to deal with whatever situation they are perceiving as problematic, clients have run through all the possible responses available to them from their current behavioral and perceptual repertoires. What is more, they have created a reality in which their responses have become a part of the pattern within which the problem situation is being maintained (Watzlawick et al., 1974). As counselor/therapists, therefore, I believe that our role is to provide new information, to be a source of the random, so that a new and, we hope, more satisfactory reality may be created.

To this point we have considered many such sources of the random. For example, in chapter 4 we noted the potential for the sharing of the counselor/therapist's story to provide a basis for questions or reflections, or both, which may enable the client to achieve new understandings that may help in attaining the desired solution to his or her problem. In chapter 5 we examined the introduction of a relative perspective on problems and the impact of viewing such problems as both crisis and opportunity. We also have looked in some depth, in chapter 6, at the exploration of dreams as well as at the use of both shamanic practices and oracles, each of which may be perceived as providing new information or a new perspective on a particular situation. Indeed, the sources of the random are endless and may be derived from a variety of domains including art, fiction and poetry, and the theater; and I don't believe we should ever underestimate the power of humor to add a new dimension to the counseling/therapy process. For example, as Jean Houston writes:

> For me laughter is the ultimate altered state. At the peak of roaring laughter, one exists, as in midsneeze, everywhere and nowhere, and is thus available to be blessed, evoked, deepened. In the bag of tricks I have used over the years to bring people to other states of mind, I still find that for most, laughter remains the easiest way to begin moving beyond that half-awake state we call "normal waking consciousness." (1996, p. 170)

However, as we think specifically about spirituality and soul healing, it also may be useful to consider the importance of a focus on the larger meaning and purpose of our lives as well as the encouragement of reading, keeping journals and meditating to access and facilitate greater awareness in this realm.

In the narration of his "contemporary quest for ancient wisdom," Paulo Coelho tells of receiving from his mentor the following important message:

> "We must never stop dreaming. Dreams provide nourishment for the soul, just as a meal does for the body. Many times in our lives we see our dreams shattered and our desires frustrated, but we have to continue dreaming. If we don't, our soul dies, and agape cannot reach it. . . .
>
> "The good fight is the one we fight because our heart asks it of us. In the heroic ages—at the time of the knights in armor—this was easy. There were lands to conquer and much to do. Today, though, the world has changed a lot, and the good fight has shifted from the battlefields to the fields within ourselves.
>
> "The good fight is the one that's fought in the name of our dreams.

When we're young and our dreams first explode inside us with all of their force, we are very courageous, but we haven't yet learned how to fight. With great effort, we learn how to fight, but by then we no longer have the courage to go into combat. So we turn against ourselves and do battle within. We become our own worst enemy. We say that our dreams were childish, or too difficult to realize, or the result of our not having known enough about life. We kill our dreams because we are afraid to fight the good fight." (1995, pp. 50–51)

Coelho's point regarding the importance of dreams is consistent with the findings of contemporary psychological research which, as noted in chapter 3, indicate that people are more likely to experience anxiety, depression, and many other physical ailments in the absence of a sense that life has meaning and purpose. What is more, it appears that the search for both meaning and a connection to a transcendent or sacred dimension not only is a basic aspect of human development but also is fundamental to mental and physical health and well-being (Jones, 1995). Thus, as we interact with our clients, it seems appropriate to be sensitive to the possibility that the problems they are experiencing may be bound up with some basic issues of meaning, purpose and spirituality.

I am reminded in this regard of a young couple with whom I worked several years ago. The presenting problem was the dissatisfaction of one spouse, who felt that the choice to marry the other spouse had been made in error, for the wrong reasons. Needless to say, the latter partner, who was working hard to be perceived as the right mate as well as to keep the marriage together, was frustrated by the fact that all attempts seemed to have been in vain. After several sessions, discussing first what reality it was that each spouse would experience as desirable and then focusing on their desired goal of improved communication, our conversation shifted. Given that one partner was a member of the clergy and that both were deeply religious, it is not surprising that we began to discuss the meaning of life, moving from there to a consideration of death. It emerged that the dissatisfied spouse had some genuine fears about death, which previously had not been addressed. In our conversations, I suggested that the couple might want to do some reading and talking. They liked the idea, so I loaned them *Who Dies?* by Stephen Levine (1982). Reading this book proved to be the turning point in our work together. Consistent with the notion that we are able to live our lives more fully once we have come to terms with our inevitable mortality, the dissatisfied spouse found that an expanded view of death as well as the opportunity to discuss together, as a couple, issues related to this topic shed new light on their relationship. Indeed, it was not long before our work together concluded, with both partners satisfied and the marriage intact. I am aware from subsequent meetings with this couple, related to child-rearing issues, that this successful outcome has been sustained over time.

The search for meaning and purpose, or perhaps a common goal that a couple can pursue, has provided the basis for many homework projects I have suggested over the years. Perhaps the most enjoyable assignment, judging from client reports, is for the couple to take advantage of a warm summer evening (after the children are in bed), to spread a blanket on the lawn and lie on their backs together, holding hands and looking up at the stars. They are then to discuss quietly whatever possibilities for their lives come to mind, and perhaps to recapture the dreams they shared when they first met and formed their relationship. No specific outcome is required or expected. Rather, the intention is that, as a function of being together in a different way and focusing on what they might create together, a new reality will emerge that the couple will experience as more satisfactory.

Similarly, as with the couple just described, I may well be aware of a book to suggest to a client if this seems appropriate. Fortunately, one of my greatest pleasures in life is reading. In fact, I received the highest score posssible on a test aimed at assessing whether or not I am a biblioholic (Raabe, 1991)! While I may read self-help books, however, I am in general most wary of recommending them, for I am concerned that they may suggest to the reader the existence of a problem that she or he previously did not have. Because of the perceived expertise of their authors as well as their tendency to describe life in terms of *shoulds* and *should nots*, such books may influence unduly the reader's perception of what is problematic and thereby participate in the creation of an undesirable reality. Therefore, I am more inclined to recommend nonfiction that focuses on exploring a particular topic in depth or fiction that I believe has the potential to offer what may be perceived as a useful perspective. Such recommendations often focus on the search for meaning and purpose as related to the solutions that clients have indicated they desire.

As we think about other sources of the random, we also may consider the personal journal. In fact, a journal may be a very useful means of getting in touch with our heart's dream, with our mission and purpose in life, with our connection to the sacred. Taggart (1994) notes that working with journals can take the form of process recordings, diary keeping, sharing journals, intentional life reviews, and audiotaped records or responses. In addition, she writes that she and others have found the journal to be powerful because:

> [It] helps us remember and gives continuity to life, it stimulates imagination, it helps us explore our emotional depths, it helps us remember and work with our dreams, it encourages personal growth, and it helps us evolve a personal relationship with God. (p. 159)

I, too, have found keeping a journal to be helpful, particularly at points of crisis in my life and when I have been searching for the meaning of it all. I therefore have recommended this process to my clients for use in a variety of situations. My belief is that, in addition to being a way to voice feelings or release pent-up emotions, a journal provides a concrete way in which to have a conversation with that which we consider to be the transcendent dimension—God, a higher power, our higher self, or the soul. While we may sometimes feel we have not been heard and that the conversation is one-sided, the outcome of such conversations can be quite remarkable. For example, as you may recall from the quote in chapter 4, Elisabeth Kubler-Ross reports using the technique of asking questions and then getting answers, which she perceives as coming from her soul, using her left, or nondominant, hand. Similarly, in his book, *Conversations with God*, Walsch (1995) shares with readers the journal created as he wrote questions and then received responses in the form of automatic writing. Regardless of whether or not we, or our clients, experience such a dramatic response, putting our thoughts into writing or speaking them into a tape recorder may help us to see things in a different light. Thus, new information may be provided that assists in the construction of a new reality.

Still another source of the random or way to access new information, especially as related to mission or purpose in life, may be found through the process of turning inward. My suggestion to clients is that, whether they prefer meditation, guided imagery using audio tapes, or prayer, they might consider taking some time to be alone, to ask questions and then to listen in silence, with as quiet a mind as possible, for whatever answers may be forthcoming. Anticipating the hesitation clients often express in response, especially about meditation, I am quick to articulate my view that there is no specific formula that must be followed, and I do not believe that we have to be disappointed if the outcome does not appear to be earthshaking. Rather, I suggest that just taking the time to slow down, in contrast to the typically hectic pace at which most of us lead our lives, may be very beneficial. As the journalist Tony Schwartz reports:

To my surprise, the practice of letting go of my thoughts and resting in a place of inner quiet proved both exhilarating and moving. For the first time, I found that it was possible to get beyond my gnawing everyday concerns and to experience instead a sense of calmness, clarity, and deep well-being. In time, I became convinced that I'd found the answer I'd been searching for—a way to fill up what was missing in my life. (1995, p. 7)

Often I also share my own similar experience: for me, things just seem to go more smoothly when I start each day by meditating. Certainly there is evidence to support my story, including studies of the benefits of certain kinds of yoga practices, transcendental meditation, and the relaxation techniques pioneered by Herbert Benson:

Physiological response and benefits [of such exercises] have been reported to include decreases in heart rate, blood pressure, and muscle tension, and increased alpha and theta activity in the EEG. The methods have been touted as an important method of controlling stress and establishing a "wakeful hypometabolic state," which can restore the body to a comfortable, healthful level of homeostatic balance. (Achterberg, 1985, p. 45).

What is more, as clients begin to take time out from their busy schedules to meditate, or pray, or listen to tapes, they generally report not only an increased sense of well-being but also that they receive information, often in the form of new perspectives or answers to their questions.

Closely associated with meditation and prayer is the process of dialoguing with one's illness or with an area in the body associated with a problem. This can be done either during the counseling/therapy session by means of a guided meditation, or clients can be asked to experiment on their own. One way to help clients connect with the inner wisdom or knowing of their bodies has been described as follows:

Often I lead them to call forth a personification of this wisdom as a being whom they are invited to call "The One Who Knows Health." The personification makes it possible for their inner knowings to assume recognizable form and to communicate with the conscious mind as directly and unambiguously as possible. (Houston, 1996, p. 191)

As I guide clients within, I invite them to take an imaginary journey throughout their body, noticing particularly any places of discomfort. I then suggest that they request that the organ or area involved provide information about what can be done to facilitate healing. I also may suggest that they envision healing energy in the form of white light pouring into their body, or that they hold in their mind's eye an image of their body as totally healed, or both. At other times, I may make use of visualizations specific to the problem being experienced (Epstein, 1989), a practice that is consistent with the belief that the mind and body are one and thus that healing may be facilitated through imagery (Achterberg, 1985).

The idea is to allow the client to access new information that will aid in the creation of a new, more satisfactory reality. For, whatever is received, the experience may provide the basis for another story. Indeed, regardless of how it is accessed, understanding of the illness story may play an important part in the search for solutions. Or, as noted by Kleinman, relative to chronic health problems:

> [I]llness has meaning; and to understand how it obtains meaning is to understand something fundamental about illness, about care, and perhaps about life generally. Moreover, an interpretation of illness is something that patients, families, and practitioners need to undertake together. For there is a dialectic at the heart of healing that brings the care giver into the uncertain, fearful world of pain and disability and that reciprocally introduces patient and family into the equally uncertain world of therapeutic actions. That dialectic both enhances the therapy and makes of it and the illness a rare opportunity for moral education. (1988, p. xiv)

The dialectic of which Kleinman speaks brings us to what I consider to be the extremely important issue of system perturbation and the creation of realities through the use of questions and reflections. That is, every question on the part of the counselor/therapist will have an impact on or will perturb the system as a whole. It thus constitutes an intervention, a behavior that will be given meaning by the client. Therefore, I believe that our ability to frame questions and to offer reflections out of sensitivity to and respect for clients' belief systems is crucial both to their impact as well as to their effectiveness.

FRAMING QUESTIONS AND OFFERING REFLECTIONS

Consistent with the assumptions of second-order cybernetics (Becvar & Becvar, 1996), my story is that as we interact with clients, the system is engaged in a mutual, recursive process of perturbation and compensation and, ideally, through this process new, more satisfactory contexts, or realities, are cocreated. Consistent also with the postmodern, narrative approaches to family therapy, questions and reflections represent two important forms of system perturbation. In accord with a soul-healing approach, some of these questions and reflections, particularly as they relate to mission and purpose and a connection to the sacred, would speak to a spiritual orientation. However, I am convinced that there is a real art to their creation and delivery.

Following the advice of Tom Andersen (1991), I believe it is important that questions and reflections be offered tentatively as suggestions, thoughts, or ideas, or all three, so that they may be accepted or rejected. Further, I believe in order to be useful, they must be embedded in a story that enables the client to hear them. Accordingly, the counselor/therapist must have a good understanding of the client's worldview, his or her unique circumstances, and the language that is meaningful to him or her. The questions or reflections include words and metaphors that are most likely to structurally couple with, or be receivable and believable by, the client.

I therefore attempt to match the visual, auditory, or kinesthetic mode according to which my clients primarily operate (Bandler & Grinder, 1975). I also will speak very differently, for example, to a computer programmer than I would to an artist, and I attempt to be sensitive to gender differences (Gray, 1992; Tannen, 1990). Further, I do not hesitate when necessary to say something like, "I am struggling to find the right words to use" as I pause and take time to figure out how best to phrase a query or comment. Thus, at all times, rather than being the expert who has the answers, the counselor/therapist becomes the participant in a respectful dialogue. Such a dialogue emphasizes the client's strengths and is focused on facilitating the elimination of problems through the achievement of the client's goals.

I also am sensitive to moments when it seems appropriate to include in the dialogue the realm of spirituality. Questions and reflections that are designed to participate in the creation of new realities related to meaning and purpose and that are consistent with a spiritual orientation point to the future and to solutions that would be constructive for the client at a soul level. As noted previously (Khan, 1982), the basic focus concerns the particular qualities that, according to a larger, spiritual plan, are at issue; qualities that in all likelihood must be developed in order to meet the current challenge. Some of the questions and reflections that emerge for me from such a focus include the following:

- In what way does this situation, or in what way could this situation, add meaning to your life?
- I wonder how we might look at and understand this situation differently.
- What opportunity for learning does this situation provide for you?
- I wonder whether there are themes or patterns that link this situation to others in your life.
- How do you think this situation might facilitate your growth?
- Suppose you had chosen this situation, knowing that it would be useful for you. I wonder what the usefulness of it might be.
- What resources do you possess that might be stimulated by this situation?
- I wonder about the timing of this situation and how it may be significant for you.
- How might you use this situation to benefit yourself or others in your world?
- I wonder in what direction this situation might be helping to point you.
- How could you use your creative energies to make something useful out of this situation?
- I wonder if the choices you are making reflect what you truly value.
- If you were to view this situation as representing the middle of an important aspect of your life story, a story whose outcome you knew was going to be positive, how might this story end?
- I wonder, if this situation could talk, what it might be trying to tell you.
- If you thought of this situation as a map given to you by your higher power, where do you think you might look for the buried treasure?
- I wonder whether your soul might be trying to communicate something to you through this situation.

There are many stories that might be used as a context for questions and reflections such as these. The counselor/therapist might make recourse to Biblical or other relevant spiritual references that speak to the transformation that may emerge out of crisis. For instance, the Egyptian myth of the phoenix is the story of a bird that rises from the ashes of destruction. There are countless examples, many of them made into movies, of ordinary people who have achieved extraordinary victories despite major tragedies and setbacks. In addition, there is one's own personal story as well as the stories of the unsung heroes and heroines. I refer here to other clients who have overcome significant obstacles and dealt successfully with personal problems in such a way that, in retrospect, the crisis is understood as a positive, life-changing watershed. As always, however, such stories must be selected with care and must not be Pollyannaish trivializations of the client's reality.

All of these questions, reflections, and stories obviously are variations on a theme. They all address, at least implicitly, the importance of perception in seeking understanding of and resolution for problems. They all point to the possibility that however great the pain of a given situation, there may be alternate ways of viewing that situation. Further, there is a recognition, perhaps a suggestion, that the client may be experiencing one of those moments which hold the potential for spiritual growth and healing at a soul level. Thus they all represent ways to engage with the client in an attempt to think differently and thereby to create new realities. Moreover, building on the responses that emerge as a function of such questions and reflections, as well as the stories in which they are embedded, the conversation may then turn more specifically toward a focus on solutions.

FOCUSING ON SOLUTIONS

The search for solutions (e.g., de Shazer, 1988; O'Hanlon & Wiener-Davis, 1989) is another important aspect of the postmodern approach to family therapy. Given the assumptions that reality is comprised of multiple perspectives and that there is no one right way to live or be, clients are encouraged to define for themselves their personal goals. Emphasis is given to the importance of language in constructing stories about problems as well as about their deconstruction and their solutions. In addition, from a soul-healing perspective, the focus on solutions involves articulating outcomes that enable clients not only to rewrite the local narratives in which their problems are embedded but, where possible, to expand their larger stories in such a way that the potential for ongoing, long-term growth is enhanced. That is, as we create with our clients an awareness of the spiritual gifts that may be hidden within their problems, we also may help them create and begin to walk a path toward a sense of greater wholeness and well-being. Taken to its furthest limits, the potential of such an outcome for each of us is indeed great, for example:

[W]e can experience the inpouring of light or grace, a sense sublime of living in a felicitous universe whose ground is love and whose gift is utter forgiveness for what we have or have not done. We open then to a reality larger than any particular path—open to the dazzling glory and wonder of it all, a wonder that exceeds all known boundaries of time and space. (Houston, 1996, p. 277)

However, while I believe it certainly may be helpful to keep such a grand goal in mind, I also am mindful of the fact that achievement of even the greatest of outcomes usually begins in small ways. I also therefore believe it is important to search for solutions or experiences of success, however modest, that are attainable or realistic for the client. In the process, I may request information about moments in the past when she or he achieved that which is sought in the present.

To illustrate this process, I will describe another person with whom I have worked. This is a man whom I will call Jim, who was dealing with the death of his wife after a prolonged illness. The losses Jim was experiencing included not only his spouse but also the system of support that had sustained him through the many months of his wife's repeated hospitalizations. As is often the case, even after what may be only a brief interval, he was now getting the message from both family members and friends that it was time to stop grieving and get on with his life. Such a message tapped into previous accusations that he was overly sensitive and too emotional. However, contrary to his usual behavior, which had been to assume that it was he who had a problem and to apologize, he had begun to refuse to accept such charges and to confront those who made them. While a part of him was aware that it was healthy to recognize not only that his sensitivity was not necessarily bad but that he had the right to choose what he would accept from others in this regard, he now felt more alone than ever and wondered if perhaps the others were right after all.

I validated not only Jim's perception that sensitivity is not a fault but also his decision about choosing those behaviors he would and would not accept from his well-intentioned friends and family members. Then, in response to his question regarding what he was supposed to learn from all of this, we considered many possibilities. After a time we agreed that perhaps the message was that it was important for him to "go it alone" for a time. I then asked him, "What belief system do you make recourse to, or what gives meaning to your life?" His answer was that part of the problem he was dealing with was that he no longer had a meaningful belief system. Upon further questioning, he revealed that until he reached early adulthood, he had been a regular churchgoer. However, he had come to a point in his life when the tenets of the belief system in which he had been reared no longer fit, and he therefore had gone on a search for something else with which he would be more comfortable. After exploring many different denominations, he had selected one that seemed to provide what he was looking for. He subsequently changed his affiliation to this new church, eventually becoming a very active participant in its administrative structure. However, after his wife's death, he found that the belief system of this church also had been "blown out of the water" for him.

Building on the process that had been successful for him in the past, I suggested to Jim that perhaps it was time to go on another search. When he replied that he just didn't have the energy to start all over again by visiting different churches, I proposed that there might be another way, that perhaps he could conduct his search through books. I encouraged him to go to a library or a bookstore and do some browsing, just seeing what books appealed to him or seemed to be crying out to him to be read. I shared my experience of sometimes feeling that a book had just jumped into my hand, and that I couldn't put it back even if I tried. In addition, I encouraged him in the meantime to revisit one of the churches that had appealed to him in his previous search.

Taking small steps, such as those just indicated, Jim began to regain a sense of peace. After much soul searching, both literally and figuratively, he decided that his choice was to be part of a nondenominational spiritual community in which he felt support for his belief system, which had evolved from a variety of frameworks. He also parlayed his sensitivity into a focus on humanitarian efforts as part of his work as an urban planner and developer. And having come to a point where he fully accepted himself in the context of a meaningful belief system, he realized that it no longer was important that he be alone. Thus, he could once again think about creating new relationships with friends and family members. Ultimately he also found a new marriage partner, a woman of similar beliefs and interests who desired to walk with him on his now-transformed path of life.

I chose to use Jim's story because I believe it illustrates well not only the way in which small, careful steps may evolve into large changes but also the potential for joy that may be hidden in even the moments of greatest despair. In resolving the tragedy of his wife's death and its repercussions in his life, Jim also experienced what is possible in terms of a focus on solutions, particularly as related to meaning and purpose in life. Though I doubt that at the outset he could have heard the following words, I suspect that in retrospect he would agree wholeheartedly that their message about creating a new, more comfortable reality rings true:

> Let the power of joy pervade your soul and lift you above the tribulations of your life with a sense of ease. In the last resort it will be all right. A defeat can avert itself to be a victory. Going through the darkness you reach into the light. Suffering will open the way to the exaltation of joy. (Khan, 1994, p. 132)

While I certainly did not use such words or attempt to speak to Jim of "silver linings," I nevertheless believe that out of darkness can come great light. Such has been not only my experience but also that of many others I have known and with whom I have worked. Therefore, at an implicit level, I am certain that this potential exists, and I tend to be sincerely optimistic with my clients. Indeed, consistent with my assumption that this perspective of mine undoubtedly influences the counseling/therapy process, I believe that another important aspect of the creation of new realities is the belief system of the counselor/therapist.

THE IMPACT OF THE COUNSELOR/THERAPIST'S BELIEFS

As you may recall from chapter 3, according to Dossey (1993) studies examining this issue reveal that physicians' beliefs can have a powerful influence in terms of the realities they participate in creating with their patients and thus, ultimately, in terms of the outcome of the therapy process. As I have noted, it is therefore his stance that in the ideal situation, the beliefs of doctor and patient are consistent; that in the best of all possible worlds both believe in the efficacy of the treatment and trust that the outcome will be positive; and that in the worse-case scenarios, the beliefs of the patient and the doctor conflict or neither the patient nor the doctor believes that the therapy will be successful. A stance like Dossey's is consistent with the findings of a study, made more than two decades ago, that hope engendered in the client seemed to be the single most important ingredient in any recipe for healing (Frank, 1974). And more recently, Norman Cousins has written in a similar vein:

> People tell me not to offer hope unless I know hope to be real, but I don't have the power not to respond to an outstretched hand. I don't know

enough to say that hope can't be real. I'm not sure anyone knows enough to deny hope. I have seen too many cases these past ten years when death predictions were delivered from high professional station only to be gloriously refuted by patients for reasons having less to do with tangible biology than with the human spirit, admittedly a vague term but one that may well be the greatest force of all within the human arsenal. (1989, pp. 65–66)

Thus I believe that it behooves us to be sensitive, at many levels, to the messages we communicate to our clients. Indeed, it is my position that it is vitally important to recognize the transforming power of our thoughts as we participate in the alteration of perceptions. More specifically, we might also be aware of the power which may emerge as we invoke our own belief in a transcendent dimension, regardless of whether or not this dimension is addressed explicitly. And while recognizing that the most any of us can be is a cocreator of a new reality, we might acknowledge that our role is nevertheless significant. In other words:

In therapy we do not supply a family's spirit. However, we can participate in it, and perhaps even kindle new energy and determination if we join our own spirit to theirs. Therapy calls for us to recognize a family's spirit, draw it out, and fly with it. It is our own spirit that allows us to see and speak to a family's spirit. (Aponte, 1994, p. 146)

Accordingly, it makes sense for many reasons to focus on strengths and solutions, on possibilities and potentials, and to have faith in the process. As we do so we influence, however implicitly, the creation of a reality that is a context supportive of positive outcomes. What is more, to do otherwise may be far more serious than we often may realize. In the first place, as we engage in negativity regarding expectations, we may be undermining the potential of anything else we do to succeed: we may be sending incongruent messages that are at best confusing and at worst may be received by clients as information about the inevitability of failure. For the analogical level, or nonverbal message plus context, of communication is the relationship-defining mode (Watzlawick, Beavin, & Jackson, 1967). Not only does it provide a commentary about how a message is to be received, it also is the mode to which people tend to pay the most attention. Secondly, by expressing limited expectations, we may participate in maintaining a problem, joining clients in their patterns of negative thinking. Third, and perhaps most important:

It is very difficult to reverse the effects of negative thinking once they have taken physical form. Not impossible—but very difficult. It takes an act of extreme faith. It requires an extraordinary belief in the positive force of the universe—whether you call that God, Goddess, the Unmoved Mover, Prime Force, First Cause, or whatever. (Walsch, 1995, p. 189)

Therefore, while I believe that we must be sincere, I think it is essential that we embody a "positive force" that may enable clients to overcome whatever negativity they may be experiencing. To do so requires a sense of optimism about what is possible, so that our communication is congruent. Moreover, it requires acute sensitivity to the language we employ to convey our message, especially when our intentions are to encourage and to emphasize what is possible.

By contrast, as alluded to in chapter 2, I have experienced the impact of negative language and have been challenged by the need to resist the implicit message regarding possible dire outcomes. For example, my internist has often said to me things like, "We don't want you to survive breast cancer only to die from heart disease" in his efforts to convince me to undergo yet another diagnostic procedure. My dentist has on several occasions communicated a message that I experience as negative programming: "You have reached the age when you can expect your fillings to start breaking." But my personal favorite was shared by a client who, after receiving a bone marrow transplant, was told by an oncologist, "You know that your body is your own worst enemy." While I believe that in all cases the communications were well-intended, the messages sent were very different from the ones received. All had a very negative connotation, and none expressed much faith in either the patient or the patient's ability to facilitate or maintain health and well-being.

On the other hand, it has been noted that those who are true healers have a faith that is wide and deep:

It is a faith that crosses over into Absolute Knowing. They *know* that you are meant to be whole, complete, and perfect in *this moment now*. This knowingness is also a thought—and a very powerful one. It has the power to move mountains—to say nothing of molecules in your body. That is why healers can heal, often even at a distance. (Walsch, 1995, p. 189)

Such a faith emerges, for me, from my spiritual orientation. As I wrote in chapter 5, I do believe in what Jean Houston (1995) defines as the "possible human." As I have indicated, I see each of us as an aspect of the divine or sacred dimension and thus trust in our potential for perfection. And, as outlined in chapter 6, trusting the universe seems as natural and appropriate to me as breathing. While I have an awareness of the limits of what is possible in any given situation, it is to such beliefs that I refer when I say that I am sincerely optimistic and therefore am able to have faith in my clients and the potential for success in the counseling/therapy process.

In addition to trust on the part of the therapist, there is another, equally important aspect of the role of beliefs in the creation of a reality. That is, we cannot ignore the impact of the client's belief system relative to what is possible. Accordingly, I believe that counseling and therapy are much more likely to be effective to the extent that we can support clients by helping them evolve positive beliefs, or a faith both in themselves and in the process.

SUPPORTING CLIENTS

Indeed, one of those limits of what is possible with a particular client often lies in his or her negative beliefs. I therefore often find it appropriate to focus directly on these beliefs, and particularly on the related messages that may be influencing the client's functioning in a less than desirable manner. Although, as mentioned at the beginning of this chapter, I do not often recommend self-help books, there is one which I have found extremely useful in this regard. Written by Shad Helmstetter (1986), this book is entitled *What to Say When You Talk to Yourself*. Helmstetter addresses the issue of what he calls "self-talk," particularly the often negative messages we, as well as our clients, may have internalized and then tend to repeat as part of a never-ending commentary on our abilities, our behavior, and ourselves.

Helmstetter's suggestion is that we reprogram our internal dialogue, replacing the negative with positive, self-affirming messages. He recommends to readers that they create their own audiotapes, using their own voices, and provides some sample scripts that can be employed in this process. While one does not have to use these scripts, Helmstetter emphasizes the importance of using them as a model by putting whatever messages are chosen, related to one's particular goals, in the present tense (e.g., "I am losing weight;" "I am a good person;" "I am healing"). He also suggests that readers play their tapes every day, for repetition is understood to be an important part of the change process.

A similar theme is found in the book *Your Body Believes Every Word*

You Say (Levine, 1991). The focus of this book is on choosing attitudes and beliefs as well as words and images in order to influence physical healing. Like Helmstetter, Levine also emphasizes the importance of ongoing repetition; further she notes that:

> Our beliefs about the way things are shape the way we see things. The notion that prophecy can be self-fulfilling has some scientific truth. Researchers in perception have demonstrated that we often see what we expect to see, hear what we expect to hear, and feel what we expect to feel. (1991, p. 95)

Clients also may be supported in the process of changing beliefs through the use of positive affirmations. Indeed, the construction of a particular reality through change in the language of our self-talk is similar to the procedure described, for example, by Shakti Gawain (1978) as creative visualization. Gawain explains this creative visualization as "the technique of using your imagination to create what you want in your life" (p. 2). Having visualized the desired situation, one is then encouraged to add verbal affirmations such as the following (Gawain, 1978, p. 41):

> *God is working through me now,*
> *or*
> *I am filled with divine light and creative energy,*
> *or*
> *The light within me is creating miracles in my life*
> *here and now,*
> *or whatever phrase has meaning and power for you.*

In addition to her spiritual emphasis, Gawain also focuses on issues of both physical and emotional health and stresses the importance of repetition. For it is her belief that we may create our reality by mentally picturing, two or three times a day, the outcome of a particular situation for which we are striving. Moreover, she writes that:

> There is nothing at all new, strange, or unusual about creative visualization. You are already using it every day, every minute in fact. It is your natural power of imagination, the basic creative energy of the universe which you use constantly, whether or not you are aware of it. (Gawain, 1978, p. 2)

What is important about the processes espoused by all three of these authors is the invitation to make use, consciously, of an inherent ability to facilitate the creation of our desired reality. A belief in this ability is based on the assumptions that thought is energy, and that anything created is created first as a thought. The more energy we put into the thought, the more likely it is that we will attract that reality to ourselves—a variation on the theme of "As you sow, so shall you reap."

We find a similar message repeated often and in a variety of spiritual contexts. For example, regarding the beliefs of the New Thought Christian we learn:

Affirmations are statements of truth by which you build a conscious awareness of God which results in an existence of good. They are very positive and orderly statements made silently or audibly so that the ideas may take hold in your feeling nature. They are the "yes" attitudes of mind that result in the acceptance of your good. This actually brings ideas out of God-mind into the realm of manifestation or formed things, existence. (Warch, 1977, pp. 65–66)

In a more generic spiritual explication, we hear the same theme and underlying dynamic:

When you thank God in *advance* for that which you choose to experience in your reality, you, in effect, acknowledge that it is there . . . *in effect*. Thankfulness is thus the most powerful statement to God; an affirmation that even before you ask, I have answered.

Therefore never supplicate. *Appreciate*. (Walsch, 1995, p. 11)

And traditional Jewish sources similarly emphasize the power of affirmations to create reality. That is, while everything is understood to be part of God's plan, the choice of whether or not to buy into this plan is left to the individual (Rosenak, 1995). However, if we believe in a possibility, we will it to occur. And having experienced a particular situation, we will discern later the wisdom of the teachings. Thus reality is created through experience followed by reflections on that experience.

The same message is consistent with a postmodern perspective, and derives from both secular and spiritual domains. Life is about creation rather than discovery. Further, our beliefs, especially as manifested in language or images, are instrumental to the process of creating realities.

With the support of the counselor/therapist, therefore, clients may learn first to decide upon and articulate the reality they wish to create and then begin to engage in the process of bringing it into existence. By helping clients understand the role of beliefs, whether through the use of suggested readings, shared stories, or assigned tasks, we may participate in the construction of a reality that helps them create in their lives the realities they desire. However, given that the ultimate concern of counselors and therapists is creating realities, it becomes essential, at least from my perspective, that we consider carefully the issues of ethics in general as well as of moral and ethical behavior in particular.

ETHICS AND MORAL/ETHICAL BEHAVIOR

All mental health professions have their codes of ethical behavior with which their respective members must abide in order to maintain good standing. Such codes are designed to safeguard clients and to specify the standards of appropriate professional conduct. Thus they speak to such issues as nondiscrimination; client confidentiality; professional competence and integrity; boundary issues related, for example, to dual relationships and sexual intimacy; and other responsibilities to clients. However, in addition to the areas of concern focused upon in codes of ethics, in recent years the mental health field has been engaged in much self-reflection concerning moral/ethical issues and the behavior of counselors and therapists (Doherty, 1995).

Indeed, while codes of ethics certainly seem to be essential, when operating from the perspective of second-order cybernetics, with its assumptions of interdependence and reality as perceptually created, other areas of significance related to moral/ethical behavior also emerge. As we have noted elsewhere, "The ethical imperative . . . is to avoid pathologizing, avoid the implication that we have access to the Truth, and avoid narrowing the range of health to the point where there is little we do that is not illness" (Becvar & Becvar, 1996, p. 117). We also are reminded by this perspective of the importance of considering the larger ecology of which problems are a part as well, and of both the ramifications of change for the client's network and the influence of the larger context on problem formation and maintenance. Similar concerns are shared by postmodernists, for whom, it has been noted that "the *entire therapeutic venture* is fundamentally an exercise in ethics" (Efran, Lukens, & Lukens, 1988, p. 27). When the assumptions of these two perspectives are transposed into an orientation according to which therapy is understood as a spiritual process, moral/ethical behavior becomes the basic element without which soul healing could not occur.

To explain this last statement, let us begin with the assumption that is the subject of this chapter. If we assume that reality is created as a function of our beliefs and perceptions, and that our role with clients is basically one of participating with them in the creation of newer, more satisfactory realities, we cannot overestimate the significance of our role and the necessity for the highest standards of behavior. However, I also assume an optimistic outcome to be inevitable as I consider the question and reflections offered by Paul Watzlawick (1984, p. 326), who asks, "What would the world of a person be like who managed to accept reality fully and totally as his or her own construction?" It is Watzlawick's belief that such acceptance would lead a person to tolerance, both in beliefs and in behavior, and the natural assumption of total ethical responsibility. In Watzlawick's view, total responsibility equals total freedom, for "whoever is conscious of being the architect of his or her own reality would be equally aware of the ever-present possibility of constructing it differently" (1984, p. 327). I share a similar perspective based on the notion of freedom with responsibility. To this is added awareness of the sacred trust involved as I engage with clients, at their request, in the creation of new realities.

To explain further, let us look next at the assumption of interdependence in the context of a spiritual orientation. If our behavior is based on the belief that everyone and everything are part of an interconnected whole, then it is understood that each person affects and is involved in the destiny of every other person, that no thought or behavior occurs in isolation, and that whatever we give out comes back to us. Not only do our actions become models ideally reflecting for our clients that to which we each aspire (Walsh & Vaughan, 1980), but also we are left with no choice but to recognize the magnitude of our participation and our responsibility. In other words,

> True spirituality also is to be aware that if we are interdependent with everything and everyone else, even our smallest, least significant thought, word, and action have real consequences throughout the universe. . . . We come to realize we are responsible for everything we do, say, or think, responsible in fact for ourselves, everyone and everything else, and the entire universe. (Sogyal, 1992, p. 39)

Thus, while this is a shared responsibility, our part in it cannot be taken lightly. Similarly, if a fundamental premise is that each of us is a manifestation of the divine, and that as counselors and therapists we are participating in the creation of a context in which growth and healing at the level of the soul ultimately may be facilitated, how can we do otherwise than respect the sacredness and value of all life? How can we not recognize how crucial is the impact of our interactions with clients? Indeed, once again we come to the fundamental importance of relationship:

> It is the interrelationship between beings—between all beings, whether they be animals, vegetables, or even the planets or the sun, but particularly between people—that triggers off unfoldment. The beauty of our life is in the extraordinary encounter between the different parts of the totality. . . . God meets Himself in the meeting of each person with each person. This is the most sacred thing that can ever happen—like the meeting of two worlds. (Khan, 1982, pp. 58–59)

This acknowledgment and acting out of an awareness of the sacredness of the encounters between counselors/therapists and clients may be understood as a process of witnessing. Indeed, as noted here, particularly in the discussions related to suspending judgment (chapter 5), "Empathic witnessing is a moral act, not a technical procedure" (Kleinman, 1988, p. 153). That is, the counselor/therapist as witness shares some of the moments of the client's greatest pain, considers with him or her some of life's most fundamental questions, perhaps even engages in discussions of moral/ethical issues, but refrains from making judgments. Once again, the process is the creation of a context in which the divinity of each individual is acknowledged. Or, in the words of Wayne Dyer, "As a Witness, you can begin to participate in the 'quantum mechanics of creation.' You become a creator because everything that you observe is affected by the fact that you are observing it. The act of witnessing becomes a creative act" (1995, p. 120).

The act of witnessing also is characterized by compassion, the attribute that seems to appear most frequently in the list of qualities that counselors and therapists, with or without a spiritual orientation, ideally would embody. For example, for the family therapist William Doherty:

> A central virtue for therapists, then, as well as for other health professionals, is the ability and predisposition to care for those who entrust their pain to us. Perhaps even more than in other health care settings, the caring bond therapists offer to clients is the heart of the process and the central vehicle for our effectiveness. The empirical evidence for this

assertion lies in many decades' worth of research showing that the therapist's ability to create a warm, accepting atmosphere is a principal healing component in all forms of psychotherapy. Its absence is a primary cause of therapeutic failure. (1995, p. 118)

I concur with Doherty, who believes that in addition to caring and compassion, a counselor/therapist ideally is characterized by courage, prudence, a willingness to use moral language, and respect for both the interpersonal and community commitments and responsibilities of clients. He also emphasizes the importance of justice and truthfulness. Similarly, the teacher, psychologist, and meditation master Jack Kornfield notes that:

The community is created, not when people come together in the name of religion, but when they come together bringing honesty, respect, and kindness to support an awakening of the sacred. True community arises when we can speak in accord with truth and compassion. This sense of spiritual community is a wondrous part of what heals and transforms us on our path. (1993, p. 241)

Thus, given a spiritual orientation, the counseling/therapy process is synonymous with the highest standards of moral/ethical behavior. Accordingly, the counselor/therapist acts in the manner prescribed by appropriate codes of ethics. In addition, the counselor/therapist recognizes, as well as acts in a manner that is consistent with, the assumptions upon which the practice of soul healing is based. That is, there also is an emphasis on interconnectedness and on the attainment of the highest good of all involved through the mutual creation of realities. And there is acknowledgment of the sacredness of the process. All of which may be summed up in the notion that the counselor/therapist is committed to finding and walking a path with heart, the fifth principle of soul healing and the subject of the next chapter. Chapter 8 also provides the conclusion to Part II of this book.

The seat of the soul is where the outer and inner worlds meet.

—NOVALIS

CHAPTER 8

Walking the Path with Heart

INTRODUCTION

In this chapter we consider the fifth and final principle of soul healing, walking the path with heart. We will be examining first what is meant by the path with heart, including the characteristics by which it is known, its requirements, and its related challenges. Our focus will then shift to the means by which all of us—counselors/therapists and clients—may discern our personal paths, may make appropriate decisions relative to walking such a path, and may find support for the choices we make. It is important to be aware that in the course of such a process we are likely to come face to face with such fundamental issues as ultimate meaning as well as finding satisfaction in life, the soul's purpose, illness, death, loss and grief, and making difficult decisions in the context of both the material and the spiritual dimensions of our lives. Therefore, each of these issues will be addressed, with a particular emphasis on the challenge of dealing with death. The desired outcome of these discussions is information about ways to create a context supportive of the achievement of a deeper level of awareness and fulfillment, of soul healing. The chapter concludes with suggestions for helping ourselves and our clients seek resolution to the challenge of living at two levels, the material and the spiritual, and particularly the tension involved with successfully integrating these realms of our lives as briefly discussed in chapter 6. All of which describes a process, at whatever point we may be on life's journey, that may be understood and undertaken as the path with heart.

THE PATH WITH HEART

In his book *What Really Matters*, Tony Schwartz describes his personal search for wisdom in America. Schwartz's quest evolved out of a sense that something in his life was missing, despite the fact that, at least outwardly, he had achieved much. He writes that at the age of 35, with the publication of a best-selling book:

> I was about to earn more in a few weeks than I had in the whole of my working life, giving me a financial cushion that few people are ever lucky enough to enjoy. Publishers were eager to sign up whatever book I chose to do next. My marriage of ten years was strong and stable. My wife had her own challenging career, and our two young daughters, ages two and six, were healthy and mostly happy. I jogged several miles a day and played tennis at least twice a week. I had several close friends, and I felt I contributed to my community.
>
> Why, then, wasn't I happier? (1995, p. 3)

Indeed, despite his apparent success, Schwartz relates that underneath it all he was experiencing a sense of "inner turbulence and discontent, a muted but chronic sense of anxiety" (1995, p. 4). Although not drawn to organized religion, he had chosen a life of integrity and had placed his faith in achievement as well as in several years of psychoanalysis, which he had anticipated would lead to a sense of inner peace and self-satisfaction. He was understandably mystified when the desired state of mind was not forthcoming despite his achievements. Therefore, when the opportunity, in the form of time and money, presented itself, he began an intensive investigation in the hope of finding what was missing from his life. In the course of a four-year odyssey he interviewed and worked with numerous teachers in such areas as meditation, biofeedback, drawing, tennis, body work, dream work, and personality assessment. He notes, "I was looking for people who embodied wisdom and completeness—role models for my own search" (1995, p. 13). Often Schwartz thought he had uncovered the answer for which he was searching only to find that, with the passage of time, his initial exhilaration was replaced by disillusionment as the effectiveness of a technique decreased or a particular teacher's behavior was found to be inconsistent with his or her message.

Having posed two basic questions regarding who he was and why he was here, ultimately Schwartz decided that the answers are interrelated. Further, he found the inescapable conclusion to be that, in the end, we must take whatever we learn in response to such questions and weave the information together in a way that is personally meaningful as each of us participates in a journey that continues throughout life. Accordingly, he closes the introduction to his book with the following thoughts:

> I found that the way people define the nature of the self dictates how they envision the purpose of life. For some, the highest aspiration is self-improvement, for others it is self-discovery, and for others it is self-transcendence and selfless service. By one view, the goal is to achieve our potential through conscious, disciplined action. By another it is simply to know ourselves better, to be more conscious and aware, less defensive and automatic in our behaviors. By yet another view, wisdom is derived from moving beyond rational intention and surrendering to an intuitive knowing that arises from within, when the mind and body quiet down. Finding a way to integrate these often contradictory perspectives into everyday life became my own central challenge. The book that follows, the story of my search for wisdom, is a work in progress. So am I. (Schwartz, 1995, p. 15)

Schwartz's search for higher-order meaning and purpose may be understood not only as a natural phenomenon but one that is "central to human life and is the goal of human development" (Jones, 1995, p. 12). Although this search is not necessarily apparent in every life, Jones notes further that:

> [S]tudies of human development reveal a natural drive within us to make sense of our experience and a groping toward a more universal and encompassing vision. The struggle to find meaning by connecting or reconnecting with a universal, cosmic, moral, and sacred reality represents not a failure of nerve, the onset of premature senility, or a lapse into neurosis but is rather a natural part of the unhindered developmental process. The denial of this quest for the transcendent debilitates and impoverishes our life. (1995, pp. 9–10)

Schwartz's search for wisdom seems to provide an apt illustration of the natural developmental process described by Jones. What is more, from my perspective what both authors are referring to, though neither uses these words, also may be described as a search for the path with heart. For such a path is known not in terms of specific structures or in terms of where it leads but rather by certain qualitative characteristics of the process involved with the search. Indeed, this path may take as many forms as there are people who choose to walk it, and all paths go the same place, which is no place. As the Yaqui Indian Don Juan explains to his apprentice, the anthropologist Carlos Castaneda:

> "Therefore you must always keep in mind that a path is only a path; if you feel you should not follow it, you must not stay with it under any conditions. To have such clarity you must lead a disciplined life. Only then will you know that any path is only a path, and there is no affront, to oneself or to others, in dropping it if that is what your heart tells you to do. But your decision to keep on the path or to leave it must be free of fear or ambition. I warn you. Look at every path closely and deliberately. Try it as many times as you think necessary. This question is one that only a very old man asks. My benefactor told me about it once when I was young, and my blood was too vigorous for me to understand it. Now I do understand it. I will tell you what it is: Does this path have a heart? All paths are the same: they lead nowhere. They are paths going through the bush, or into the bush. In my own life I could say I have traversed long, long paths, but I am not anywhere. My benefactor's question has meaning now. Does this path have a heart? If it does, the path is good; it if doesn't, it is of no use. Both paths lead nowhere; but one has a heart, the other doesn't. One makes for a joyful journey; as long as you follow it; you are one with it. The other will make you curse your life. One makes you strong; the other weakens you." (Castaneda, 1968, pp. 106–107)

A path with heart thus speaks to several dimensions. According to such a description, a disciplined life is required in order to achieve clarity about one's path—about what is appropriate or not at each step along the way. The essential discipline refers to the need to be focused, to be self-aware and to be diligent in attending to the self-control that is entailed. Given such clarity and the willingness to make a commitment, one may then select the particular path that seems most compatible with one's unique goals and desires while rejecting those which are not, despite the concerns and reactions of others. Therefore, the path with heart is to be chosen carefully and with a great deal of reflection, neither out of fear nor because one sees it as a way to achieve material success. It leads nowhere because what is crucial is the nature of the journey rather than any particular destination. However, when one has found and is walking such a path, one knows it by the way one experiences life. When one is filled with a sense of joy, a sense of being in tune, a feeling of at-oneness with all that is or a transcendent dimension, no matter how it is defined, one may perceive oneself to be on the path with heart.

For me, the ability to trust the universe, as described in chapter 6, goes hand in hand with walking the path with heart. Similarly, for Bolen, "To know how to choose a path with heart is to learn how to follow the inner beat of *intuitive feeling*" (1979, p. 87). Further, having chosen the path, one becomes aware of qualitative differences in every area of life. Bolen also describes these inevitable changes in a way that rings true for me:

> [W]hen a person is following a path with heart, his or her dreams are usually nourishing; they seem interesting and pleasant, often imparting a sense of well-being. Synchronistically, opportunities seem to open fortuitously, the people we should meet accidentally cross our path, a flow or ease accompanies our work. Each facilitating, unsought event then begins to confer a feeling of being blessed, each serving as a lantern along the way, illuminating the path with heart.
>
> To travel this path with heart, a person has an inner world in which the ego is filled with a spiritual abundance from its connection with the Self. There is generosity and freedom from fear within the psyche and in the world. Synchronistically, people cross our path and events unfold, facilitating rather than hindering the course we are on. The sense of fullness and flow influences the sense of time; there seems to be enough time to do whatever we are here for; even parking places synchronistically materialize. (Bolen, 1979, p. 94)

Thus, from the magnificent to the mundane, life is infused with awareness of a spiritual level of reality.

Although using different terms, Raheem (1991) defines a similar process in which the individual soul seeks to align itself with universal spirit. Referring to Jung's claim that each of us carries within us an "archetype of wholeness" that urges us to grow to our fullest potential, she sees such development as requiring a complete commitment that moves beyond a desire to fulfill our society's goals for us. The objective is a return to soul awareness as each person identifies his or her unique path, a path that is consistent with the larger spiritual dimension of which all are a part. What is more, it is her belief that:

> One who knows the soul will also know the Great Spirit, or the Tao—that vitalizing, benevolent wave of the universe which interpenetrates All That Is, including the individual soul. Personal wholeness brings a feeling of unity with that Spirit. A sense of separateness—from oneself, others and the environment—is replaced by an inner attunement to a great Natural Order. (Raheem, 1991, p. 178)

This phenomenon also has been portrayed as living archetypically as a function of the ability to tap into essence, or the ground of one's being. And similar changes in perception and experiencing have been noted. According to Houston:

> A Buddhist statement expresses wonderfully well what it means to live archetypically. In this state, "one sees all beings as Buddha, hears all sounds as mantra, and knows all places as nirvana." To me this means every moment has its magic, every action however small is stellar in its consequences ("stir a flower and bestir a star"), and each word that one speaks is creation. (1996, p. 324)

In each instance what we hear is a sense of awe and wonder as one opens up to the universe, to awareness of the whole, to the possibility of magic and miracles. To do so, however, often requires a great shift in perception relative to the way we ordinarily view the world. While this may be a challenging process requiring a basic change in attitude, we may be compensated well for our efforts. In the words of one who made such a shift:

> Once I suspended my a priori academic disbelief about miraculous phenomena, and followed a more open-minded approach that was nonjudgmental, nonreductionistic, and phenomenological in investigating these phenomena, then things began to open up for me. It was as if the universe was somehow rewarding me for simply being ready

to listen without the usual debunking mind-set reducing everything to materialistic explanations characteristic of mainstream modern and postmodern intellectualism. (Markides, 1995, pp. 126–127)

Based on personal experience I can only reiterate what the authors cited above, as well as many others, have described. For me, walking the path with heart, although certainly filled with challenges, is constantly reaffirming. Indeed, while I do rely on miracles as I have noted, I never cease to be delighted at the way things work, at the impact upon my life of the choice to trust the universe. Sometimes the unfolding of events is so complex that there hardly seems any connection. And yet, in retrospect, I am able to perceive a set of patterns that comprise a beautifully complete and meaningful mosaic that is astounding in its magnitude. However, I must hasten to add that finding and walking a path with heart was and continues to be a lifelong project involving ongoing assessment and the evaluation of challenges and choices, both large and small.

DISCERNING THE PATH WITH HEART

From my perspective, each of us is engaged, whether consciously or not, on a journey toward wholeness, toward soul healing. As we become aware of a desire for greater meaning and purpose in our lives, as we entertain considerations of what life is all about, as we undertake explorations of the transcendent or spiritual domain, we begin to make this journey toward wholeness a conscious process. It is at this point that our explorations may be labeled as a search for the path with heart.

Just as there are as many paths as there are seekers, there are many, many routes to awareness, many paths to the path with heart. Not the least uncommon of these routes to awareness is the experience of ill health, psychological pain, or tragedy. Thus we counselors/therapists are in a unique position to assist our clients with their search as they are confronted with questions about the deeper meaning and purpose of life. Hence the need, at least according to my story, to be cognizant of and sensitive to issues in this domain. This may be particularly true when the client previously has storied his or her life in a manner that is devoid of hope.

For example, Lawrence LeShan, who has spent more than 35 years working with people whose cancer was considered terminal and beyond all medical help, found that in most cases his patients viewed life from a perspective of general despair:

> Its verbalization often came as a surprise to the patients, followed swiftly by a realization that "this is how I always felt." All the evidence from long-term individual psychotherapy with these people indicated that the emotional orientation of despair predated the appearance of the cancer by many years. It had been the person's basic life-feeling, their *lebensgefuhl* for most of their lives. There had been periods in each life when this background music was very loud and periods when it was quite low, but always it had been there. (1990, p. 105)

As he worked with such despairing people, LeShan became aware that what he terms a "holistic psychology approach" had much to offer. In fact, he found that by helping his clients create a full, rich life, one with a sense of meaning and purpose, their immune systems' effectiveness was enhanced to the point that many instances of healing, including total cures, occurred. He notes:

> Over and over again I have seen one of two things happen when the total environment of the person with cancer is mobilized for life and his or her inner ecology is thereby changed in a positive way. For some, the patient's life is prolonged, not in an arbitrary way, but in order that there may be more experience of the self, self-recognition and the recognition—and often fulfillment—of dreams. And then there were the genuine miracles—not magic, but dedicated devotion and hard work which made the cancer a turning point in the person's life rather than a sign of its ending. (1990, p. xi)

The crucial issue in LeShan's work appears to be the focus on the individual's dreams or aspirations, and on creating a life that is experienced as meaningful in accordance with each individual's personal goals and desires. For, as noted by Norman Cousins after ten years of research to validate his own experience of miraculous healing:

> The immune system is a mirror to life, responding to its joy and anguish, its exuberance and boredom, its laughter and tears, its excitement and depression, its problems, and prospects. Scarcely anything that enters the mind doesn't find its way into the workings of the body. Indeed, the connection between what we think and how we feel is

perhaps the most dramatic documentation of the fact that mind and body are not separate entities but part of a fully integrated system. (1989, pp. 35, 37)

There are many lessons we may learn from the work of both LeShan and Cousins. First of all, we may understand the potential healing involved with helping each client see any painful situation with which he or she may be dealing as a turning point, bringing with it the opportunity to consider how to create a reality that will be experienced with greater satisfaction. Secondly, we may recognize the degree to which the story we are telling ourselves and according to which we are living our lives may be helping to maintain a problem (Griffith & Griffith, 1994). Thus, third, we may be sensitive to the fact that a client's feeling that his or her life lacks meaning may be participating in the creation of a context within which both emotional and physical problems make sense. And fourth, we may become aware of the level of significance, for all of us, that may be associated with pursuing our dreams, or with finding and walking the path with heart.

However, while a serious illness, such as cancer, or other traumatic experiences may be the catalyst for the search for such a path, they certainly are not the only route. People who, like Schwartz (1995), are aware of a lack of fulfillment and who desire something more also may be experiencing the birth pangs of a spiritual quest. By way of illustration, let me tell you about a client, whom I will call "Sam," who has just turned 40 and who has attained many of his personal goals. However, he continues to feel a kind of vague emptiness and has said repeatedly, "I know something is missing; I just don't know what it is." Sam has considered a career change but knows that is not the answer, having already gone through this process twice before. He is not entirely satisfied with his relationship with his partner but also is aware that even if it were more stable his unease would not be resolved. Lately he has begun to doubt his worth and invariably finds himself lacking even though he knows that basically he is a good person. In addition, with the deaths of the parents of several of his friends, he recently has become more sensitive to the needs and realities of his own aging parents as well as the inevitability of their death in the not-too-distant future. In response to Sam's expressed concern about the possibility that he was being unduly morbid, I pointed out that until the age of 40 we tend to think in terms of the years since our birth. After 40, however, our attention tends to shift to a consideration of the years until our death (Eisdorfer & Lawton, 1973).

Indeed, according to my story, Sam's dilemma may be described as a spiritual issue that makes perfect sense given his age and stage in life. However, I am careful not to speak in such terms to Sam for it would not fit his belief system. Nevertheless, I have suggested that he might do some experimenting, both through reading and participating in activities in new areas. In addition to recommending Schwartz's book, I also have discussed with him the possibility of doing some volunteer work, keeping a journal, recording dreams, and taking a class in an area of great interest. It seems to me that he, too, is searching for what it is that really matters, and I have framed the possibility of his doing the suggested explorations in just those terms. However, while I suspect that we will have many conversations related to this area and believe that I can offer some avenues for consideration, ultimately it is Sam who will need to determine the answers to his questions as well as find the related sense of satisfaction that currently eludes him. I see my role in all of this as a participant, as cocreator of a context that supports my client in his search.

As part of this process, I am mindful of the fact that the path with heart does not necessarily entail the pursuit and attainment of monumental goals. Rather, it means hearing and responding to our heart's desire, being true to ourselves, or marching to the beat of our own drum in whatever way seems most appropriate for us. And we may take our cues from a variety of sources. According to Hammerschlag:

> The primary task in the pursuit of salvation and healthy living is to choose to respond to the summons of life's journey. The truth is that you don't have to take somebody else's path or identify with an established heroic figure. *You* are the principal character in your own life's drama.
>
> Our culture provides clues on which to base our journeys; so do our families, communities, and religions. All of us have a unique identity, something that binds us to our history. We also borrow from other tribes to forge our own heroic paths. We can follow existing trails or create new ones. Growth and personal truth are found on many paths. (1993, p. 41)

For Kornfield (1993), in order to discern the path with heart, it is essential that we consider what we might do to enhance our ability to be open, and honest. He also emphasizes the need to increase our capacity to love and to be compassionate, both toward ourselves and others. In addition, he believes that:

> A path with heartIt will also include our unique gifts and creativity. The outer expression of our heart may be to write books, to build buildings, to create ways for people to serve one another. It may be to teach or to garden, to serve food or play music. Whatever we choose, the creations of our life must be grounded in our hearts. Our love is the source of all energy to create and connect. If we act without a connection to the heart, even the greatest things in our life can become dried up, meaningless, or barren. (1993, p. 17)

As an example, I would like to tell you about another client, who has given me permission to share parts of a letter I recently received. After an unwanted divorce, this client, whom I shall call "Sydney," was faced with the challenge of continuing to maintain a long and successful career as an architect with a well-known firm while at the same time taking over as custodial parent of two young children. Our work together focused on helping Sydney, a deeply spiritual person, through this transition and ended when things definitely seemed to be back on an even keel. At our termination meeting, which occurred about three years ago, I remember being asked to keep Sydney in my prayers, especially as related to the ability to make good life decisions, and particularly those involving career choices.

In the intervening years, I have been aware that Sydney has been very successful both in terms of career and in working out a viable co-parenting relationship with the former spouse. However, the letter to me indicates that Sydney now has decided not only to take an early retirement option offered by the architectural firm but also to return to school to pursue a career as a chaplain. In spite of the potential of further work as an architect, which would have produced substantial financial rewards, and in the face of great dismay on the part of family and friends, Sydney has chosen to follow what I would describe as the path with heart. An excerpt from the letter follows:

> I am really so pleased to have this opportunity to study. . . . I came very close to being offered a *fabulous* job in architecture, and I was praying and praying to the Holy Spirit to let me know if I should turn it down (with my father and others not understanding how I "could walk away

from all that money"), so I told the firm I wanted to work 20–25 hours a week only; they thought hard about it and then politely said, "no." I have some great ideas (I think!!) about working with patients and am energized with the thought of beginning my courses!!

In Sydney's case, what had become important by the end of our work together was to begin to focus on doing what would provide the most satisfaction. However, the decision to change careers was a long, slow process and was made only after careful reflection and requests for guidance. What emerges for me from this letter is a sense of the rightness of the decision, now that it has been made. Indeed, this internal sense that one is doing the right thing is one of the key issues in discerning a path with heart. Another key issue is awareness that we are creating rather than discovering the person we wish to be and the life we desire to lead (Raheem, 1995; Walsch, 1995). Basic to the perspective of soul healing, it is most important to make choices that are supportive of our well-being and our growth at the deepest level of our being.

In discerning the path with heart, it thus may be useful to consider our basic principles and values and whether or not we are living in a manner that is consistent with them. We might look at our personal networks with a focus on whether or not we are with those we experience as supportive and of like mind when it comes to being true to oneself. Kornfield suggests further that we ask ourselves questions such as the following:

> Have we let ourselves love the people around us, our family, our community, the earth upon which we live? And, did we also learn to let go? Did we learn to live through the changes of life with grace, wisdom, and compassion? Have we learned to forgive and live from the spirit of the heart instead of the spirit of judgment? (1993, p. 15)

Indeed, as I have mentioned, walking the path with heart is no small undertaking. While there is a great deal to be gained in terms of personal satisfaction, we truly must be committed, for we may find repeatedly that we are tempted by other options and are not always understood by those around us. This is especially true if following our heart's dream takes us in directions not usually chosen. In either event, however, rather than being a one-time decision, I find it an ongoing process of choice in response to constant tests and challenges.

CHOOSING TO WALK THE PATH WITH HEART

Several years ago I heard the following quote, which I immediately wrote down because it seemed to me to speak volumes: "The strongest are those who renounce their own times and become a part of those yet to come—the strongest and the rarest." As the wise author of these words (whose name I don't know) surely was aware, it is difficult to be different. Sadly, from my perspective, pursuing one's dreams in accordance with one's principles and values is not the prevailing modus operandi and when one does so, life does not suddenly become problem free. Indeed, as Sydney's letter testifies, it is not unusual for others to be confused by decisions that fall outside the norm. Also common are accusations that one is making a mistake as well as challenges regarding who one is and what one is about. Indeed, to walk the path with heart may be to go against the grain. Thus, as Raheem notes,

> [Such a choice] requires taking risks, venturing into unfamiliar territories. It brings a massive shift in perspective which must be accommodated by new ways of being with oneself and the world. For example, . . . great energy intensity, the sometimes searing awareness of facing the unveiled truth, the insecurity of following one's own truth and loneliness of standing apart from the collective—these aspects and more accompany the journey of being true to the soul. (1991, p. 179)

What is more, as we have seen, this choice tends to be a recurring one. At each new crossroads one may be faced again with the need to weigh alternatives and evaluate how best to proceed. While the appropriate choice may at times seem perfectly obvious, at other times the issues may not be so clear-cut or the pulls of old habits may be hard to resist. And such a choice involves not only life-changing decisions but also the smallest issues of daily living. As an example of the former, several years ago I was offered two teaching positions, both of which were very attractive to me. In one of the positions I would have been working in a well-established program in an urban area with people I knew and respected and with whom I would love to have worked. The other position entailed working with people I did not know to create a new program aimed at serving a rural and rather impoverished area. Despite my awareness of the challenges involved, I chose the latter because it seemed to me to provide an opportunity to be of greater service, to do something more meaningful in the larger scheme of things. This was my value, and I felt that being consistent with it was the right choice for me. What is more, my current choice to work with clients in the way that I have described represents a major life decision relative to what I consider to be my path with heart. Similarly, I have found that it is not at all uncommon for those persons with whom I work in therapy to be faced with the same kinds of situations and decisions.

For example, a client recently described an experience of rectifying a situation that, in retrospect, was felt to have been created by having listened to the wrong voices. Initially this client decided to leave one job and take another because the new position seemed to be more consistent with the "appropriate" professional career path. The new job ultimately was short lived, however, because the client's mother became terminally ill, and the client chose to resign and to care for the mother on a full-time basis until her death. After taking some time off for rest, recuperation and reevaluation, the client took another position very similar to the original job. My client is extremely happy with the decision and recently has realized that, regardless of lower professional status and reduced income, it is this kind of position that makes best use of the client's particular gifts and talents. My client also has become aware that the right choices invariably are made when internal, rather than external, voices are heeded. This process and its related awareness are remarkably consistent with the story as well as the advice offered by Kubler-Ross:

> It is very important that you only do what you love to do. You may be poor, you may go hungry, you may lose your car, you may have to move into a shabby place to live, but you will *totally* live. And at the end of your days you will bless your life because you have done what you came here to do. . . .
>
> If . . . you listen to your own inner voice, to your own inner wisdom, which is far greater than anybody else's as far as you are concerned, you will not go wrong and you will know what to do with your life. (1995, p. 38)

However, while these examples illustrate some of life's larger decisions, smaller issues daily present us with choices that are no less significant in terms of their challenge to our ability to remain committed to our chosen path. Once again, let me use myself as an example, and tell you about a situation with which I currently am dealing.

In the course of writing this book, which has taken the better part of a year, my computer and I have become very close indeed. I repeatedly have marveled at the convenience of word processing, which enables me to handle a great deal of data with tremendous ease. And in an otherwise rather solitary period of my life, E-mail has allowed me to maintain contact with friends all around the country and to have access to needed information at a moment's notice. However, much to my dismay and with great frustration at the required change in process, this chapter is being written by hand.

To explain, about six weeks ago, my modem malfunctioned. I waited until the end of the month, and the completion of the previous chapter, to send my computer out for repair. Knowing that I would be out of town for a long weekend and with the assurance of my repair person, who is a family friend, that I would have the computer back in a week, it seemed like a reasonable decision to make. However, it has now been two weeks and I still don't have the computer. Needless to say, I have not been particularly happy about either the delay or the unkept promise. In response, there is a part of me that would like to decrease, or at least stall payment for services, which also has been increased beyond the original estimate. At the same time, I am sensitive to the fact that two wrongs don't make a right. Further, I wonder if perhaps I am being presented with an opportunity both to prevent someone else from being treated similarly in the future and to live in a manner that is consistent with the kind of person I would like to be. Therefore, I have decided that once I receive my computer, I will pay my bill in full and on time. But I also intend to send a letter explaining my feelings about the way in which I have been treated and what I believe would have been more ethical behaviors, thereby putting the burden of responsibility for making amends on the repair person. Regardless of the outcome, I will have done what I consider to be appropriate for me. I will have stayed on my path with heart, the one that calls me to live according to my principles and values.

Indeed, for me, the tensions of mainstream attitudes and behaviors are constant, and I am aware of the way in which they may challenge my ability to see clearly and act accordingly. I often experience myself as living at two levels, or with one foot in each of two different worlds. As described in Nancy Wood's poem in chapter 6, on the one hand there is the material world, the world of technology, and the quest for status and success at all costs. On the other hand, there is the world of spirit, of the soul, of transcendent concerns, values, and meaning. From my perspective, successfully choosing and walking the path with heart requires integrating, or at least maintaining an appropriate balance between, these two worlds. Indeed, as Ram Dass has written, this may be a major turning point on one's journey:

> So eventually you begin to realize that you can't push away your incarnation. And that's the beginning of progress. Instead of pushing it away, you look for ways to regain the balance, to come back into your incarnation without forgetting about your soul. You begin to learn how to integrate the two planes, to keep your awareness open to your incarnation and your soul at the same time. (1995, p. 71)

Before considering this challenge further, there are some other issues in need of attention, for learning to integrate the two planes, or worlds, inevitably leads to a consideration of some of life's most basic questions. In other words, if we are to walk the path with heart we must at some point deal with our concerns about who we are and why we are here. And I believe that in order to do so, we must create a story which enables us to come to terms with death, as well as with the many other pains and losses that are a part of life. In the words of Pelletier, "To see beyond the constraints of disease and death itself is to 'follow the path of the heart,' according to the teachings of Don Juan" (1977, p. 322). Indeed, I believe that it is in the context of the answers to our most basic questions about death, and thus life, that we are able to become clear about our principles and values and thereby fully to create and pursue our dreams.

THE CONUNDRUM OF DEATH

At the same time, it also is my belief that each individual must deal with the issues of the meaning and purpose of life and respond to such questions as "Who am I?" and "Why am I here?" in his or her own unique way and in his or her own time. Similarly, facing and overcoming the fear of death as well as dealing with loss and tragedy are not things we can do for our clients. Rather, our role as counselors/therapists is to facilitate the process, as appropriate, and to do so in as supportive a manner as possible. However, I would maintain that to the extent that we, too, are engaged in such explorations, we will be better able to make suggestions, share resources and stories, and point out possible pitfalls along the way. This section therefore focuses on what is perhaps the most fundamental issue for all of us—death and the opportunities it provides for the facilitation of growth. For, as Cousins has written:

> Hope, faith, love, and a strong will to live offer no promise of immortality, only proof of our uniqueness as human beings and the opportunity to experience full growth even under the grimmest circumstances. The clock provides only a technical measurement of how long we live. Far more real than the ticking of time is the way we open up the minutes and invest them with meaning. Death is not the ultimate tragedy in life. The ultimate tragedy is to die without discovering the possibilities of full growth. The approach of death need not be denial of the growth. (1989, p. 25)

Similarly, according to Jung, "To the psyche death is just as important as birth and, like it, is an integral part of life" (Wilhelm, 1962, p. 124). If Jung and others are correct in their assessment of the importance of death, and I believe they are, we in the West are particularly challenged by the fact that we live in what has been called a death-denying society (Becker, 1973). Thus, while awareness of death has no doubt existed as long as human beings have had the capability for self-reflection, "In our own era . . . death has come to have a hideous face and most of us accordingly have learned to turn reflexively away from it as a means of blunting our terror of it" (Foos-Graber, 1989, p. xi).

Nevertheless, whether through the loss of a loved one, working with grieving clients, or coming face to face with our own mortality as we experience serious illness, ultimately we all are challenged to find or create a story about death that enables us to make sense of this great mystery. Indeed, I believe it is important to be aware that, as Pelletier writes, "A strong belief system can ease the fear of death and lend a sense of direction to our passage through life" (1977, p. 89). Furthermore, many believe that the more comfortable we become with death, the more fully we may live life. For example, it has been said that, "By rejoining death with the rest of life, all of us will experience a joy and a release of the energy that is currently locked up in our fear and evasions" (Foos-Graber, 1989, p. 5). Similarly, the surgeon Bernie Siegel observes that:

[I]n many cases, people who've become aware of their mortality find
that they've gained the freedom to live. They are seized with an appreciation for the present: every day is my best day; this is my life; I'm not
going to have this moment again. (1995, p. 39)

The Catholic priest Henri Nouwen also points out the ramifications
for the others in our world of our coming to terms with death:

Befriending our death is a lifelong spiritual task but a task that, in all its
different nuances, deeply affects our relationships with our fellow human beings. Every step we take toward deeper self-understanding
brings us closer to those with whom we share our lives. As we learn,
over time, to live the truth that death does not have a sting, we find
within ourselves the gift to guide others to discover the same truth. We
do not first do one of these things and later the other. Befriending our
own death and helping others to befriend theirs are inseparable. (1994,
p. 51)

Sogyal Rinpoche, a Tibetan lama, who notes that paradoxically the
only thing permanent about our life is its impermanence, also suggests
that we ask ourselves the following questions:

Do I remember at every moment that I am dying, and everyone and
everything else is, and so treat all beings at all times with compassion?
Has my understanding of death and impermanence become so keen
and so urgent that I am devoting every second to the pursuit of enlight-
enment? (1992, p. 27)

These reflections are not intended to inculcate a morbid focus or a
constant sense of impending doom. Rather, such awareness and such
questions encourage us to live in a more vital and honest manner
which, over the long term will change the way we relate to others and
to our lives. Likewise, in this manner we will be better equipped to
handle not only death but also all of the ups and downs, the pains and
losses, of life. And it is with such a perspective that the importance of
living life as the path with heart is underlined.

By contrast, I know from my own experience how devastating it
can be to live without a heightened awareness of our impermanence,
to be caught unprepared and to have to deal with a loss of great magnitude without a belief system that sufficiently enables one to make

sense of the situation. I also know from experience, as I wrote in chapter 1, how important and life-changing the process of searching for meaning in life can be. And further, I know not only from my own experience but also from that of my clients how much one may be helped to deal with serious illness and other problems and losses when one is able to story them in a meaningful way. At the same time, I also believe it is important to remember that no matter how seemingly solid our belief system, death may shake it and us to the very roots of our being. Let me use as a case in point the well-known scholar and Christian writer C. S. Lewis, whose poignant tale was chronicled in the movie *Shadowlands.*

Lewis was born to Irish parents who were members of the Church of England, but he had rejected all religions as invented mythologies by the time he was a teenager (Hooper, 1996). However, after many years of soul searching, study, and reflection, during which he frequently was aware of "something more," he found himself, at the age of 31, a reluctant convert to Christianity. He subsequently became best known for his books, articles, and lectures on this religious belief system and so influential a spokesperson was he that many considered him "a latterday [sic] G. K. Chesterton" (Walsh, in Lewis, 1976, p. 129). This stature is all the more significant as we read Lewis's account, *A Grief Observed*, of his experience during the days and months that followed his wife's death. He writes early on in this process:

> Meanwhile, where is God? This is one of the most disquieting symptoms. When you are happy, so happy that you have no sense of needing Him, so happy that you are tempted to feel His claims upon you as an interruption, if you remember yourself and turn to Him with gratitude and praise, you will be—or so it feels—welcomed with open arms. But go to Him when your need is desperate, when all other help is vain, and what do you find? A door slammed in your face, and a sound of bolting and double bolting on the inside. After that, silence. You may as well turn away. The longer you wait, the more emphatic the silence will become. There are no lights in the windows. It might be an empty house. Was it ever inhabited? It seemed so once. And that seeming was as strong as this. What can this mean? Why is He so present a commander in our time of prosperity and so very absent a help in time of trouble? (1976, pp. 4–5)

Lewis was 54 and a confirmed bachelor when in 1952 he met Joy Davidman Gresham, then a woman of 37 with two small children. And

while their marriage, which took place in 1956, lasted only four years
because of Gresham's death from cancer, it was one of great love and
devotion. Further, according to Joy's son Douglas (Gresham, 1988),
Lewis never really recovered from her death. He did, however, find his
way back to the faith that had been such a strong support for so many
years. As Chad Walsh notes in the afterword to *A Grief Observed*:

> In the midst of an agonized bereavement, Lewis records new insights
> that modify the neat certainties in his earlier books. It is implacably
> honest, and the tentative reassurances toward which it moves—the in-
> tuition of Joy's continued reality in another dimension of existence, the
> reality of God's presence and love—are modestly stated, more sug-
> gested than stated. But as the book comes to an end, the reader finds
> himself sharing the first timid movement of Lewis back toward a
> world that makes sense. The night of loneliness and emptiness may
> plot further assaults, but the worst is, perhaps, over. (Lewis, 1976,
> pp. 149–150).

Lewis's story illustrates several important points. Despite a very
strong belief in God, he found that a confrontation with the reality of
death and the loss of a great love provoked serious questions not only
about his faith but about the story according to which he previously
had lived his life. Although he ultimately appears to have come to
terms with his wife's death and regained his faith, he perhaps never
truly "got over" her loss. According to his stepson, Lewis "was never
again the man he had been before Mother's death. Joy had left him and
also, so it seemed, had joy" (Gresham, 1988, p. 130). Indeed, I don't believe we ever truly "get over" the death of a loved one. Rather, I believe
that the challenge that each of us faces is to revise our life/faith story,
or our fundamental assumptions, in such a way that we are able to understand death as meaningful and in this process to regain, or perhaps
attain for the first time, a real sense of joy in life. Often, as appears to
have been the case for Lewis, this may involve reconciling beliefs that
make sense at two different levels of reality.

That is, on the one hand, Lewis seems to have gained at least an intuitive sense of his wife's continued existence in another dimension.
Similarly, despite the fact that his belief system changed, he regained
his faith in God. Thus at the spiritual level he has recreated a meaningful story. However, he seems to have been only partially successful in
translating this story into the everyday material reality in such a way

that he was truly comfortable. Once again we hear a stepson's view of Lewis, who was known to his close associates as Jack:

It has been said that Jack's years at Cambridge after Mother's death were happy. That is not true. Jack, when in company with his friends and colleagues, was (after a while) again the jovial, witty intellectual they had known for years, but only Warnie [his brother] and I knew what effort that cost him. . . . Jack's colleagues and friends never saw him as he turned from waving a cheery good-bye at the door of The Kilns [his home] and casting some pearls of a parting witticism to a departing guest; they never watched him suddenly slump, his whole body shrinking like a slowly deflating balloon, his face losing the light of laughter and becoming grey, until he became once more a tired, sick and grieving man, old beyond his years. (Gresham, 1988, pp. 132–133)

From my perspective, it appears that Lewis was experiencing the very real tension that characterizes much of life in our society. And nowhere is this more evident than where death is concerned. By contrast, Lenz recounts the message he received from a Buddhist master on the subject of death:

"When you can see the other side of life, the world you refer to as death—the mysterious undiscovered universe that lies just beyond our mind and senses—all of the pain and frustration of your life will go away. You will see that everything and everyone you love, who may appear to have been destroyed, are still just fine. They have simply moved from the world of moment to moment, back into the world of emptiness. They have returned to the reservoir of life that we call *nirvana*." (1995, p. 233)

However, it does not seem to be quite that simple for those of us whose belief systems are more Western. And my reading suggests that grief and the pain of loss are universal experiences, even for those who are more open to and accepting of death. Thus, even though it may be reassuring to know that life continues in some form beyond death, there is still the absence of a physical presence that must be accommodated. Similarly, even though we may find new ways to understand and experience life as meaningful, the changes in our belief systems and behaviors reverberate throughout the various other systems in which we live.

Not surprisingly, therefore, I believe that our role as counselors and therapists may well involve much more than helping clients as they attempt to recreate their lives and make appropriate adjustments in the face of death and other problems and losses. Our role perhaps also may need to include a focus on successfully resolving the tension of living at two levels. Such a focus may be particularly relevant, as noted in the previous section, as one moves to a consideration of walking the path with heart.

LIVING AT TWO LEVELS

As we have seen, it is hard to be different. As one attempts to live one's life consistent with a story that includes a spiritual dimension, or in accordance with values and principles outside the mainstream, no matter how worthy, one may have difficulty finding support. While life ultimately may be about meaning, that is not the prevailing discourse in our society. Indeed, there are many who have spoken of the division between the realms of the spiritual and the material. For example, Sogyal, who also cites the quantum physicist David Bohm on the matter, writes:

> One of the reasons I have written this book is to show I believe what Melvin Morse says is possible: Technology and the spirit can and must exist side by side, if our fullest human potential is to be developed. Wouldn't a complete, and completely useful, human science have the courage to embrace and explore the facts of the mystical, the facts of death and dying as revealed in the near-death experience and in this book? (1992, p. 335)

Certainly I would not be writing this book if spirituality had not for so long been considered outside the purview of science and thus of the mental health disciplines. And despite this book and others currently available, I am keenly aware of the fact that many will find my views nontraditional at best and not worthy of consideration at worst. Particularly suspect will be the inclusion of material on and derived from intuitive knowing, from trusting the universe, in addition to an acknowledgment of the importance of more traditional ways of knowing. Paradoxically, however, it is this ability which enables me to make the choices I do, even as I attempt to live in and make sense of a physical reality that, for the most part, functions according to values and principles to which I do not subscribe. As LeShan writes:

If however, instead of the necessary, practical goals of the biological and physical world which we can work toward so well in the Sensory Reality, we wish to work toward another type of goal, we need the Clairvoyant Reality. If we wish to choose as our goals a sense of serenity, peace, joy in living, being fully at home in the cosmos, a deeper understanding of truth, our fullest ability to love, we need the world of the One. (1974, p. 60)

Thus mine is a holistic viewpoint that assumes an interconnectedness of all that is and sees all ways of knowing as complementary and having validity. What is more, it is my belief that each person can make a difference in terms of creating a larger reality that all may experience as more supportive and meaningful, and I share such beliefs with my clients. In fact, from my perspective, a change in context occurs as a function of changes in the individuals who are a part of that context. Thus, to the extent that each of us lives in a manner consistent with the reality we desire, we have participated in creating such change:

People who have the daring and determination to live out their ideals release a tremendous beneficial power into their lives, and that power will begin to transform the world they live in. Mahatma Gandhi called this "practical idealism," which means that it can be practiced in every aspect of life. It doesn't call so much for great acts of heroism as for a continuing, persistent effort to transform ill will into good will, self-interest into compassion. (Easwaran, 1992, p. 124)

Indeed, I am aware that changes are occurring all around us as a function of individual acts of "daring and determination." For example, in addition to greater awareness of the spiritual dimension in people's lives, recent years also have seen the call for moral responsibility in psychotherapy (Doherty, 1995). Similarly, while I personally have rejected the use of diagnostic categories because of their potential to objectify clients and because they are inconsistent with my belief system, I acknowledge an increased sensitivity regarding their appropriate application. For example, as Kleinman writes:

No diagnostic rubric should be authorized to describe those individuals and their illness experiences one-dimensionally, in a look-alike caricature that is carried over into treating them as if they were the same.

> The purpose of a diagnostic system, after all, is to guide treatment of a disease through a recognition of patterns. It is not meant to be a perfect representation of types of individuals or a guide to caring for their life problems. It is also the case that the copy should not be denied, the diagnosis jettisoned, lest the disease go untreated. . . . But to provide humane care, healers must not lose sight of what is unique to each patient. (1988, p. 207)

Indeed, walking the path with heart requires respect for the unique paths others may choose to walk and an understanding that each of us will make sense and meaning of life in our own unique ways. Thus, balance is required not only in terms of understanding the different levels of reality but in terms of the different interpretations of these levels. In addition, we also must be mindful of the paradox of the path:

> The danger, then, is that we can become so preoccupied with the path that we do not go anywhere on it while all around us life goes on its way. [Meister] Eckhart concludes his warning by remarking that "whoever seeks God without any special Way, finds Him as He really is . . . and He is life itself." But how can we seek God without having a special way to do it?
>
> This brings us to a paradox compact as stone: Without a spiritual discipline we go nowhere, but a discipline intentionally followed may lead us only to the practice of the discipline. (Carse, 1995, p. 39)

It is my belief that as spiritual discipline is translated into way of life, for example as the path with heart, we transcend the paradox to which Carse refers. In this process, ideally we find our own answers to the basic questions about who we are and why we are here. Thus, life becomes meaningful, and we find ourselves able to live more or less comfortably within the tensions of different levels of reality and with the paradoxes of existence. As we do so, we experience our ability to create a more desirable reality. Accordingly, our own sense of self is enhanced, which enables us to be more caring, compassionate, and respectful of others. All of this transforms not only our lives but our work with our clients. However, another paradox is that all that anyone can do for another is to speak of this experience, of the path with heart, as I do—whether I speak to my clients or to readers of this book. In the end, each of us must decide whether or not what the author of the following passage suggests sounds inviting enough to attempt:

When you have done what you have to do, you will feel very secure, very fulfilled. As you discover the Self in your own heart, you discover it simultaneously everywhere, in the people and creatures around you. You will feel very much at home in this universe. You don't need to take my word for it. Try it and see for yourself. (Easwaran, 1992, p. 93)

PART III

Conclusion

If we wish to give philosophic expression to the profound connection between thought and action in all fields of human endeavor, particularly in science, we shall undoubtedly have to seek its source in the unfathomable depths of the human soul. Perhaps philosophers might call it "love" in a very general sense—that force which directs all our actions, which is the source of all our delights and all our pursuits. Indissolubly linked with thought and with action, love is their common mainspring and, hence their common bond.

—PRINCE LOUIS DE BROGLIE

CHAPTER 9

Continuing the Journey

INTRODUCTION

In this chapter, I explore the ramifications for counselors/therapists and their clients, and thus for society as well, of a move to undertake consciously, both in our professional and in our private lives, a spiritual journey in pursuit of wholeness. As described in this book, it is a journey that may be thought of as a process of soul healing. We mental health professionals have a unique opportunity to support such a process which, according to my story, is facilitated as we embrace the five guiding principles discussed in chapters 5 through 8: acknowledging connectedness, suspending judgment, trusting the universe, creating realities, and walking the path with heart. Before considering this opportunity, however, I begin with a brief look at the historical roots of a focus on the soul, or on curing and healing souls. From there our discussion shifts to a consideration of the current context in which we live and work. As I have indicated, this context displays signs of an increasing awareness of and interest in spirituality, greater concern with matters of the soul, and perhaps even a move to transcend the traditional division between religion and science. Some thoughts about the possible outcomes of an inclusion of spirituality in the therapeutic conversation, both in terms of discussions about counseling/therapy and in terms of discussions with our clients, then are presented. Also considered are the changes that might occur if counseling/therapy, indeed perhaps all of life, were understood as a spiritual process; the characteristics of the counselor/therapist who works from such an orientation; and the possible challenges that may be encountered along the spiritual path, as well as suggestions for how to deal with them effectively. A summary of the major themes in the book is provided as a guide for those readers who are interested in further explorations in the realm referred to as soul healing. By way of conclusion, not only to the chapter but also to the book, some final thoughts are offered regarding where a spiritual orientation in counseling/therapy ultimately may take us.

HISTORICAL AND CURRENT CONTEXT

As I said as I began discussing my personal philosophy in chapter 1, I subscribe to the notion that there really is nothing new under the sun. I would like to point out that, while a spiritual orientation in counseling/therapy qualifies as a relatively recent phenomenon in our modern era, in fact, it may be understood as representing a return to our roots, perhaps to the origins of our profession. Similarly, a perusal of our history reveals that thinking in terms of soul healing is not exactly a novel idea. That is, according to Thomas Szasz, the precursors to contemporary psychotherapy may be found in an ancient tradition, based in philosophy and religion, whose focus was on healing or curing souls:

> Actually, psychotherapy is a modern, scientific-sounding name for what used to be called the "cure of souls." The true history of psychiatry thus begins not with the early nineteenth-century psychiatrists, but with the Greek philosophers and the Jewish rabbis of antiquity; and it continues with the Catholic priests and Protestant pastors, over a period of nearly two millennia, before the medical soul-doctors appear on the stage of history. (1978, p. 26)

Thus, we learn that according to the belief system of the Greeks, health was understood as humankind's natural condition. The unnatural condition of disease was thought to occur as a function of mental disharmony created by a foreign influence and, therefore, "the essence of all therapy was spiritual healing" (Szasz, 1978, p. 27). According to Jaeger, "Euripides (ca. 485–407 B.C.) was the first psychologist. It was he who discovered the soul . . . who revealed the troubled world of man's emotions and passions" (1965, p. 353). Jaeger notes further that, "in Euripides' time (in addition to doctors of the body) there existed 'doctors of the soul.' Such was Antiphon, the sophist, who also taught and wrote about the interpretation of dreams" (1965, p. 481). Indeed, as noted in the discussion of dreams in chapter 6, it is among the ancients that we find the healing temples where dreams were analyzed as communications from the soul or the gods (Jacob, 1988). What is more, we learn that Socrates (ca. 470–399 B.C.), "was, and wished to be *iatros tes psuches*, a healer of the soul. These Greek syllables have been recast to form the word 'psychiatrist'" (McNeill, 1951, p. 320). And it was Cicero (143–106 B.C.) who suggested the utilization of "healing words," *iatroi logoi*, in his recommendations to those who would comfort the soul (Szasz, 1978).

Other well-known soul healers identified by Szasz include not only the ancient Jewish rabbis, but also Jesus, Martin Luther, and many of the Puritans. In addition, he notes that "Freud and Jung . . . claimed that their interventions were both medical curings and spiritual carings" (Szasz, 1978, p. 183). It therefore is his conclusion that:

Viewed as the cure of souls, this history of psychotherapy—from ancient Judaism and Greece through early and Medieval Christianity and the Reformation—displays a continuity and consistency quite at odds with its history as psychiatric treatment understood in the medical sense of that term. (Szasz, 1978, p. 40)

Thus, despite more recent efforts of psychology and psychiatry to separate from and even to disown their religious heritage, to operate according to the medical model, and to achieve credibility based on scientific rigor and the methodology of empiricism, thinking in terms of spirituality and of souls may be to become part, once again, of a long and noble tradition. It also may reestablish an appropriate and useful stance for us as we work to facilitate healing. Over time, such healing may occur not only in the realm of individual growth and transformation but also in that of our conceptual frameworks and larger social ideologies and discourses. It is relevant to note that, Kyriakos Markides, a sociologist, believes—idealistically and perhaps too optimistically—that:

We may be heading toward a point in history when the traditional conflict between religion and science will come to an end. It will do so through a deeper understanding of nature and reality, resulting from the lifting of the veil separating ordinary three-dimensional consciousness from super-sensible realities. (1995, p. 354)

Even in his idealism, however, Markides is anything but an anomaly for, as you may recall from the discussion in chapter 2, idealism has been defined as one of the key elements of a spiritual orientation (Elkins, 1990). Further, there are indicators that as a profession we are moving in the direction he predicts, though this movement is not yet widespread. Thus, for example, we hear from a family therapist, "People certainly suffer deprivation, but I believe that at the core they suffer a poverty of *despair*. This is a poverty that robs people of their souls—of meaning, purpose, and hope" (Aponte, 1994, p. 1). Aponte therefore calls upon us to "join the bread with the spirit," to integrate the practical with the transcendent in our work with clients.

Similarly, in her final column in *Counseling Today* as president of the American Counseling Association, Joyce Breasure writes:

> I think the reason we are seeing so many people in disharmony is because the American people have lost their hearts, souls and spirits. The struggles that people are facing today can easily bring them into disharmony unless they have a strong spiritual belief system. . . . I implore you to recognize the unity of mind, body and soul in others and yourself. It is much easier to medicate, hospitalize and ignore the items that do not fit into a treatment plan, but that's not truly helping our clients. People can easily recognize our insincerity and fear of things that cannot be put into nice little categories. (1996, p. 5)

Then there is the work of Thomas Moore (1992, 1994). Moore was one of the first psychologists in recent years to bring a focus on the soul to the forefront of our attention. The following provides a summary of his view:

> In the modern world we tend to separate psychology from religion. We like to think that emotional problems have to do with the family, childhood, and trauma—with personal life and not with spirituality. We don't diagnose an emotional seizure as "loss of religious sensibility" or "lack of spiritual awareness." Yet it is obvious that the soul, seat of the deepest emotions, can benefit greatly from the gifts of a vivid spiritual life and can suffer when it is deprived of them. The soul, for example, needs an articulated worldview, a carefully worked out scheme of values, and a sense of relatedness to the whole. It needs a myth of immortality and an attitude toward death. It also thrives on spirituality that is not so transcendent, such as the spirit of family, arising from traditions and values that have been part of the family for generations. (1992, p. 204)

More significant, perhaps, is evidence of a shift in perspective in the general population, which I believe is providing the primary impetus for change relative to spirituality. I note in this regard the extraordinary popularity of books such as *The Tibetan Book of Living and Dying*, in which Sogyal Rinpoche (1992) distills and explains in a very readable manner the esoteric wisdom of Tibetan Buddhism. One of the concluding messages of this book is that:

> Spiritual care is not a luxury for a few; it is *the* essential right of every human being, as essential as political liberty, medical assistance, and equality of opportunity. A real democratic ideal would include knowledgeable spiritual care for everyone as one of its most essential truths. (1992, p. 209)

In a similar vein, one of the number-one best-sellers in recent years is *A Return to Love* by Marianne Williamson (1992). In this book Williamson shares her reflections on the channeled work *A Course in Miracles* (1975). She explicates one basic theme, about which she writes:

> Love is what we were born with. Fear is what we have learned here. The spiritual journey is the relinquishment—or unlearning—of fear and the acceptance of love back into our hearts. Love is the essential existential fact. It is our ultimate reality and our purpose on earth. To be consciously aware of it, to experience love in ourselves and others, is the meaning of life. (Williamson, 1992, p. xxii)

Then there is James Redfield's fictional work *The Celestine Prophesy*. It is noteworthy that more than 4 million copies of this book have been sold to date, and a sequel recently was published. Obviously there is something very appealing, or at least intriguing, about the ten insights describing an alternative view of reality contained in their pages. Of his fundamental focus, Redfield writes:

> We know that life is really about a spiritual unfolding that is personal and enchanting—an unfolding that no science or philosophy or religion has yet fully clarified. And we know something else as well: we know that once we do understand what is happening, how to engage this allusive process and maximize its occurrence in our lives, human society will take a quantum leap into a whole new way of life—one

that realizes the best of our tradition—and creates a culture that has been the goal of history all along. (1993, unnumbered page)

Obviously such messages are striking a chord in the hearts of a large segment of the population. From my perspective, we must at least acknowledge that change is in the air and be sensitive to the fact that many people, some of whom are our clients, are subscribing to the kinds of ideas sampled here. Indeed, interest in and activity relative to the religious/spiritual arena, much of it outside traditional institutions, has reached unprecedented levels in recent years (Jones, 1995).

What is more, I believe it is important to become aware that we mental health professionals have a unique opportunity to participate in the healing of the soul of the world, in the creation of the kind of culture of which Redfield speaks, as we participate with others in soul healing at an individual level. For we are the ones to whom people often turn in their pain and despair; we are the recipients of that sacred trust bestowed upon us by clients when they come seeking help; and it is we who have the privilege of assisting many on their particular journey toward healing and wholeness.

Consistent with my story, I believe we take appropriate advantage of this opportunity and demonstrate the worthiness of our clients' trust in us as we include spirituality in the therapeutic conversation. This is particularly true as we do so out of an awareness of the ramifications of such discourses at various levels of the system. Indeed, from my perspective it is important that the conversation that includes spirituality occurs both at the level of public discourse about therapy and at the level of discourse that comprises the private interactions between client and counselor/therapist.

INCLUDING SPIRITUALITY IN THE
THERAPEUTIC CONVERSATION

That is, I believe that, at the macro level of the larger context, it behooves us to recognize fully the nature of the enterprise in which we are engaged as counselors/therapists. We must acknowledge the extent of the role we play in terms of influence on people's lives and accordingly behave in a manner consistent with the highest standards of moral/ethical conduct. Further, I would suggest that it is critical to be cognizant of the fact that, regardless of the content of our discussions, the process of therapy may be construed as a spiritual enterprise the outcome of which affects us all at the deepest level of our being. As a family therapist who has considered and traced the development of this field, of which I have been a part for many years, this seems a fitting place indeed at which to have arrived. To explain, let's return briefly to our history, this time with a more recent focus.

We have described (Becvar & Becvar, 1988, 1993, 1996) the 1940s as a time in which the seeds of the paradigm shift represented by systems theory and cybernetics were planted. The 1950s saw the family therapy plant take root as new ways of theorizing and practicing began to emerge and be implemented. The budding of this plant into various models characterized the 1960s, while the 1970s saw the development of organized schools of family therapy. A sense of connecting and integrating the different approaches defined the 1980s. The 1990s began with much controversy and internal conflict, primarily as an outgrowth of the feminist critique. However, the theme that seems to have evolved in the latter half of this decade is one of general concern with transcending models and developing collaborative and respectful therapeutic dialogues. As we approach the year 2000, the inclusion of ethics, morality, and spirituality in our therapeutic conversations has become an area of great interest. Apparently we see ourselves as developmentally ready to address in greater depth what may be not only some of the most significant dimensions of our holistic perspective but also some of the most crucial aspects of our work. As we have seen, however, this focus is not limited to family therapists, and certainly it has ramifications for all mental health professionals.

That is, if out of acknowledgment of our interdependence and thus the sacredness of our task, we consider ourselves engaged in a spiritual process, we must be concerned with *how* we do what we do. A spiritual orientation manifests in praxis and is characterized by a transformation of the way we live and interact with others in our world (Capra & Steindl-Rast, 1991; Elkins, 1990). Appropriate counselor/therapist behavior thus moves beyond the requirements of professional codes of ethics and into a concern with higher-order principles and moral/ethical issues. It also is not restricted to intellectual knowledge but includes as well our minds, our hearts, and our souls (Kubler-Ross, 1995). For example, as Kornfield writes:

> The therapist should not only be skilled but also demonstrate an obvious sense of integrity and kindness. It is not so important that he or she share the particular spiritual path of the client, but that he or she respect spiritual life and the principles of attention, compassion, and forgiveness that un-

derlie both therapy and good meditation. In the end, it is not the particular techniques of therapy but a deep relationship, conducted within awareness and compassion, that in itself is the source of healing. The touching of our hearts and minds in this way can be a profound channel to the understanding of the sacred and the healing of our limitations. (1993, p. 252)

Similarly, I believe we counselors and therapists would do well to heed the advice given by Sogyal (1992) to those looking for a spiritual guide or teacher. Like Kornfield, he emphasizes compassion and notes that true teachers are characterized by kindness, humility, and a commitment to serve students and the students' needs rather than their own. Thus, consistent with a spiritual orientation, there is a sense of altruism (Elkins, 1990) and a recognition that nobody wins unless everybody wins (Sams, 1993). It is in the context of a relationship defined by behaviors such as these on the part of the teacher or therapist that real trust is created. And it is such trust that enables the student or client to find meaningful support in his or her attempts to deal successfully with all the issues of both life and death. Like Kornfield (1993), we may understand this process of establishing a trusting, supportive environment as one of creating sacred space.

In addition, as we include spirituality (Elkins, 1990) in the conversations about our work, we acknowledge a transcendent dimension, we understand that our lives have meaning and purpose, and we honor the sacredness of all life. While being realistic about the degree of pain and tragedy in our world, we tend to move toward committing ourselves to changing that world through a recognition that we human beings are capable of so much more than we have as yet expressed. Indeed, from a spiritual perspective, we recognize that each of us may be understood according to the following characterization:

> You are goodness and mercy and compassion and understanding. You are peace and joy and light. You are forgiveness and patience, strength and courage, a helper in time of need, a comforter in time of sorrow, a healer in time of injury, a teacher in times of confusion. You are the deepest wisdom and the highest truth; the greatest peace and the grandest love. You *are* these things. And in moments of your life you have *known* yourself as these things. (Walsch, 1995, p. 87)

It is my belief that with a spiritual orientation the ultimate satisfaction that each of us desires (Elkins, 1990) is achieved as we choose to create our realities based on assumptions such as those just articulated. That is, as we honor the sacredness of the process in which we are engaged as well as the divinity of those with whom we work, we facilitate the emergence of both. And the more such sacredness and divinity evolve in the context of the counseling/therapeutic relationship, the more they inevitably ripple out to affect others in the lives and worlds of every individual and every relationship.

At the same time, at the micro level of the therapeutic conversation between client and counselor/therapist, we also must recognize not only that the people with whom we have the opportunity to work are spiritual beings but that religion/spirituality may be an area of great concern for many of those who choose to engage in counseling/therapy. Therefore, if we do not make room in our conversations for discussions related to this realm we are less than holistic. More important, however, by failing to privilege such a discourse, we may be doing our clients a real disservice. For it is they, I believe, who should have the right to decide whether or not it is appropriate to include or exclude religion/spirituality. It is they from whom we must take our cues if we are to be truly respectful of their knowledge and expertise. And even when such matters are deemed inappropriate as an explicit topic of conversation, we need to be aware that a lack of focus in this realm does not negate the possibility that problems being experienced influence and are influenced by what may be going on at a soul level. Stated metaphorically:

> A life in a castle of a soul is no blessing if that castle is dark, cold, damp, or filled with the musty beliefs of ancient histories; while a cottage of a soul, cozily lit, can be most pleasant and provide the self with a kindly roadside inn that makes even long journeys enjoyable and venturesome. (Roberts, 1978, p. 24)

In other words, it still may be important to be sensitive to needs and concerns at a very deep level even if this level is not the topic of interest to our clients. Given the perspective of soul healing, we might therefore operate out of awareness both of a natural and inherent inclination toward wholeness at a soul level and a desire to provide a context that will be experienced as healing and conducive to growth and development that are appropriate for the client. It is important to emphasize, however, this is done only as a part of the context within which we work to help clients to achieve their desired goals. That is, our desire to facilitate growth and development at a soul level doesn't replace the client's agenda. Rather, it becomes part of the process of helping the client to achieve his or her goals.

While I respect this proviso, I believe we also would do well to recognize the value of facilitating an experience of connectedness. For everyone involved, this might increase an awareness of the meaning to be derived from a sense of the interdependence of all that is, as that interdependence has been described by both quantum physicists and by postmodernists. Indeed, as we participate in the creation of such an experience, it is my belief that we facilitate the overall effectiveness of the counseling/therapy process.

What is more, the opportunity for and the experience of nonjudgmental acceptance can be extremely affirming and meaningful. It is such a context that I believe allows for and encourages the unfolding of our greatest potential. In addition, it may well be a unique experience for our clients. And even when it is not, it is one that may have far-reaching ramifications. That is, not only might a soul-healing context be cocreated in the moment, but when that context is emulated and perhaps generalized to other relationships, real change, both in individual lives and in the larger society, might be forthcoming. Therefore, while the primary focus of our work may be on the immediate interactions between ourselves and our clients, systemically we may recognize that we cannot do just one thing (Becvar & Becvar, 1996), and that our behaviors inevitably have an impact on and influence the various other levels of the systems in which we and our clients live.

Similarly, learning to trust the universe and experiencing the miracle of the reality that is available from such a stance may be to access a life-enhancing sense of mystery and awe. Thus, we may enable our clients to become aware that information is available to all of us on many levels. What is more, we all may learn to honor the more intuitive ways of knowing. In addition, with a story that life does indeed have meaning and purpose and the awareness that we dwell in a larger universe within which our dreams may be realized, we may find the ability to understand and cope more effectively with life's challenges, regardless of their magnitude. Indeed, we may recognize that we are the cocreators of such challenges.

Further, perhaps the context that best supports clients' ability to experience their own power is one in which it is recognized that we have the potential to influence our lives in far more significant ways than generally is acknowledged or believed. Thus, to have an epistemology that has a conscious awareness of itself (Keeney, 1983), to be aware that it is we who participate in the construction of our realities as a function of our beliefs, allows us not only to influence that reality but also to focus on and participate in the creation of the changes we desire. Such an awareness is relevant both for counselors/therapists and for our clients, who may find it a useful dimension to incorporate into their belief systems.

And finally, helping ourselves and our clients to see the potential of walking a path with heart may enable us all to bring about change not only in our individual lives but also in our world. As described in chapter 8, to walk a path with heart is to participate in the creation of a context supportive of all the behaviors and benefits just enumerated. It also is to become a role model for others, a model of what is possible relative to our personal visions (Sams, 1993). What is more, as each of us achieves a measure of success in attaining our personal vision and realizing our full potential, we may move closer to the goal of spiritual fulfillment and perhaps, ultimately, to the world peace about which many of us dream. In the meantime, as we work toward the accomplishment of lofty goals such as these, we may find that we have equipped ourselves in some of the most meaningful ways possible. Thus, as Hammerschlag writes:

> I have come to see clearly that those men and women who survive crises are those who have maintained a special connection to the way. They have walked their own walk with eyes open to the people and the truths around them, without discounting the walks of others. They have developed a special sense of who they are. They have supplemented the knowledge of science with a faith in the mysterious. The lesson they have imparted to me is unquestionably this: if you are going to greet the world as an equal, your feet have to be planted firmly in some unique, prideful recognition of Self. You must learn in a good way that what you are is okay. Then you can know that others are just fine too. (1988, p. 16)

The issue at this point, however, is how to get from here to there, and in the meantime how to live with and respond to those who reject a story such as the one I have just articulated. The way I choose is to attempt to live and work in a manner that is consistent with my frame of reference even as it continues to evolve. I remain committed and yet open, for mine is an ongoing search with far more questions than there are answers. And above all, it is one that includes having respect for belief systems and stories that are different than mine. In the following section I present a summary of the basic assumptions of my perspective, or story. I invite you to think of these assumptions as comprising my internal dialogue, or personal self-talk, as I interact with others, particularly in the context of counseling/therapy.

SUMMARY

As a therapist who operates from a postmodern stance grounded in second-order cybernetics, constructivism, and social constructionism, I make certain fundamental assumptions about the counseling/therapy process. Such assumptions are part of the context that I participate in cocreating regardless of the focus of particular interactions with specific clients. For example, assuming that you are my client, the following is the way I think about what it is you bring to our conversation when you request that I assist you with your life and some of its challenges:

- You have a story to tell, probably a problem-saturated story that has emerged, in part at least, as a function of the prevailing beliefs in society about health and dysfunction.
- There are things in your life that you don't like, that you would like to see changed, and therefore, although you may not be saying so, you have at least an implicit idea about how you would like things to be.
- Not all of your life is bad or unsuccessful, although that is what you may tend to focus on, at least as we begin our conversation together.
- The things that you describe as problematic are logical to context and thus, in some way that you probably don't understand, make sense.
- You are not a diagnostic category in spite of the fact that in order for you to get reimbursed by your insurance company, you may need me to provide a diagnosis.
- Your needs and desires, your stories, are unique, and the therapy process is designed to fit you and your uniqueness.

Given the same theoretical perspective previously described, if you are my client the following is the way I think about what it is that I bring to my conversation with you:

- I have many stories in my head that provide explanations and guidelines about individual, family, and system behavior, and the process of change, but I am not a so-called expert.
- My most important role is to listen to you, my client, as you tell

your story; to recognize your expertise; to help you articulate possible solutions in the form of your desired goals; and to search for instances in the past when you have been successful.

- When I offer reflections and ideas, I will do so in a tentative and respectful manner that acknowledges my awareness that I don't have access to the Truth. Rather, I have knowledge I can draw on that may be useful to you.
- Together we will have a conversation in which we mutually influence one another in the process of cocreating a context that is logical to and supportive of the solutions or goals you desire.
- It would be inconsistent for me to diagnose you using, for example, the categories of the *DSM-IV*. That is, I do not believe in diagnostic labels that may participate in the further creation of a problem-saturated story that may become your reality.
- I will explain my position to you, and together we will consider the ramifications of selecting a diagnosis and, if you choose to do so, which it might be. I will ask you to decide how to proceed regarding this issue.
- I will respond to you as a unique person/system to the best of my ability. Where my ability to be effective with you is compromised by the limits of a third-party payer, I will let you know, and we will discuss the issue together.

In addition to the theoretical perspective just described, given my spiritual, soul-healing orientation, the following thoughts and considerations also inevitably influence and guide my conversation with you:

- I assume that you and I are part of an interconnected whole, and we not only mutually influence each other at a physical level but have access to a level of communication and connectedness that exists at a spiritual or soul level.

- I see all of us as aspects of a larger, divine universe and I honor that perception relative both to you and to me. I therefore truly love myself, thus having more to give to you, and I honor our encounter as a holy one.

- I acknowledge the sacred trust that you bestow upon me when you come to me for professional help, and I will do everything in my power to be worthy of that trust by being respectful of you and by working in a moral/ethical manner.

- I will attempt to tune in to you, to hear you both with my ears and with my intuition. You need to know that I trust the information I receive at a "gut" level, and I may present it to you when this seems appropriate.

- I may share my stories with you or describe my journey, or both, as a means of letting you know that we are all in this together, headed in the same general direction, even though we may be taking very different paths.

- I believe that relationships may be understood as having a spiritual basis and connection, and I share my view that there are no accidents. I may try to provide you with such an awareness in the hope that it will enable you to understand your relationships in a more meaningful manner that facilitates your learning and growth.

- I will inquire about the role that religion/ spirituality plays in your life, but I will take my cues from you about how best to proceed in this area.

- I do not make judgments about your behavior or that of others in your world. I assume that all behavior is logical in context, and I will help you to understand the way in which the behaviors you do not like somehow make sense. We will work together to achieve your goals relative to the behaviors that you find problematic.

- I will attempt to help you suspend judgment of other people and of events as a way of shifting to a focus on solutions and the achievement of your desired goals.

- I accept you where you are, and I hope to facilitate your acceptance of others in your world in a similar manner.

- I assume that you and the others in your world are all doing the best you can, given your particular circumstances.

- I will work to help you achieve your goals, but I also will recognize the limits of what may be possible. I acknowledge the appropriateness of the outcome, whatever that may look like.

- I will attempt to keep our focus on the here and now. I may ask about the past in order to get a better understanding of your context. I also may ask about your desired future state. However, I am aware that all we really have to work with is the present moment, and that it is only by changing in the here and now that past and future events and their interpretations may be influenced.

- Given my trust in the universe, I look for the magical, synchronistic events in my life and world. I probably will point them out to you when it appears that you, too, may have experienced them.

- I may ask you about your dreams, and if you are interested we may spend some time exploring them together. As we do so, however, I will encourage you to reach your own conclusions about their possible meanings and messages.

- I may encourage you to explore some areas that are new for you relative to consciousness and the accessing of information, for example through meditation or even by means of oracles or shamanic practices. At the same time, I will encourage you to keep your feet planted firmly on the ground and to maintain, wherever possible, a sense of humor.

- I also may encourage you to explore various sources of the random, or new information, through reading and other activities in order to help you facilitate the creation of new, more useful realities.

- I may frame questions and offer reflections that encourage you to understand problems and crises as opportunities for growth and learning. We may even consider the possibility that they represent healing moments that are fruitful for you at a soul level.

- I may suggest that, as we focus on solutions, we attempt to cocreate realities that enable you to become the person you would like to be and to achieve the kind of relationships you desire.

- I am aware that my belief in your ability to achieve your desired goals will have an influence on the outcome of our work together. I therefore will make every effort to support you, to validate you, to accept you, and to affirm my belief in your potential to succeed. At the same time I will be realistic about what does not appear to be possible.

- I also am aware that your belief in your ability to achieve your desired goals will have an influence on the outcome of our work together. I will remind you of the influence of your beliefs on the creation of your reality.

- I am grateful for my view of life as a spiritual journey that may be undertaken as a path with heart, and I may speak to you about its importance for me in terms of attaining a sense of meaning and purpose.

- I may encourage you to consider your heart's dream and the possibility of pursuing this dream, even if only in small ways, if this seems appropriate or of interest to you.

- I will help you discern and choose a path with heart that seems right for you if that is your desire. I also will explain and help you find ways to avoid possible stumbling blocks and I will support you in the best way I know.

- I do not fear death or conversations about death, and I will be happy to talk with you about your thoughts and fears related to this topic. I also will invite you to experience the way in which life may be enriched as we come to terms with our own mortality and that of others.

- If our conversation includes religion/spirituality, I may talk to you about the challenge of living at two levels, and we may have conversations about how to integrate the spiritual and the material aspects of our lives. While I probably won't have any definitive answers, we certainly may come up with some interesting questions.
- I will attempt to send you positive energy in the form of love.

With me, as I am with you in a manner consistent with these assumptions, my hope is that your experience of the counseling/therapy process will include the following:

- You will have a sense of connectedness and will feel accepted, validated, respected, and supported.
- You will feel not only that you have been heard but also that you have your own expertise as well as some other resources of which you previously were unaware.
- You will have a clearer idea about what it is you would like as well as a sense of what is possible, and you will feel hopeful about the attainment of your goals.
- You will have a new understanding of the degree to which you may influence the creation of your reality and will have new information about or perspectives on how to proceed.
- You will feel that healing at a very deep level is being facilitated, and that your growth and development, or the unfolding of your vast potential, are being encouraged.
- You will experience the power of love and feel energized and renewed.

In considering whether or not I have been successful, either in my own life or that of my clients, I also like to take note of and have my clients be cognizant of the twelve "Warning Signs of Health," which I have posted in my office waiting room. They were collected from a bulletin board in Waldport, Oregon, but unfortunately, no author's name was given. However, they seem to provide another useful set of benchmarks worthy of our attention as we think about the outcomes of our work. That is, if we have been successful, perhaps you, my client, also will notice the following:

1. Persistent presence of support network.
2. Chronic positive expectations; tendency to frame events in a constructive light.
3. Episodic peak experiences.
4. Sense of spiritual involvement.
5. Increased sensitivity.
6. Tendency to adapt to changing conditions.
7. Rapid response and recovery of adrenaline system due to repeated challenges.
8. Increased appetite for physical activity.
9. Tendency to identify and communicate feelings.
10. Repeated episodes of gratitude, generosity or related emotions.
11. Compulsion to contribute to society.
12. Persistent sense of humor.

These summaries both of my internal dialogue and of the desired outcomes describe, in a nutshell, the process I think of as counseling/therapy with a spiritual orientation, the process of soul healing. As noted at the outset and repeated throughout, it is just my story. However, my hope is that what I have written also speaks to you and that you will find your work validated and perhaps enhanced as a function of my sharing it.

You may find it interesting to note that in several places I have made reference explicitly to love and implicitly to its transformative power. I have done so because that is the place my thinking, as well as that of many others, takes me as I ponder not only where it all seems naturally to lead but also how to wrap up my discussion of counseling and therapy with a spiritual orientation. And so we turn now to a final consideration of some of the sources of, as well as some conclusions to, my soul healing story.

FINAL THOUGHTS

I am well aware of the great disdain with which the New Age is regarded, particularly within academia and the scientific community. Further, I recognize that I may be perceived by some as having fallen under its sway. Indeed, perhaps awareness of such perceptions explains the need I felt to outline in such great detail the origins of my theoretical and spiritual perspective as well as to provide so many references to and quotes from reliable and credible sources. I also am cognizant of the bad rap that the New Age emphasis on love has had as a function of the way it has been perceived and employed. I also acknowledge that some of the criticism of people calling themselves "New Agers" does in fact seem to be valid. However, not everyone or anything associated with this movement represents quackery or fraud, or both. For example, I applaud its emphasis on spirituality, and I support the goal of creating a reality that would be experienced by all as more loving and humane. I also applaud its contributions to a heightened awareness of ecological and environmental issues. I therefore caution us not to throw the baby out with the bathwater, not to assume guilt by association and certainly not to discard some very important information that has emerged within the context of this movement.

At the same time, I also offer a word of warning as we move to a consideration of the topic of love. That is, I do not believe that in order to be a good counselor/therapist, all we have to do is love our clients. Just as it takes more than love on the part of parents for their children to grow into healthy adults, it takes more than love on our part for our work with clients to be perceived as effective or successful. However, as an overarching frame of reference, the idea of creating a context based on love does not seem to me to be a bad place to begin. Or end. It is with such a proviso in mind that I share some thoughts relative to the role of love in our life, our work and our world.

Many variations on the following theme have been offered by professional healers working in diverse settings and from different perspectives: "There is a physiology of love. It is not just an emotional experience, but a whole soul experience. Love is the golden thread that unites all the forms of healing" (Warter, 1994, p. 224). In addition to what has been written, I also suspect that many of us have had our own personal experiences with the role of love in facilitating healing, both for ourselves and for others with whom we live or work, or both. Indeed, love seems to be the glue that holds the parts of who we are and what we do together. And it is the experience of a loving, compassionate context that may seem to our clients to have provided the magic ingredient that enabled a successful outcome of our work together.

Elisabeth Kubler-Ross, who is well known for her work with terminally ill patients, has reached a similar conclusion. However, public responses to her and to her work also provide, from my perspective, a sad commentary on what may be experienced even when, or perhaps because, we choose to behave in a loving manner. In fact, it has not been very long since Kubler-Ross's Virginia farm, which was home to numerous otherwise unwanted AIDS babies, was the target of arson. Nevertheless, at the end of a long and brilliant career during which she has received both adulation and condemnation, Kubler-Ross states:

> Here we will know that the absolutely only thing that matters is love. Everything else, our achievements, degrees, the money we made, how many mink coats we had, is totally irrelevant. It will also be understood that *what* we do is not important. The only thing that matters is *how* we do what we do. And the only thing that matters is that we do what we do with love. (1995, p. 73)

Most significant to me, however, are the conclusions of the Chilean biologists Humberto Maturana and Francisco Varela, whose book *The Tree of Knowledge* (1992) is subtitled and describes "the biological roots of human understanding." Many of those who espouse the perspectives of second-order cybernetics, constructivism, or social constructionism have based their assumptions regarding our inevitable subjectivity and the reality-creating role of perception, rooted in biological processes, on the findings of Maturana and Varela. Theirs is not only a radical view but also one that has had a profound impact on our understanding of what it means to be human. From their perspective, it is through our mutual interactions that we bring forth a world, which accordingly exists only as a function of our social structural coupling. In addition, through the lens of biology, these researchers have provided a scientific perspective that also may alter the way we think about love:

> This is the biological foundation of social phenomena: without love, without acceptance of others living beside us, there is no social process and, therefore, no humanness. Anything that undermines the acceptance of others, from competency to the possession of truth and on to ideologic certainty, undermines the social process because it undermines the biologic process that generates it. Let us not deceive ourselves: we are not moralizing, we are not preaching love. We are only revealing the fact that, biologically, without love, without acceptance of others, there is no social phenomenon. If we still live together that way, we are living indifference and negation under a pretense of love. (Maturana & Varela, 1992, pp. 246–247)

As we compare these statements with the remarks of those who espouse a spiritual perspective, we find some striking similarities. For
example, you might want to reread the quote from Marianne
Williamson cited earlier in this chapter. In addition, the following assertion made in the context of a "metaphysical adventure" certainly
seems to offer a related message:

> In our present time, the closest we get to peace is trying to resolve con-
> flict. This is not peace. Even the absence of war in society is not peace;
> peace is the absence of any trace of malice within each person. Peace is
> an experience of the soul, not an intellectual statement of nonconflict.
> Peace cannot be experienced by the mind; it can only be witnessed by
> the mind as the soul Self—who we are—experiences Unconditional
> Love. (Roads, 1995, p. 142)

In fact, from such a perspective we may understand that at a soul
level we are all expressions of such love. Therefore, our role, or our
soul purpose, involves becoming aware of and manifesting this highest or spiritual self. It also involves recognizing and facilitating awareness of the same divinity in all that is, and in all with whom we
interact. That is:

> The soul is very clear that its purpose is evolution. That is its *sole* pur-
> pose—and its *soul* purpose. It is not concerned with the achievements
> of the body or the development of the mind. These are all meaningless
> to the soul. (Walsch, 1995, p. 82)

However, as we all certainly are aware, it is hard to break out of old
patterns. Indeed, I doubt that anyone knows more about how difficult
change may be than we counselors/therapists. And we are no more
immune to the challenge of change than are our clients. From my perspective, such change necessarily includes acceptance of the spiri-
tual/religious dimension in our work and a willingness to expand our
thinking about consciousness, about human potential, and about the
nature of reality. More important, it requires that we behave differently,
that we act in a manner consistent with the reality we desire to create:

> *You each create your own reality* [italics in original]. If you create separa-
> tion, then your reality will give birth to fear, and you will live fearfully,
> experiencing its wide range of consequences. If you create judgment,

then you will live with being judged. All negativity you express toward other people will always reflect back into your own life. It has been most aptly said, 'What you sow, you must reap.' Now is the time to sow Love, reaping the rich and abundant harvest of soul fulfillment. (Roads, 1995, pp. 246–247)

In a recently published book entitled *An Ethic for the Age of Space*, Lawrence LeShan notes that the age of space was born with the dropping of the bomb on Hiroshima and moved into adolescence with man's landing on the moon. However, he believes that since the beginning of this new era we have moved inexorably toward the creation of a reality that threatens the survival of mankind. For each advance we have made in the realm of technology has brought with it new problems in need of solution. However, we have failed miserably in terms of a code of moral and ethical behavior that would enable us to deal with the challenges of the space age and prevent the suicide of the human race. He writes:

We have made great and almost unbelievable progress in the last three centuries, in physics, chemistry, in the arts, and in all the sciences except one—we have not learned how to live better with each other and with the general nature of which we all are a part. The science of human consciousness and behavior has been a dismal failure. The information and technology explosions have changed everything about the way we live except the ways we interact with each other and with the ecology. Indeed, as far as the ecology goes, our new technology has made things far worse. (1996, p. ix)

LeShan believes that the crux of the problem, "the deadliest idea human beings have ever developed" (1996, p. 18) is that:

1: Any genuine question must have one and only one true answer. All other answers are necessarily errors.
2: There is one and only one dependable path toward the discovery of this truth.
3: The true answer, when found, must necessarily be compatible with all other truths and form a single whole. One truth cannot be incompatible with another. (1996, p. 20)

He laments the decision made many years ago to exclude values and ethics from the field of psychology and calls for new ethical guidelines for human behavior and for an educational system consistent with these guidelines. For him, ensuring the future of mankind requires the creation of a new reality that takes into consideration not only individual needs but also respects other constructions of reality as well as the needs of the larger community and the cosmos.

For Huston Smith (1992) we have created a dilemma through our extreme reliance on science, with its emphasis on objectivity, prediction, number and control. Thus we have overvalued the pursuit of the "power-to-control" and its related utilitarian epistemology. In the process we have devalued knowledge generation through nonscientific means and thus have limited our ability to acknowledge what it means to be fully human. He quotes the sociologist Manfred Stanley, who writes:

> The world, once an "enchanted garden," to use Max Weber's memorable phrase, has now become disenchanted, deprived of purpose and direction, bereft—in these senses—of life itself. All that which is allegedly basic to the specifically human status in nature comes to be forced back upon the precincts of the "subjective" which, in turn, is pushed by the modern scientific view ever more into the province of dreams and illusions. (Smith, 1992, p. 105)

Smith believes that the ultimate adversary is the idea that we live in a lifeless and indifferent universe without larger meaning and purpose—"Newton's great mechanism of time, space and inanimate forces operating automatically or by chance" (1992, p. 125). He believes instead that the notion that we are part of a unitary whole, dwelling in a spiritual domain, cannot be denied if one truly considers both the ramifications of the former view and the profound evidence for the latter. He writes:

> Matter and energy are one. Time and space are one, time being space's fourth dimension. Space and gravity are one: the latter is simply space's curvature. And in the end matter and its space-time field are one; what appears to us as a material body is nothing but a center of space-time's deformation. Once again: If we could be taken backstage into the spiritual recesses of reality in the way physics has taken us into its physical recesses, might we not find harmony hidden there as well—earth joined to heaven, man walking with God? (1992, p. 129)

Obviously, I concur with the conclusions of LeShan and Smith, and particularly so considering what failure to change the beliefs according to which we operate currently may mean. Thus, I state that it is the reality of love, of soul healing and of soul fulfillment, that I wish to create. However, I truly do not want to convey the idea that I have found the answer, that my story is the correct story regarding how to do it. Rather, it is just one way, a way that right now is working for me. I would like to repeat my belief that what is vitally important is that we make room for and respect everybody's stories. Ideally, such respect would accommodate the differences in perceptions and belief systems not only between individuals, but also between groups, between competing ideologies, between nations.

As mentioned throughout this chapter, we counselors/therapists are uniquely situated to influence the creation of such a reality given the number of people with whom we daily come into contact. Thus, relative to counseling/therapy, one way in which we may participate in the process of transcending dichotomies is by assuming a spiritual orientation. Along the way we might heed the following seven points of wisdom distilled from a Native American spiritual perspective:

1: There are no rules on how to grow or change.
2: All self-imposed rules or judgments are limiting illusions.
3: The Great Mystery cannot be solved, so don't try.
4: Everything you seek can be found inside of you.
5: Laughter and irreverence dissolve the illusions and fear.
6: Unseen worlds exist within the tangible and cannot be separated.
7: You ARE, the moment you decide to BE. (Sams, 1993, p. 307)

For, as this perspective is translated into the language of counseling/therapy, I believe we create a healing context, one that nurtures our souls, the souls of our clients, and the soul of the world. As socially sanctioned agents of our culture, I wonder how we can do any less. And as individuals who have chosen to work with and help others, I know of no better reward than to be part of a process in which our clients' perceptions and thus their lives are shifted in such a way that they and we experience soul healing.

By compassion the soul is made blessed.

—MEISTER ECKHART

Afterword

The creation of this book has been characterized by an interesting and evolving process of mutual influence, perturbation, and feedback, such that the final product has continued to emerge right up to the last moment. Although I was aware from the beginning of the general message I wanted to convey, its ongoing articulation shifted and was shaped not only by each new author whose work I read but also by the reflections, critiques, and suggestions of my many readers. I would like to acknowledge with great gratitude all those who have contributed to this enormously exciting and rewarding experience.

In particular, I am most appreciative of the professional and personal feedback and encouragement I constantly receive from my best friend and most biased supporter, my husband, Ray. And the life we share is daily enriched and made more meaningful by the presence in our world of my beautiful daughter, Lynne. To my son, John, whose death was the catalyst for my spiritual journey, goes a prayer of thanksgiving for our continuing relationship.

Significant contributions to the preparation of this manuscript, at various stages, were made through the thoughtful reading and commentaries of Milo Benningfield, David Hilditch, Margaret Hoopes, and Roberta Tonti. I am grateful to Bellaruth Naperstek and her sister, Carol Ingall, for their consultation and assistance with the Jewish spiritual perspective. I also wish to offer special thanks to Leah Friedman, who not only agreed to read the final version but did so in the manner of a copyeditor, finding the most minute typos and offering me straightforward suggestions about how the manuscript might be improved.

Finally, I am grateful to the folks at Basic Books, first Jo Ann Miller, then Eric Wright, and finally, Juliana Nocker, who as my editors helped to make this book a reality. I also would like to thank the members of the production staff, particularly Michael Wilde, for their work in seeing it through to publication.

References

Abraham, R., McKenna, T., & Sheldrake, R. (1992). *Trialogues at the edge of the West: Chaos, creativity, and the resacralization of the world.* Santa Fe, NM: Bear & Co.

Achterberg, J. (1985). *Imagery in healing: Shamanism and modern medicine.* Boston and London: New Science Library.

Achterberg, J. (1988). The wounded healer. In G. Doore (Ed.), *The shaman's path.* Boston: Shambhala.

Adams, J. L. (1976). *Conceptual blockbusting.* New York: W. W. Norton.

American Psychiatric Association. (1994).*Diagnostic and statistical manual of mental disorders* (4th ed.). Washington, DC: Author.

Andersen, T. (1991). *The reflecting team: Dialogues and dialogues about the dialogues.* New York: W. W. Norton.

Anderson, H. (1993). On a roller coaster: A collaborative language systems approach to therapy. In S. Friedman (Ed.), *The new language of change* (pp. 323–344). New York: Guilford.

Anderson, H., & Goolishian, H. A. (1988). Human systems as linguistic systems: Preliminary and evolving ideas about the implications for clinical theory. *Family Process, 27,* 371–393.

Aponte, H. J. (1994). *Bread and spirit: Therapy with the new poor.* New York: W. W. Norton.

Arrien, A. (1993). *The four-fold way: Walking the paths of the warrior, teacher, healer and visionary.* New York: HarperCollins.

Bach, R. (1977). *Illusions: The adventures of a reluctant messiah.* New York: Delacorte Press.

Bandler, R., & Grinder, J. (1975). *The structure of magic I.* Palo Alto, CA: Science and Behavior Books.

Barasch, M. I. (1993). *The healing path: A soul approach to illness.* New York: G. P. Putnam's Sons.

Bateson, G. (1972). *Steps to an ecology of mind.* New York: Ballantine Books.

Bateson, G. (1979). *Mind and nature.* New York: E. P. Dutton.

Bateson, G., & Bateson, M. C. (1987). *Angels fear: Towards an epistemology of the sacred.* New York: Macmillan.

Becker, E. (1973). *The denial of death.* New York: Free Press.

Becvar, D. (1995). The gift of cancer. *Creative lifelines for survivors, 1* (2), 7–8, 10.

Becvar, D., & Becvar, R. (1987). Family traditions. *Marriage Encounter, 16* (7), 23–24.

Becvar, D., & Becvar, R. (1988). *Family therapy: A systemic integration*. Boston: Allyn & Bacon.

Becvar, D., & Becvar, R. (1993). *Family therapy: A systemic integration* (2nd ed.). Boston: Allyn & Bacon.

Becvar, D., & Becvar, R. (1994). *Hot chocolate for a cold winter's night: Essays for relationship development*. Denver, CO: Love.

Becvar, D., & Becvar, R. (1996). *Family therapy: A systemic integration* (3rd ed.). Boston: Allyn & Bacon.

Becvar, R., & Becvar, D. (1982). *Systems theory and family therapy: A Primer*. Lanham, MD: University Press of America.

Becvar, R., & Becvar, D. (1995). *Crazy-making culture tales*. St. Louis, MO: Unpublished manuscript.

Becvar, R., Becvar, D., & Bender, A. (1982). Let us first do no harm. *Journal of Marital and Family Therapy, 8* (4), 385–391.

Benningfield, M. (in press). Addressing spiritual/religious issues in therapy: Problems and complications. *Journal of Family Social Work*.

Bergin, A. E. (1988). Three contributions of a spiritual perspective to counseling, psychotherapy, and behavior change. *Counseling and Values, 33*, 21–31.

Bernstein, R. J. (1978). *The restructuring of social and political theory*. Philadelphia: University of Pennsylvania Press.

Bertalanffy, L. von. (1968). *General system theory*. New York: George Braziller.

Blocher, D. H. (1974). *Developmental counseling*. New York: Ronald Press.

Blum, R. (1987). *The book of runes*. New York: St. Martin's Press.

Bohm, D. (1980). *Wholeness and the implicate order*. London: Routledge & Kegan Paul.

Bolen, J. S. (1979). *The Tao of psychology: Synchronicity and the self*. San Francisco: Harper & Row.

Borysenko, J. (1995). Ensouling ourselves. In R. Carlson & B. Shield (Eds.), *Handbook for the soul* (pp. 45–48). Boston: Little, Brown.

Boscolo, L., Cecchin, G., Hoffman, L., & Penn, P. (1987). *Milan systemic therapy: Conversations in theory and practice*. New York: Basic Books.

Bowman, E. S. (1989). Understanding and responding to religious material in the therapy of multiple personality disorder. *Dissociation, II* (4), 231–238.

Breasure, J. M. (1996). The mind, body and soul connection. *Counseling Today*, March, p. 5.

Briggs, J. P., & Peat, F. D. (1984). *Looking glass universe*. New York: Simon & Schuster.

Bronfenbrenner, U. (1979). *The ecology of human development*. Cambridge, MA: Harvard University Press.

Bronowski, J. (1978). *The origins of knowledge and imagination*. New Haven & London: Yale University Press.

Broyard, A. (1990). Doctor, talk to me. *New York Times Magazine*, August 26, pp. 33, 35.

Campbell, D. G. (1989). *The roar of silence: Healing powers of breath, tone & music*. Wheaton, IL: Theosophical Publishing House.

Capra, F. (1975). *The tao of physics*. Berkeley, CA: Shambhala.

Capra, F. (1983). *The turning point*. New York: Bantam Books.

Capra, F., & Steindl-Rast, D. (1991). *Belonging to the universe*. New York: HarperCollins.

Carroll, L. (1995). *Alchemy of the human spirit*. Del Mar, CA: Kryon Writings.

Carse, J. P. (1995). *Breakfast at the Victory: The mysticism of ordinary experience.* New York: HarperCollins.

Castaneda, C. (1968). *The teachings of Don Juan: A Yaqui way of knowledge.* New York: Simon & Schuster.

Chopra, D. (1991). *Unconditional life.* New York: Bantam Books.

Coelho, P. (1993). *The alchemist.* New York: HarperCollins.

Coelho, P. (1995). *The pilgrimage.* New York: HarperCollins.

Condron, D. R. (1993). *Dreams of the soul: The yogi sutras of Patanjali.* Windyville, MO: SOM.

Cousins, N. (1989). *Head first: The biology of hope.* New York: E. P. Dutton.

Dass, R. (1995). The pilgrimage of awareness. In R. Carlson & B. Shield (Eds.), *Handbook for the soul* (pp. 67–73). Boston: Little, Brown.

Davies, P. (1983). *God and the new physics.* New York: Simon & Schuster.

Dell, P. F. (1983). From pathology to ethics. *Family Therapy Networker, 1* (6), 29–64.

Deloria, V. (1994). *God is red: A native view of religion.* Golden, CO: Fulcrum.

Demos, J. (1979). Images of the American family, then and now. In V. Tufte & B. Myerhoff (Eds.), *Changing images of the family* (pp. 43–60). New Haven, CT: Yale University Press.

de Shazer, S. (1988). *Clues: Investigating solutions in brief therapy.* New York: W. W. Norton.

de Shazer, S. (1991). *Putting difference to work.* New York: W. W. Norton.

Does Therapy Help? (1995). *Consumer Reports,* November, pp. 734–739.

Doherty, W. J. (1995). *Soul searching: Why psychotherapy must promote moral responsibility.* New York: Basic Books.

Dossey, L. (1989). *Recovering the soul.* New York: Bantam Books.

Dossey, L. (1993). *Healing words.* New York: HarperCollins.

Dyer, W. (1995). Becoming a waking dreamer. In R. Carlson & B. Shield (Eds.), *Handbook for the soul* (pp. 119–125). Boston: Little, Brown.

Easwaran, E. (1992). *Your life is your message: Finding harmony with yourself, others & the earth.* Tomales, CA: Nilgiri Press.

Efran, J. A., Lukens, R. J., & Lukens, M. D. (1988). Constructivism: What's in it for you? *Family Therapy Networker, 12* (5), 27–35.

Eisdorfer, C., & Lawton, M. P. (Eds.). (1973). *The psychology of adult development and aging.* Washington, DC: American Psychological Association.

Elkins, D. (1990). On being spiritual without necessarily being religious. *Association for Humanistic Psychology Perspective,* June, pp. 4–5.

Elliott, W. (1995). *Tying rocks to clouds.* New York: Image Books Doubleday.

Epstein, G. (1989). *Healing visualizations: Creating health through imagery.* New York: Bantam Books.

Fields, R., Taylor, P., Weyler, R., & Ingrasci, R. (1984). *Chop wood carry water: A guide to finding spiritual fulfillment in everyday life.* Los Angeles: Jeremy P. Tarcher.

Flemons, D. (1991). *Completing distinctions.* Boston: Shambhala.

Foos-Graber, A. (1989). *Deathing: An intelligent alternative for the final moments of life.* York Beach, ME: Nicolas-Hays.

Foundation for Inner Peace. (1975). *A course in miracles.* Tiburon, CA.

Frank, J. (1974). *Persuasion and healing.* New York: Schocken.

Franz, M. L. von. (1980). *Projection and recollection in Jungian psychology.* LaSalle, IL: Open Court.

Fulghum, R. (1995). *From beginning to end: The rituals of our lives*. New York: Villard Books.

Gale, J. E., & Long, J. K. (1995). Theoretical foundations of family therapy. Athens, GA: Unpublished manuscript.

Gawain, S. (1978). *Creative visualization*. New York: Bantam Books.

Georgia, R. T. (1994). Preparing to counsel clients of different religious backgrounds: A phenomenological approach. *Counseling and Values, 38*, 143–151.

Gergen, K. (1985). Social constructionist movement in psychology. *American Psychologist, 40*, 266–275.

Gergen, K. (1991). *The saturated self*. New York: Basic Books.

Goldsmith, J. S. (1959). *The art of spiritual healing*. New York: HarperCollins.

Gray, J. (1992). *Men are from Mars, women are from Venus*. New York: HarperCollins.

Gray, J. (1995). Love vitamins for your soul. In R. Carlson & B. Shield (Eds.), *Handbook for the soul* (pp. 54–60). Boston: Little, Brown.

Gresham, D. H. (1988). *Lenten lands: My childhood with Joy Davidman and C. S. Lewis*. New York: HarperCollins.

Griffith, J. L., & Griffith, M. E. (1994). *The body speaks: Therapeutic dialogues for mind-body problems*. New York: Basic Books.

Haley, J. (1963). *Strategies of psychotherapy*. New York: Grune & Stratton.

Haley, J. (1973). *Uncommon therapy*. New York: W. W. Norton.

Hammerschlag, C. A. (1988). *The dancing healers*. New York: HarperCollins.

Hammerschlag, C. A. (1993). *The theft of the spirit*. New York: Simon & Schuster.

Harner, M. (1990). *The way of the shaman* (3rd edition). New York: Harper & Row.

Hayward, J. (1984). *Perceiving ordinary magic*. Boston: New Science Library.

Heisenberg, W. (1971). *Physics and beyond*. New York: Harper & Row.

Helmstetter, S. (1986). *What to say when you talk to yourself*. New York: Pocket Books.

Hoffman, L. (1985). Beyond power and control. *Family Systems Medicine, 4*, 381–396.

Hoffman, L. (1993). *Exchanging voices: A collaborative approach to family therapy*. London: Karnac.

Holmes, T. (1994). Spirituality in systemic practice: An internal family systems perspective. *Journal of Systemic Therapies, 13* (3), 26–35.

Hooper, W. (Ed.). (1996). *C. S. Lewis: Readings for meditation and reflection*. New York: HarperCollins.

Hoopes, M. M., & Harper, J. M. (1987). *Birth order roles and sibling patterns in individual & family therapy*. Rockville, MD: Aspen Publications.

Houston, J. (1996). *A mythic life: Learning to live our greater story*. New York: HarperCollins.

Horrigan, B. (1995). Candace Pert, Ph.D.: Neuropeptides, AIDS, and the science of mind-body healing. *Alternative Therapies, 1* (3), 71–76.

Howard, G. S. (1991). Culture tales. *American Psychologist, 46*, 187–197.

Howe, Q. (1974). *Reincarnation for the Christian*. Wheaton, IL: Theosophical Publishing House.

Husserl, E. (1965). *Phenomenology and the crisis of philosophy*, translated by Quentin Lauer. New York: Harper & Row.

Illich, I. (1976). *Medical nemesis: The expropriation of health*. New York: Pantheon Books.

Imber-Black, E., & Roberts, J. (1989). *Rituals for our times: Celebrating, healing and changing our lives and our relationships*. New York: HarperPerennial.

Ingerman, S. (1991). *Soul retrieval*. New York: HarperCollins.

Ingerman, S. (1993). *Welcome home*. New York: HarperCollins.

Jacob, W. L. (1988). *Interpreting your dreams: Nature's path to self-knowledge*. Coraopolis, PA: J. Pohl Associates.

Jaeger, W. (1965). *Paideia: The ideals of Greek culture* (Gilbert Highet, Trans.) (Vols. I–II). New York: Oxford University Press.

Jones, J. W. (1995). *In the middle of this road we call our life*. New York: HarperCollins.

Kabat-Zinn, J. (1995). Soul work. In R. Carlson & B. Shield (Eds.), *Handbook for the soul* (pp. 108–116). Boston: Little, Brown.

Keeney, B. P. (1983). *Aesthetics of change*. New York: Guilford.

Kelly, G. A. (1955). *The psychology of personal constructs: A theory of personality*, (Vols. I–II). New York: W. W. Norton.

Khan, P. V. I. (1982). *Introducing spirituality into counseling and therapy*. New Lebanon, NY: Omega.

Kleinman, A. (1988). *The illness narratives: Suffering, healing & the human condition*. New York: Basic Books.

Koestler, A. (1978). *Janus: A summing up*. London: Pan Books.

Kornfield, J. (1993). *A path with heart: A guide through the perils and promises of spiritual life*. New York: Bantam Books.

Krieger, D. (1993). *Accepting your power to heal*. Santa Fe, NM: Bear & Co.

Krippner, S., & Welch, P. (1992). *Spiritual dimensions of healing*. New York: Irvington.

Kryder, R. P. (1990). *Gaia matrix oracle*. Mount Shasta, CA: Golden Point Productions.

Kubler-Ross, E. (1995). *Death is of vital importance: On life, death, and life after death*. Barrytown, NY: Station Hill Press.

Kuhn, T. S. (1970). *The structure of scientific revolutions*. Chicago: University of Chicago Press.

Kushner, H. (1995). God's fingerprints on the soul. In R. Carlson & B. Shield (Eds.), *Handbook for the soul* (pp. 18–24). Boston: Little, Brown.

Lasch, C. (1979a). *The culture of narcissism*. New York: Warner Books.

Lasch, C. (1979b). *Haven in a heartless world*. New York: Basic Books.

Lederer, W. J., & Jackson, D. D. (1968). *The mirages of marriage*. New York: W. W. Norton.

Lenz, F. (1995). *Surfing the Himilayas: A spiritual adventure*. New York: St. Martin's Press.

LeShan, L. (1974). *The medium, the mystic, and the physicist*. New York: Penguin Books.

LeShan, L. (1990). *Cancer as a turning point: A handbook for people with cancer, their families, and health professionals*. New York: Penguin Books.

LeShan, L. (1996). *An ethic for the age of space*. York Beach, ME: Samuel Weiser.

Levine, B. H. (1991). *Your body believes every word you say*. Lower Lake, CA: Aslan.

Levine, S. (1982). *Who dies? An investigation of conscious living and conscious dying*. New York: Doubleday.

Lewis, C. S. (1976). A grief observed. New York: Seabury Press.

Lovelock, J. E. (1979). *Gaia: A new look at life on earth*. Oxford: Oxford University Press.

Maier, S. F., Watkins, L. R., & Fleshner, M. (1994). Psychoneuroimmunology: The interface between behavior, brain, and immunity. *American Psychologist, 49* (12), 1004–1017.

Markides, K. C. (1995). *Riding with the lion: In search of mystical Christianity*. New York: Arkana.

Mathieu, W. A. (1991). *The listening book: Discovering your own music*. Boston: Shambhala.

Maturana, H. R., & Varela, F. J. (1987). *The tree of knowledge*. Boston: Shambhala.

Maturana, H. R., & Varela, F. J. (1992). *The tree of knowledge: The biological roots of human understanding* (Revised Edition). Boston: Shambhala.

May, R. (1967). *Psychology and the human dilemma*. Princeton, NJ: D. Van Nostrand.

May, R. (1989). The empathic relationship: A foundation of healing. In R. Carlson & B. Shield (Eds.), *Healers on healing* (pp. 108–110). Los Angeles: Jeremy P. Tarcher.

McNeill, J. T. (1951). *A history of the cure of souls*. New York: Harper & Row.

Meador, B. D., & Rogers, C. R. (1984). Person-centered therapy. In R. Corsini (Ed.), *Current psychotherapies* (pp. 142–195). Itasca, IL: F. E. Peacock.

Medicine Eagle, B. (1989). The circle of healing. In R. Carlson & B. Shield (Eds.), *Healers on healing* (pp. 58–62). Los Angeles: Jeremy P. Tarcher.

Mehta, R. (1967). Introduction. In A. W. Osborn, *The expansion of awareness*. Wheaton, IL: Theosophical Publishing House.

Miller, G. A. (1992). Integrating religion and psychology in therapy: Issues and recommendations. *Counseling and Values, 36*, 113–122.

Miller, J. A. (1989). Wonder as hinge. *International Philosophical Quarterly, 29* (1), 53–66.

Moore, T. (1992). *Care of the soul*. New York: HarperCollins.

Moore, T. (1994). *Soul mates*. New York: HarperCollins.

Morgan, E. S. (1944). *The Puritan family*. Boston: Trustees of the Public Library.

Moss, R. (1989). The mystery of wholeness. In R. Carlson & B. Shield (Eds.), *Healers on healing* (pp. 35–41). Los Angeles: Jeremy P. Tarcher.

Motoyama, H., & Brown, R. (1978). *Science and the evolution of consciousness*. Brookline, MA: Autumn Press.

Nouwen, H. J. M. (1994). *Our greatest gift: A meditation of dying and caring*. New York: HarperCollins.

O'Hanlon, W. H., & Wiener-Davis, M. (1989). *In search of solutions: A new direction in psychotherapy*. New York: W. W. Norton.

Ornstein, R. E. (1975). Contemporary Sufism. In C. L. Tart (Ed.), *Transpersonal psychologies*. New York: Harper & Row.

Ornstein, R. E. (1976). *The psychology of consciousness*. New York: Penguin Books.

Pelletier, K. R. (1977). *Mind as healer, mind as slayer*. New York: Dell.

Pert, C. (1986). Emotions in body, not just in brain. *Brain/Mind Bulletin, 11* (4), 1.

Peteet, J. R. (1994). Approaching spiritual problems in psychotherapy. *Journal of Psychotherapy Practice and Research, 3*, 237–245.

Pirsig, R. M. (1975). *Zen and the art of motorcycle maintenance*. New York: Bantam Books.

Prest, L., & Keller, J. (1993). Spirituality and family therapy: Spiritual beliefs, myths and metaphors. *Journal of Marital and Family Therapy, 19* (2), 137–148.

Polanyi, M. (1958). *The study of man*. Chicago and London: University of Chicago Press.

Pribram, K. H. (1971). *Languages of the brain*. Englewood Cliffs, NJ: Prentice Hall.

Prigogine, I. (1980). *From being to becoming*. San Francisco: W. H. Freeman.

Raabe, T. (1991). *Biblioholism: The literary addiction*. Golden, CO: Fulcrum.

Raheem, A. (1991). *Soul return: Integrating body, psyche & spirit*. Lower Lake, CA: Aslan Publishing.

Redfield, J. (1993). *The celestine prophesy*. New York: Warner Books.

Remen, R. N. (1989). The search for healing. In R. Carlson & B. Shield (Eds.), *Healers on healing* (pp. 91–96). Los Angeles: Jeremy P. Tarcher.

Roads, M. J. (1995). *Into a timeless realm: A metaphysical adventure*. Tiburon, CA: H. J. Kramer.

Roberts, J. (1974). *The nature of personal reality*. New York: Bantam Books.

Roberts, J. (1978). *The afterlife journal of an American philosopher*. New York: Prentice Hall Press.

Rogers, C. R. (1939). *The clinical treatment of the problem child*. Boston: Houghton Mifflin.

Rogers, C. R. (1942). *Counseling and psychotherapy*. Boston: Houghton Mifflin.

Rogers, C. R. (1951). *Client-centered therapy*. Boston: Houghton Mifflin

Rogers, C. R. (1959). Client-centered therapy. In S. Arieti (Ed.), *American handbook of psychiatry*, Vol. 3 (pp. 183–200). New York: Basic Books.

Rogers, C. R. (1961). *On becoming a person*. Boston: Houghton Mifflin.

Rosenak, M. (1995). *Roads to the palace*. Providence, RI: Berghahn Press.

Ross, J. L. (1994). Working with patients within their religious contexts: Religion, spirituality, and the secular therapist. *Journal of Systemic Therapies*, 13 (3), 7–15.

Rossbach, S. (1987). *Interior design with feng shui*. New York: Arkana.

Rossi, E. L. (1986). *The psychobiology of mind-body healing*. New York: W. W. Norton.

Rossman, M. (1989). Illness as an opportunity for healing. In R. Carlson & B. Shield (Eds.), *Healers on healing* (pp. 78–82). Los Angeles: Jeremy P. Tarcher.

Saleebey, D. (1989). The estrangement of knowing and doing: Professions in crisis. *Social Casework: The Journal of Contemporary Social Work*. November, pp. 556–563.

Sams, J. (1993). *The 13 original clan mothers*. New York: HarperCollins.

Sams, J., & Carson, D. (1988). *Medicine cards: The discovery of power through the ways of animals*. Santa Fe, NM: Bear & Co.

Sardello, R. (1992). *Facing the world with soul*. Hudson, NY: Lindisfarne Press.

Satir, V. (1972). *Peoplemaking*. Palo Alto, CA: Science and Behavior Books.

Sawin, M. M. (1979). *Family enrichment with family clusters*. Valley Forge, PA: Judson Press.

Sawin, M. M. (1982). *Hope for families*. New York: Sadlier.

Schrodinger, E. (1967). *What is life? & Mind and matter*. New York: Cambridge University Press.

Schwarz, J. (1989). Healing, love, and empowerment. In R. Carlson & B. Shield (Eds.), *Healers on healing* (pp. 18–21). Los Angeles: Jeremy P. Tarcher.

Schwartz, T. (1995). *What really matters: Searching for wisdom in America*. New York: Bantam Books.

Selvini Palazzoli, M., Boscolo, L., Cecchin, G., & Prata, G. (1978). *Paradox and counterparadox*. New York: Jason Aronson.

Shah, I. (1970). *The way of the Sufi*. New York: E. P. Dutton.

Sheldrake, R. (1981). *A new science of life: The hypothesis of formative causation*. Los Angeles: Jeremy P. Tarcher.

Siegel, B. (1995). Love: The work of the soul. In R. Carlson & B. Shield (Eds.), *Healers on healing* (pp. 39–44). Los Angeles: Jeremy P. Tarcher.

Simonton, O. C. (1989). The harmony of health. In R. Carlson & B. Shield (Eds.), *Healers on healing* (pp. 48–52). Los Angeles: Jeremy P. Tarcher.

Smith, H. (1992). *Beyond the post-modern mind*. Wheaton, IL: Theosophical Publishing House.

Sogyal, R. (1992). *The Tibetan book of living and dying*. New York: HarperCollins.

Solfvin, J. (1989). The healing relationship. In R. Carlson & B. Shield (Eds.), *Healers on healing* (pp. 100–103). Los Angeles: Jeremy P. Tarcher.

Sontag, S. (1977). *Illness as metaphor*. New York: Doubleday.

Stander, V., Piercy, F. P., MacKinnon, D., & Helmeke, K. (1994). Spirituality, religion and family therapy: competing or complementary worlds? *The American Journal of Family Therapy, 22* (1), 27–41.

Stewart, S. P., & Gale, J. E. (1994). On hallowed ground: Marital therapy with couples on the religious right. *Journal of Systemic Therapies, 13* (3),16–25.

Szasz, T. (1978). *The myth of psychotherapy: Mental healing as religion, rhetoric and repression*. Syracuse, NY: Syracuse University Press.

Taggart, S. R. (1994). *Living as if*. San Francisco: Jossey-Bass.

Tannen, D. (1990). *You just don't understand*. New York: William Morrow.

Todeschi, K. J. (1996). Our future as co-creators. *A.R.E. Community, 5* (1), 10–13.

Tomatis, A. A. (1991). *The conscious ear*. Barrytown, NY: Station Hill Press.

von Glasersfeld, E. (1984). An introduction to radical constructivism. In P. Watzlawick (Ed.), *The invented reality* (pp. 17–40). New York: W. W. Norton.

Walsch, N. D. (1995). *Conversations with God: An uncommon dialogue*. Charlottesville, VA: Hampton Roads.

Walsh, R., & Vaughn, F. (1980). *Beyond ego: Transpersonal dimensions in psychology*. Los Angeles: Jeremy Tarcher.

Warch, W. (1977). *The new thought Christian*. Marina del Ray, CA: DeVorss.

Warter, C. (1994). *Recovery of the sacred: Lessons in soul awareness*. Deerfield Beach, FL: Health Communications.

Watson, J. (1995). Nursing's caring-healing paradigm as exemplar for alternative medicine? *Alternative Therapies, 1* (3), 64–69.

Watts, A. W. (1963). *The two hands of God: The myths of polarity*. New York: Macmillan.

Watts, A. W. (1972). *The book*. New York: Vintage Books.

Watzlawick, P. (1978). *The language of change*. New York: Basic Books.

Watzlawick, P. (1984). *The invented reality*. New York: W. W. Norton.

Watzlawick, P., Beavin, J., & Jackson, D. (1967). *The pragmatics of human communication*. New York: W. W. Norton.

Watzlawick, P., Weakland, J., & Fisch, R. (1974). *Change: Principles of problem formation and problem resolution*. New York: W. W. Norton.

Weiss, B. (1995). The soul's legacy. In R. Carlson & B. Shield (Eds.), *Handbook for the soul* (pp. 63–66). Boston: Little, Brown.

Webster's New Collegiate Dictionary (1959). Springfield, MA: G. & C. Merriam.

Weil, A. (1995). *Spontaneous healing*. New York: Alfred A. Knopf.

Wheeler, J. (1973). From relativity to mutability. In J. Mehra (Ed.), *The physicist's conception of nature*, pp. 242–244. Holland: D. Reidel.

White, M., & Epston, D. (1990). *Narrative means to therapeutic ends*. New York: W. W. Norton.

Wilhelm, R. (Trans.). (1962). *The secret of the golden flower*. San Diego, CA: Harcourt Brace Jovanovich.

Williamson, M. (1992). *A return to love: Reflections on the principles of a course in miracles*. New York: HarperCollins.

Winter. (1988). *Intuitions: Seeing with the heart*. Norfolk, VA: Donning.

Wood, N. (1993). *Spirit walker*. New York: Delacorte Press.

Worthington, E. L. (1994). A blueprint for intradisciplinary integration. *Journal of Psychology and Theology, 22* (2), 79–86.

Young, A. (1988). *Cosmic healing*. Marina del Rey, CA: DeVorss & Co.

Zukav, G. (1990). *The seat of the soul*. New York: Simon & Schuster.

Index